Leith Scotfow.

GW00371301

# CRUISING

*J D Sleightholme*

# Cruising

A manual for the small sailing boat owner

ADLARD COLES LIMITED
**GRANADA PUBLISHING**
London Toronto Sydney New York

Published by Granada Publishing in
Adlard Coles Limited 1977
First published 1963
Second edition 1970
Second impression 1971
Third impression 1972
Fourth impression 1974
Third edition 1977
Second impression 1980

Granada Publishing Limited
Frogmore, St Albans, Herts AL2 2NF
and
3 Upper James Street, London WIR 4BP
Suite 405, 4th Floor, United Nations Plaza, New York, NY 10017, USA
Q164 Queen Victoria Buildings, Sydney, NSW 2000, Australia
100 Skyway Avenue, Toronto, Ontario, Canada M9W 3A6
PO Box 84165, Greenside, 2034 Johannesburg, South Africa

Copyright © 1963, 1970 and 1977 J. D. Sleightholme

ISBN 0 229 11591 8

Printed in Great Britain by
Fletcher & Son Ltd, Norwich

# Contents

# Contents

# Photographs

# CRUISING

# Introduction

Edwardian yachtsmen might well look with amazement at the sort of cruisers we sail today and not least would they be amazed at the smallness of them. It is no longer valid to relate the size of the boat to the sort of sailing she can do; small, even tiny craft regularly and safely cross oceans and around our inshore waters they proliferate. Offshore racing over the years has pruned away the old, heavy gear, simplified rig and sail plan and refined the hull shapes to a point where the modern offshore cruiser is a sort of distillation of the essentials for seagoing. Synthetic materials, providing strength with light weight, combined with factory production has produced the class system to replace what was once largely a one-off production. The yachtsman no longer (or seldom) goes to a designer with his ideas; nowadays he can pick from a range of production boats all of which are already known and tried. This doesn't mean that there are no longer bad boats to be bought but it does mean that a man can have a better idea about what he is buying—provided he takes the trouble to find out.

Perhaps the only real drawback to the very small cruisers of today is that the crews they can carry are so much depleted; there is less scope for carrying dead-heads. In an average four-man/woman crew there must be at least a 50 per cent backbone of skill and stamina. In a crew of, say ten, an awful lot of people can take to their bunks before the working of the ship is affected too badly. Small boats too are tougher on their crews, if not in muscle then in their quicker motion which makes navigation, cooking and so forth much more difficult, and because of their slower relative speed they are at sea longer on passage.

But sheer size is no guarantee of safety if the gear is bad or the crew inefficient. Accidents in any case are overwhelmingly attributable to mistakes, ignorance, panic, unwise decision due to exhaustion and badly installed machinery. Left to herself the boat is rarely overcome by the sea—at least in normal sailing waters and weather. A well-designed small modern sailing cruiser, well battened down, all sail stowed and with her light, buoyant hull lying half beam-on, has preserved many an exhausted crew during a bad gale—mainly perhaps because she is virtually a bottle tossed hither and thither by the sea rather than a heavy object upon which the seas can break solidly.

In this book I have left out a great many of the old favourites usually to be found in books of this kind. I have assumed that the reader can sail a boat, or a dinghy at least, and that he understands the general nautical terms well enough. I don't teach him how to make a sheep-shank or how to carry out repairs, neither do I explain charts and compasses in any detail. Instead, I have tried to deal with the problems which arise in sailing and navigating on the assumption that it is better to learn the look of the water over a shoal patch than it is to be deeply versed in the intricacies of terrestrial magnetism—to begin with at any rate.

Ordinary common sense is the root of seagoing, that and a fair talent for practicalities. It is my belief that you could put a sensible, practical person aboard a boat and leave him to think it out for himself—and ultimately he would learn to sail, albeit at some risk. An impractical ass would never learn; it is he and his fellows who fill the lifeboats.

The hallmark of the good seaman is the event-free cruise, which does not mean that it is dull, just that his judgement is sound and that he avoids unnecessary trouble. We may have scaled down our boats but the sea and the winds remain as they always were, vast and powerful. The seas are for sailing though and the head shaking and barometer tapping which is mistakenly hailed as wisdom in some folk simply means that sooner or later they will be caught at sea, but will *lack the hard weather experience to deal with it.*

The sea is like a heavyweight boxer with a savage left hook. Stand up straight and you find yourself laid flat but duck a little, side step a little and you can survive. Weight-for-weight you cannot hope to win. Avoid the fight where you can but do not be panicked if you cannot. To stay at close grips with the sea and to love it is unlikely, to fight it is impudent, but to go out upon it with respect is to marvel at the sheer size of it and to go back again and again.

*Chapter One*

# The Small Cruiser

THERE are some very confused ideas about what constitutes a seagoing craft, and for the newcomer to cruising at sea it is all rather perplexing.

The development of the miniature three- or four-berth sailing cruiser and its appearance offshore in all kinds of weather has given rise to a good deal of head-shaking by the owners of larger and more conventional yachts, but to what extent they are justified isn't always easy to say.

Quite obviously the small modern cruiser of light construction and an overall length of under 20 feet is not a boat for taking to sea without careful study of the weather. The margin of safety for the larger modern cruiser–racer is a great deal higher; and this means that the margin for mistakes is wider too, but the small cruiser—assuming that it is well designed and built, and properly sailed with due regard to its limitations—can be safe enough in all ordinary weather including the typical 'summer blow'. It is extremes of weather and badly broken water coupled with a greater strain on an inexperienced and over-ambitious crew that pose the serious threat.

It is probably safe to say that a big percentage of much larger cruisers are unfit to be out in bad weather at sea. Size alone means far less than people choose to believe. The 18-foot cruiser in proper condition and sailed with skill is far safer at sea than just *any* ten-tonner which may have ripe sails and hull, plus a poor crew. The important truth about the much smaller craft is that she has no reserve power to allow for bad weather and she must be sailed with special care in order to keep within her margins of safety. Allowing that almost anything can be sailed almost anywhere by the right people, it remains to hit upon the safe minimum of seamanship required of the yachtsman and the safe minimum of seaworthiness required of the yacht.

The miniature or 'pocket' cruiser of around 18 foot overall length is, strictly speaking, an estuary or coastal cruiser but it must not be assumed that because she is small she is necessarily less safe at sea than a larger cruiser. Indeed, estuaries are often far rougher places to sail than the waters offshore where tidal currents may run less fiercely. Coasting in close proximity to land, despite the illusion of shelter close at hand in

1. *Above left*. The Kingfisher 20, a tried favourite severely tested over the years and nowadays also available with Chinese lug rig.
2. *Above right*. The Ridgeway Marine Ltd Pirate offers dinghy performance with night-away accommodation.
3. *Below left*. Vivacity 20-foot. A simple, efficient example of the modern breed.
4. *Below right*. Snapdragon 21, a case of designing for glassfibre—clean, functional, yet pleasing to the eye.

*(Photo: Trevor Davies)*

the form of rivers, bays and harbours, may in fact be a riskier undertaking which calls for a good deal more careful chartwork and attention to depth than the average offshore course demands. In truth, a boat is either *at sea* or *not at sea* and she is as much at sea when two miles offshore as when she is twenty miles out.

Again, in the nature of things, there are far more beginners at sea as skippers in very small boats than there are in large ones and if these smaller craft feature more frequently in the rescue it is not necessarily due to their size so much as to the lack of experience of their crews.

Being small boats they are comparatively slower ones, they are also affected sooner by any rise of wind and sea; the point at which they cease to make good ground to windward comes earlier too. A move up the size scale to 22–24 foot overall length sees dramatic improvement in performance due to increased waterline and better sail-carrying power, but it is in the region between 24 and 30 feet that family cruisers suddenly become floating homes rather than seagoing pup-tents. The happy average for many sailing families is the 25–27 footer. She has standing headroom in at least part of the accommodation, a fair measure of privacy and of course a far greater passage-making potential. She can afford to have a proper galley and suitable chart table, moreover her crew strength goes up to the point where it is more likely to have a safe reserve in the event of general seasickness.

## A Boat with a Lid

One of the favourite and mildly contemptuous sobriquets for the truly miniature cruiser is 'a boat with a lid'. Perhaps this is the easiest definition of the purely inshore cruiser, certainly it is a valuable guide to the correct attitude in sailing them. The term 'estuary cruiser' which used to be used for them implied that here was a boat for sheltered waters and notwithstanding earlier remarks about estuaries and rough water, such sailing is usually within sight of assistance.

In general these craft are around sixteen foot in length overall, probably with a centreboard, and with the open after end of the hull doing duty as a cockpit. There may be no form of fixed outside ballast, and the hull form is simply that of a large dinghy. Generous beam and firm bilge section give good initial stability, but the importance of crew weight in sitting out is still very much a part of the sailing technique in fresh winds. These little cruisers *are* safer to take offshore than dinghies, simply because there is decking to keep the water out when they are heeled or when a short sea is running; the extra beam and rather slower speeds give an impression of sturdiness, too, and it is easy to get the idea

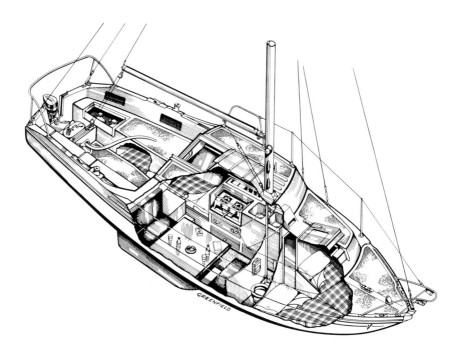

VIVACITY 24. This exploded view shows the thinking behind a typical modern layout in a plastic hull. The berths are arranged to give a private fore cabin with a separate toilet serving both fore cabin and saloon. The dinette arrangement converts to a double berth and aft, tucked under the cockpit port bench, is a quarter berth—this berth will come into its own at sea for watch-keeping. There is good stowage and ventilation. This layout, with variations, is a favourite with designers in craft of this size and type.

5. A twin keel Mystic comfortably aground while conventional hull in the background lies on her ear.

6. This Leisure 17 fitted with wind vane steering is heeling to a smart puff and lifting her weather bilge keel—the leeward keel is now deeply immersed and providing good lateral resistance.

*(Photo: Yachting Monthly)*

that they are in their element at sea. It takes more than a couple of bunks, a stove, and a sanitary bucket to make an offshore cruiser.

I have seen such an estuary cruiser, well reefed, sailing from the Essex to the Kent shore in the Thames Estuary on a day when the westerly wind was close on gale force. The proven point though was not that she could stand up to a 25-knot wind, but that she could stand up to it *in an estuary*, with the wind blowing offshore. Ten miles out at sea she might have been in dire trouble. The estuary cruiser is never under way for many hours at a time, which means that she is unlikely to be caught out. She is of generous tophamper, though, and once she is deep-reefed the windage of her flush topsides adds to the heeling forces. In any-thing of a sea, and with a wind strong enough to make deep reefing necessary, there may well be a tendency for her to bounce rather than sail. The crew's gymnastics cannot make up for what amounts to a great light box blowing on the drifting surface of the water.

All this may sound harshly critical of a class of boat which has been known to make all manner of extended cruises, and no doubt there will be some howls of wrath. Not criticism, but assessment, is intended here. In character these boats most nearly resemble the fishermen's skiffs of years ago, save that skiffs had the disadvantage of being open boats, but the advantage of being free of heavy drift-encouraging tophamper. Fishermen, for all their dire pessimism about weather, each other, and yachtsmen in particular, knew exactly what they could expect of their boats in any weather. If they were to be seen seven miles offshore (as the Bretons may still be seen) it was because they had weighed up the odds and decided that conditions were fit for the boat, and not that the boat was fit for whatever might come along. It might be added that very often they were tragically *wrong*.

Very frequently these small estuary cruisers are sold purely on the merits of the number of bunks which have been worked into the design—they are in fact sailing bedsteads, the corpulent compromise stuffed with Dunlopillo. The magic of getting away for a night, of lighting a little lamp and frying something, doesn't depend on mileage covered to get there. Few yachtsmen who started their sailing on a modest scale did not spend a night or two in a dinghy camped in some creek. The endless exploratory twists to discover a soft lodging for the hip-bone were the price to be paid. That it is possible for four people to spend a night away in a 15-footer and sleep is a tribute to ingenuity, but this sort of cruising is very much the prerogative of the teenager.

It must also be noted that there is a vast difference between sailing on the Broads, where the cruiser can stop and tie up alongside, when-ever the cramped conditions become irksome, and sailing in tidal waters where this is often impracticable.

Every type of craft has its proper element. The canal barge and the coaster, the Arctic trawler and the dredger. No professional seaman makes the mistake of expecting any one type of craft to be suitable for use beyond its scope. The little estuary cruiser is an inshore boat, and to take it to sea is to perform a stunt—stunts can only come off if the person concerned is sufficiently experienced to take a carefully calculated risk—or if he is dead lucky.

## The Small Offshore Cruisers

While our boat-with-a-lid is somewhere in the region of 16 feet overall length, a boat for offshore passage-making may be bigger by only a small margin; at 18 feet she may have the ballast ratio to carry sail in a stiff blow, the self-draining cockpit and the compact accommodation needed to conserve the strength of a couple of fit young sailors at sea. She is more likely to be a shade bigger than this; she is still to be classed as a pocket-size cruiser though and my reference to 'fit young sailors' is made by design.

A boat of this size may equally well suit an elderly retired couple who no longer need a bigger boat but if it comes to driving her into the teeth of a rising sea (and she may be equal to it) it will be crew stamina which really counts. Of the many 18–22 footers on the market most are sailing bedsteads in performance but a few are designed to give good windward results and of necessity they are wild and wet. Whether she goes well to windward or not, if she is a true offshore boat she needs to meet certain requirements.

She must of course be self-righting. She must have sturdy hatches fore and aft which could withstand a sudden heavy fall of sea upon them. Her cockpit should drain overboard; here let us pause for a moment and consider the self-draining cockpit myth. By saying that it should drain I mean that the drains should be able to cope with the effects of a heavy slop of water. Perhaps not one cockpit in fifty drains fast enough to rid the boat of a dangerous overload of water in the time for the boat to recover her full buoyancy before the next big one comes aboard. In truth, the wild motion likely to prevail at the time will most likely shift most of this water and the old saying that the most effective of all pumps in a boat is a frightened man with a bucket should be remembered.

The real virtue of the average draining cockpit lies in the fact that repeated wave slops and accumulating rainwater go overboard instead of gradually filling the bilges. Such bilgewater below can go unnoticed in times of stress; it could be dangerous, it is certainly demoralising.

FIG. 2. Small cruiser design. The four designs shown are chosen as representative of most modern craft which have cruising as the main objective. Left to right a 22-foot loa fin keel design which combines full headroom with improved windward performance. Disadvantages are the discomfort experienced when running aground and drying out and the vulnerability of the spade rudder which, lacking the protection of a skeg, could be damaged by a hard knock. The 24-foot loa twin keel design next to her may be marginally less efficient to windward, but scores on the two points mentioned and also offers full headroom below; both have an efficient high aspect rig.

Perhaps what is more important is that the cockpit area should not be too large. In most cases it will consist of a small footwell and the seating is in reality on the deck, surrounded by a coaming as a backrest. Cockpits which extend at full depth for the whole beam of the boat *could* be dangerous, although the risk of being pooped or overwhelmed is really slight for the average family yachtsman.

Additionally, she should have sails which can be deeply and properly reefed on a strongly stayed mast, and, preferably some form of auxiliary power which will drive her in rough water should sails alone prove inadequate to the task. We will deal with engines later on.

### Twin, Fin or Centreboarder

Many production classes offer the choice of twin keels, fin keel or centreboarder. The arguments for and against are not always too clear

The centreboarder, 23-foot loa offers good directional stability with her long ballast keel and should be effective to windward with her plate down. She has less headroom below and carries her sail on a shorter mast, possibly to offset the fact that her ballast cannot be carried at quite such an effective depth. The little 17-foot loa hull shown far right has proved both stiff and handy. With four berths (three in use is the comfortable maximum) she has good sitting headroom provided by the reverse sheer deckline. Her twin keels and skeg rudder provide good lateral resistance and an outboard is used as an auxiliary. Note the small mainsail which, when deeply reefed and set with a small storm jib, reduces sail area to an effective plan.

because a good twin keeler may sail the pants off a poorly designed fin-keel hull. Even when the basic hull remains the same, the performance may vary widely in one class and be only marginal in another class. Usually, though, the fin-keel version has the sailing edge on the others, especially to windward; next comes the centreboarder and third down the list the twin-keel hull.

Let us not knock twin keels though. If a boat has been designed from scratch expressly for twin keels her performance to windward, even when cruiser-racing against fins of similar size may be superior. However, if we were to take a twin and a fin, on the same basic hull and rig, and race them to windward, the odds are that the fin-keeled boat would be around 10 per cent better.

Centreboarders which have a stub ballast keel slotted to take a steel plate sometimes tend to be a bit tender in a breeze. This is due to the

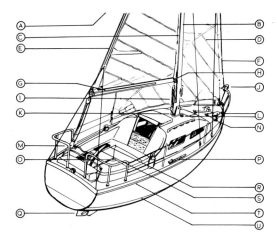

FIG. 3. *Extras, additions and useful features.* When buying new the inventory and state of readiness for sea varies boat to boat and many items are available as extras. Here are some of the design features to look for by way of fittings and some of the more worthwhile extras.

*A.* Masthead light (may be combined tri-colour), plus other navigation lights. *B.* De-luxe soundproofed mast (at anchor halliard noise at night can be hard to control); will also have spinnaker gear. *C.* Luff *track,* a luff groove means that the sail cannot be lowered temporarily without removing it from the track. Luff toggles to fit groove are an alternative. *D.* Genoa *and* spitfire jib. Performance often sluggish in light airs. Drastic reduction of sail area makes small jib imperative. *E.* Topping lift. Reefing at sea far easier if boom is allowed to swing and feather the sail while rolling down. *F.* Spinnaker halliard. Valuable as a spare headsail halliard, etc. *G.* Tapered battens or 'whelps' on boom (owner fitted, glued Araldite, prevents sagging of boom when deeply reefed). *H.* Effective roller reefing with spare handle. *I.* Tack downhauls on main and jib (better than halliard winches in small cruisers—these often too powerful and overload the spar). *J.* Fitted navigation lights. *K.* Tabernacle. Allows owner to step/unstep own mast, reducing yard charges, etc. Allows easier repairs if needed while away cruising. *L.* Electric deck plugs. Important to reliable operation of navigation lights. *M.* Novex mainsheet jamming block. Helmsman has instant control of sheet in an emergency gybe, etc. *N.* Anchor deck chocks. Essential protection of glassfibre decks. *O.* Recessed cockpit drains. Allows small quantities of water to drain without wetting feet. *P.* Sliding sheet fairleads. Greater sail trimming efficiency. *Q.* Skeg. Protects spade rudder from grounding damage, gives better directional stability. *R.* Draining locker for gas bottle. *S.* Hinged tiller, easier when going about with crowded cockpit. *T.* Cove line. Improved appearance, small cruisers often look 'boxy' unless relieved in this way. *U.* Moulded-in boot-top. Greatly aids painting or anti-fouling.

fact that the ballast weight has less leverage and although it may be heavier in order to compensate for this, the power of a fin keel with its deeply slung ballast weight is lost; once again, if she was expressly designed to take a plate this tenderness may not occur. In any case centreboarders sail well. Even better are the drop-keel designs in which a massive keel is raised or lowered either by a worm and pinion or a hydraulic lift. The ability to snatch up the plate in haste may be lost, though, and for owners who sail in shallow waters this is the great joy of a centreplate—a rumble as it knifes into a sandbank and it lifts itself, ere the crew can get to the winch.

An owner in deep water does not need either twin keels or a centre-board boat unless it is his delight to explore the shallow creeks. There is of course the advantage that with either of these shoal-draft types he can find an anchorage in places too shallow for deeper keeled yachts, also he can (with twin keels) dry out nicely upright when it suits him. Again, it is easier to road trail the shoal boats and if his mooring dries out, the owner of a twin can enjoy sitting in or working on his boat when the water has left her.

Boat for boat, they are all equally well able to cope with the open sea; it is just a matter of choice, influenced by a man's home sailing waters.

## Multihull Cruisers

Much unfair publicity has stuck to the multihull image. In cruising terms the seagoing cruising multi, particularly the catamaran, has a great deal in its favour. Accidents, by which we usually mean capsizes, have attracted a lot of attention but it is less well realised that almost all of them have happened while racing and usually to designs which had speed rather than ultimate stability as the basic purpose.

A conventional yacht with a heavy ballast keel sinks like a lead duck if she is holed; a non-ballasted multihull, even capsized, floats safely and while the conventional yacht cannot be capsized, the two factors—capsize and float or be holed and sink—tend to balance out in favour of the multi. Having said that, the fact remains that there is no good reason why a modern cruising multi should capsize. They are designed for great stability and provided that a complete blithering idiot is not allowed near the helm on a strong and squally day they will not cap-size. Blithering idiots can with equal aptitude ram a ballasted boat into dock, rock or fellow yachtsman and sink as promptly.

A sturdy family cruising cat can carry a lot of weight by way of crew and stores without losing stability by being over-laden, but a racer is

7. This Ericson 27 interior shows how practicality can be combined with 'country cottage' comfort below decks. The settees convert to comfortable berths and the table is sturdy enough to take the weight of crew lurching against it in a seaway.

8. *Right.* Luffing for the buoy in a Mystic. Note that although the breeze is quite fresh, the helmsman has luffed from a position barely a length to leeward. For the record he tended to overshoot a little, but within reason this is a good fault.

liable to be rendered unstable by over-loading; another reason for some of the capsizes read about. Cruising multis are not particularly fast. Their speeds average out in terms of being a bit slower to windward and a fair bit faster off the wind on a reach than conventional yachts of similar capacity. Their big attraction for cruising lies in the generous spread of deck space, the subdivision of their (usually) capacious accommodation into small separate cabins, which allows children to be tucked away to sleep or play without inconveniencing their elders, and the tremendous asset of not heeling more than a few degrees while sailing. Additionally they can be grounded wherever there is a level patch of sand or mud, or even beached for swimming parties.

The question of heeling or rather not heeling is important in family sailing. It means that both work on deck and down below is immeasurably easier, therefore less tiring and less taxing on parents in charge of young children. The motion of a multi is, however, quicker and jerkier, so the need for vigilance on deck is just as great. The sailing techniques differ little from those of a conventional sailing cruiser but there are certain new instincts to acquire. A multi will not always tack as smartly, especially in a short chop of sea and a light wind. Under power, in a stiff breeze, a multi-hull may prove rather a handful when trying to dock in a tight space and of course she needs a good deal more room. She may also lie less quietly to her anchor in a wind. More important though is that the helmsman's attitude must change. In a conventional, ballast keel craft the arrival of a squall simply means that the helmsman may luff a little to spill wind, confident that at the worst she will be laid over on her ear to the detriment of loose articles below decks. Such a squall calls for a more alert approach in a multi.

To begin with, the helmsman's reaction to angle of heel must change. I remember causing a catamaran owner to project himself from his bunk below in wild-eyed haste when I was on the helm at night. The breeze had hardened a little and to me, on my first offshore passage in a cat, we seemed to be going splendidly at a modest angle of heel. To the owner the angle was a subconscious danger signal and it was high time to ease her. The same angle in a ballasted boat would have meant nothing. Admittedly, this particular cat was one of the faster types and a beamier, heavier, less well canvassed cruiser would have shown us no cause for alarm.

## The Man and the Boat

It is easy enough for an author to hold forth about the sort of boat his reader should or should not buy, the kind of gear he should equip her with and the schools he should attend to learn the essential arts; it is the reader who has to write the cheques. *Of course* it is foolish for a complete novice to go tearing out to sea in an ill-equipped and an old or maybe unsuitable boat. It is also unrealistic to suppose that every reader has a bottomless pocket and that some of the boats they buy will not be a bit 'parish rigged' or a bit long in the tooth.

There is one piece of equipment that costs nothing. Gut-sense. It is gut-sense that makes a man think twice before climbing a creaking ladder with a heavy bag of tools and gut-sense that gives him his critical inward eye for the weaknesses of his boat and of himself. It isn't timidity or pessimism, it is the careful and calculating eye of the natural seaman and it is a gift that can be active in an owner from his very first day as a total novice. In due course he will take chances but they will be calculated chances and the odds are that they will come off. A man buys the boat he can afford and then he does in her the things he reckons he can cope with safely. It is as vain to suppose that a bit of reckless dash can make up for deficiencies in boat and man as it is to tackle the Matterhorn in sandshoes.

# Chapter Two

# Choosing a Cruiser

THERE is no better fun than boat-hunting and no chill of despair more alarming than the moment which follows handing over the cheque. There are always some after-thoughts and doubts, but if you have some knowledge of the small cruiser class as a whole and base your choice upon finding a particular kind of boat for a particular set of circumstances, it will take most of the risk out of it. There are very, very few downright bad boats on the market which cannot be spotted by a careful buyer. Price range is usually the first hurdle. With all the available brochures on hand it is easy to see that cruisers of similar size and type are closely competitive in price. Where one seems to undercut the others some close research is needed. One cruiser may be sold ready for sea, but lacking pulpits, guard rails, compass, warps and so on at an attractive quoted price, while another cruiser may be priced to include these and many other essential items. Most builders supply with their literature a list of extras which may include toilet, reefing gear and even engine. The only way in which a realistic price can be arrived at is by adding up a complete inventory in addition to the basic cost of the boat in each case and then passing judgement.

The buyer today has become far more realistic in his approach. While he may sign up at a Boat Show for a new and even untried cruiser, he is less likely to ignore the absence of say a Lloyd's specification for glassfibre construction.

Some builders still turn out glass hulls to their own set of standards (which may be perfectly acceptable too), but the buyer usually wants to know why. Most new craft are of glassfibre these days and very few are below standard; if they are at all lacking in this respect they are usually shoddy in other more obvious respects as well.

The main consideration in choice of hull form is one of good accommodation versus sparkling performance. One cannot often have both in a small cruiser. On the other hand it is an acceptable compromise to settle for a 4 berth 22 footer which sails smartly in all conditions save for the slam to windward in a fresh breeze and a short sea. Few plump family cruisers will cope efficiently with this test and it is here that a good auxiliary which will run smoothly despite a sharp angle of heel comes into its own—it is the penalty of the roomy little boat that an owner must be prepared to pay.

Chine-built planked or ply hulls, if properly built, are every bit as good at sea, size for size, as their round-bilge sisters, but the freedom from maintenance costs is steadily swinging in favour of glassfibre and if a boat needs to be yard stored in winter and partly at least fitted out by professionals this cost, over the years, must be considered at the time of purchase.

## What Sort of Sailing?

The average busy sailing family may spend a total of 50–60 days aboard their boat in any typical season. This includes a two-week cruise and about three weekends out of four. By far the most time will be spent at anchor or berthed; 80 per cent of the cruising will be in local home waters and the very minimum will be spent under way actually at sea on a passage outside local home waters. The hours spent under way at night will be least of all.

This sounds rather dull but far from it; this is the sort of gentle, happy cruising, shorn of anxiety and hardship, that should appeal to learners and those with small children. It has scope for being adventurous and practising navigation and seamanship and it does not become a weekend ritual of wifely apprehension. Naturally, some owners are more active and they make regular offshore passages safely and happily but cruising is of all things a joy to be shared and if everybody aboard is not equally anxious to be away and to see the land drop astern below the horizon, it can cease to be a thing shared and become a joyful challenge to one or two and a pain in the neck to the rest of the crew.

All this greatly affects the choice of a first boat. The ultimate ambition may be to world-cruise but the immediate use could be modest local cruising and it is better to buy a boat with that in mind and over the ensuing years to graduate through a series of boats to the one best suited. Having bought the first boat and provided she is readily marketable, an owner has overcome the main finance hurdle in buying successive ones.

So, a beginner's first boat might be a chubby, comfortable little thing that sails like a sentry-box but gives endless delight in his modest local wanderings. She teaches him the importance of being able to get upwind in worsening weather and his next boat, a shade larger, has better performance and an engine big enough to punch into a head sea. Why not buy this little boat right at the start? Many new owners, having sailed in boats owned by friends and tasted the delights of the open sea, may do just this but others, having had no such apprentice-ship, could end by doing the wrong thing; by frightening their families and over-stretching their own ability.

Think very carefully before deciding on the role of the boat. Do you have plenty of spare time for voyaging, is the family of the same mind, have you the confidence to tackle open-sea passages right away and more to the point have you the skills? Once again, don't be too dispar-aging of the local water cruising; you can find plenty of challenge any windy weekend you care to go out.

## Stability

Stability is the engine of the sailing vessel. A dinghy is powerless with-out her crew sitting to windward, and a small cruiser depends upon her stiffness to carry sufficient sail to get her out of trouble. Perhaps this analogy might be modified by saying that stability is her *gearbox*, it enables her to transmit the power of sail into forward drive. At all events it is not enough to rely on the crew's weight to provide stiffness. In fact, a pocket cruiser that must be sat out is either of poor design or is carrying too much sail. Reefing down to the sail number is only half the answer for she must be able to *carry* sail.

Stability is gained in two ways, by the shape of the hull and by the ballast carried on the keel or keels. Over-reduction of sail means lost power.

If a fin-keel is deep enough, in theory at least, it would be possible to give maximum stability with the minimum of actual ballast weight. The keel racing classes do literally derive their stability from their deep

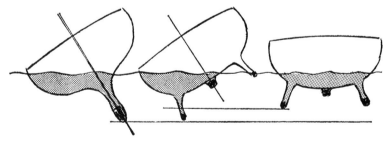

Fig. 4. When heeled the twin-keel hull increases her draft. If the keels are ballasted there will be some advantage gained by the deeper immer-sion of the leeward keel and the greater righting effect of the windward keel.

keels in just this way. Although many of them are excellent little cruisers, the disadvantages of such keels and the cost of the hulls puts them well beyond consideration here. The light displacement ply, moulded or glassfibre hulls, with their twin keels and short ends, must then be something of a compromise between the power from beam and power from weight.

If they have overhangs they will certainly gain stability and performance. There is lift to be had from a flared bow, and stability builds up fast as they heel.

The keel racer may have a ballast–weight ratio which is equal—hull weight and keel weight being about the same figure. The twin-keeler may be ballasted to something like a third or less of her dry hull weight and, as the ballast is placed high by reason of her shallow keels, it can be seen that its function is auxiliary to hull shape. Such hulls may be self-righting but they lack the power of the deeper keel and consequently must be sailed with due regard to this fact. When the ballast is divided between each keel there is an added advantage in that as one keel is more deeply immersed by a heeling boat, and therefore doing more work, the other and windward keel is stuck out at an angle which creates an increased righting moment (Fig. 4). It is a mistake to assume that because a ballast fin-keel hull is steeply heeled she will of necessity sail better. The advantages mentioned should be regarded as reserve power. Certainly most small cruisers sail best when reasonably well

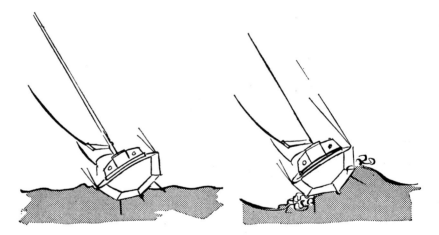

FIG. 5. Stability is affected by a beam sea. In smooth water the hull may resist sail pressure without being over-powered, but the off-balance lurch of a sea under the exposed bilge renders the same boat over-canvased for the conditions.

9. The Westerly Cirrus is a 22-foot fin keel design of glassfibre construction which has been outstanding both in performance and accommodation. Sleeping four adults she has a separate toilet and a full-size galley. With close on 50 per cent ballast ratio and a generous beam, she is a powerful sailer. *(Photo: Eileen Ramsay)*

upright and it does not pay to press them too hard. The ballasted bilge keel with its asymmetric hydrofoil shape also promises a lifting effect to windward which is noticeable to some extent, but it must be remembered that such a keel must be bolted to the hull extremely securely to offset added strain. From the point of view of getting to windward the twin-keeler may not have the overall performance of the single-keeler, as I have already mentioned, though provided the waves do not exceed a certain height she is often better. Area for area the keels total as much or more than a centreplate, and only if the centreplate is of deep, narrow section, is it likely to be much more efficient to windward.

What must be borne in mind on this matter of stability is that resistance to heeling in smooth water is one thing, but recovery from a sharp squall when sailing athwart a steepish sea is another (Fig. 5). A hard-pressed hull can be caught off-foot and knocked down hard. What will save her then will be the general design of the hull and cockpit.

A small, light displacement cruiser is easily brought to a complete standstill in such conditions. She lurches, heels and staggers from one wave to the next, each crest bringing her up and leaving her without headway until she gathers speed again in time to meet the next shock. A heavier boat carries the momentum to keep going. Lightly built craft have to be sailed in such a way that their light design is an advantage; there is less hull to be pushed through the water but they must not be allowed to stop.

## Hull Shape

With any short-waterline cruiser, hull performance to windward is bound to be no better than adequate, particularly if she lacks overhang. A racer of similar length and using her heeled hull to increase waterline length would do far better, but then she wouldn't be much of a cruiser. Design in small cruisers is one long compromise. The first major consideration is the relation of seaworthiness and handiness to ultimate safety. This sounds a bit confused. By a seaworthy hull one means one that can be handled at sea and sailed to wherever she may be going in any conditions deemed fit for a craft of her size. A handy boat is one that can be manoeuvred easily at close quarters and that answers her helm sweetly whether heeled or upright. Ultimate safety is just a matter of whether a boat will become a safe floating object after conditions (stormy seas or even loss of her mast) have knocked her out as a seaworthy craft. Many designers have played with the idea of incorporating some system of automatically inflating buoyancy; it has never proved to be practicable. But it is more important that the boat be so designed that when on her side the access to the cabin is well above the water level and the cockpit small enough to make the water in it relatively unimportant. This is achieved by building enough buoyancy into the topsides to give the hull lift as she comes on to her side and by providing wide side-decks and high enough cockpit coamings. A hull which has a pronounced dip to her sheerline around her open cockpit may well fill at this point if she is laid on her side. The advantage of beam is lost at once unless it continues to lift and, being the most deeply immersed part of the hull in this position, only the wide side decks can save the hull from filling. In passing it must be mentioned that built-in buoyancy should never be more than a last resort. First comes design and a hull which just cannot be swamped in a knock-down. A hull which is afloat by virtue of her built-in buoyancy and awash fore and aft is certain to lurch dangerously in a seaway. The weight of the crew in the cockpit may make it impossible to bale her and she will be constantly swept by the seas. As an extra safeguard built-in buoyancy has its place, but to rely on it is risky.

Many cockpits go the full depth of the hull and there is no possible way of making them self-draining. The hull on its side exerting lift is the only possible safety factor for a boat of this sort. Some have a form of bridge-deck dividing the cockpit from cabin and this contributes a lot to ultimate safety since it keeps the cabin door high. The hull which has a watertight bulkhead sealing off the cabin from the cockpit is even better provided for, as long as there is a means of pumping out both compartments. Incidentally, pumping can be a problem in the modern flat-floored hull which has no pump well in which bilge water can collect. The rolling and pitching of a boat in a seaway sends the water swilling everywhere and the pump intake pipe is sucking air much of the time.

A famous designer once remarked that any fool could design a bow —it was a stern that took some ingenuity. The small cruiser brings this lesson home hard. She has a shifting cargo of crew positioned in the cockpit most of the time. To maintain any sort of sailing trim with all the weight aft it might seem that the hull should have extra beam or sharper after sections to hold her tail up. A sailing hull presents a symmetrical shape to the water only when she is completely upright. Heeled, the shape of the immersed hull alters constantly to each puff of wind and becomes an asymmetrical shape. The line of the keel runs between a slim wedge of immersed hull on the windward side and a fat bulge of hull to leeward. The position of this bulge and its effect upon steering determine whether the boat will continue to answer her helm sweetly or steer like a stuck pig.

It is practically impossible to design a small hull which will have

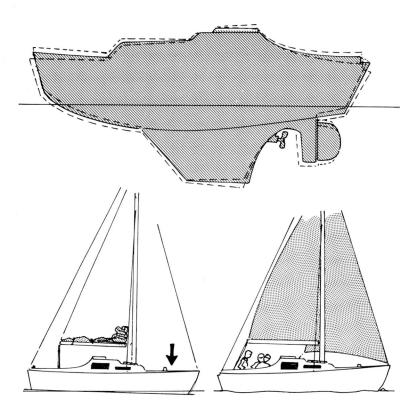

Fig. 6. Crew movement fore and aft causes considerable alteration in trim in small cruisers. Crew weight in the cockpit may mean that the boat never sails on her proper marks and it is worth trimming her a shade by the bow so that when the crew is aboard she lies correctly to her LWL.

day-sailing cockpit proportions, sleeping and living accommodation as well, and also steer with light helm when the hull is heeled down. Most of them tend to gripe up to windward and need a good deal of rudder to hold them straight. They should not be so hard-mouthed that they get away from the helmsman. This is a sign of either too much mainsail, too much weight in the *bows*, or a badly designed hull. With the chine hull, too much weight aft can make the after end of the chine slew the bows up, and, of course, a mainsheet hardened in too far has a similar effect. It all proves once again that these boats must be kept as upright as possible to get the best out of them.

34

## Crewing Considerations

Freedom is the secret of happy cruising. Freedom to come and go according to wind and tide and freedom to stay at anchor or to push a bit harder. One of the enemies of such freedom is the sort of boat which a man and his family cannot sail without having to enlist outside help each time. The endless complexity of times and dates, phone calls and rendezvous can mean delay, cancellation or, at best, annoyance.

When one looks at the feats of singlehanded racing people one very powerful fact emerges: if the boat is laid out properly and the man (or woman) has the experience, the need for a crew fades to the point where extra hands simply mean easier and better watchkeeping at sea. It isn't quite as simple as this. It is one thing to carry out routine sail handling and seamanship at sea and a very different matter to berth a boat singlehanded in an awkward corner and in a fresh blow.

More to the point where family sailing is concerned is that the skipper should be capable of doing 90 per cent of the work himself *if necessary*. A man with his wife and maybe two small children aboard must leave a safe margin for a mother to give priority to her kids. There will be times when things go wrong suddenly and he will need her help, promptly. Does he really need it or is he leaning on her just because she happens to be around? The only way in which he can find out is to try a little singlehanded sailing with nobody else aboard and it is an experience that everybody should seek because everybody will benefit from it.

In choosing a cruiser though, this element of self-dependence in small emergencies should be considered. The engine is perhaps the greatest saviour of maritime mistakes and it should be reliable, easy to start without leaving the helm and powerful enough to drive the boat as fast as her hull is capable of being driven under normal sailing conditions.

Sails are next. It is important that they can be lowered easily and quickly and set again without delay. This means that mainsail luffs should have toggle slides rather than a luff rope in a mast groove and that headsails should have halyards which will run freely without snarling while the sail is being dragged down the stay. Some inside-mast and aft-leading types of halyard tend to need a second person to see that they run clear. Rigs which comprise a small mainsail with a very large headsail are also questionable in this regard. Big sails mean harder sheet winch work and more of a battle to subdue; they also leave an area of mainsail which is too small to permit the boat to be handled properly under mainsail only.

Many small cruisers are capricious to steer, spinning off course the instant the tiller is let go and while this may be a feature to accept if the boat is suitable in all other respects, it is also one to consider. A boat which will sail herself when closehauled—or nearly do so—is usually docile to handle, allowing the helmsman to let go of his tiller for long enough to do some quick job elsewhere. Thus he can steal a good look at the chart, go forward to free a snagged sheet or to unlash the anchor (or secure it) all without having to call for other assistance.

This concern for ease of handling should be an important point in the choice of a cruiser, whether the skipper is likely to be starved of crewing assistance or not. A good boat doesn't *make* work she *saves* work. This doesn't apply to racing, where speed and efficiency is worth any effort needed and indeed some modern offshore racers cannot be handled at their maximum potential without a strong and skilled crew. Even in the smaller tonners, the amount of sheet winch work required of a crew may prove beyond a woman's strength unless winches of greater power and very considerable cost are fitted.

The ideal perhaps is the boat with a sail plan that can be handled reduced or increased easily and without risk or undue effort. This means a modest fore triangle and mainsail fitted with a really efficient reefing system. Modern roller headsails offer great advantages for the short-handed skipper. There are some disadvantages in that one sail of one weight of cloth is called upon to serve as everything from storm jib to genoa and that when rolled and left out in the weather, the exposed outer layer is subject to ultra-violet damage, also that the sheet lead isn't all it might be, but the bonus in terms of sail handling is a big one.

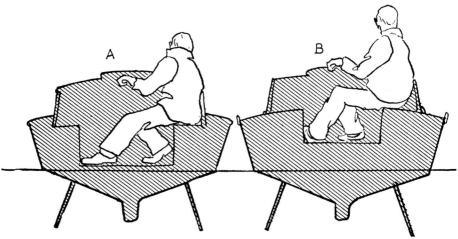

FIG. 7. Midget cruiser cockpit 'A' is too deep to self-drain, but cockpit 'B' is too shallow for leg-room and consequently the crew are not as safe in a seaway.

## Accommodation

There is a vast difference between room to sleep four and room for four people to live. Prone they take up very little room, but moving around they are another matter. Moreover, the amount of extra gear needed by four people living aboard must be put somewhere. The true test of accommodation in any yacht is a wet weekend at anchor.

It used to be said that a man needed a foot of boat to every year of his life but, while this is certainly stretching it a bit, it is true enough that the very young are more adaptable to discomfort. It is a great mistake to buy some great plywood barn or a seagoing double bed purely on the strength of accommodation. It is also foolish to try to cram too many adults into too little boat when by stretching the money just a little further a bigger boat might be bought. As we are concerned with the small cruiser, just let it be said that on any prolonged cruise it is far safer to keep one berth empty in any craft which has a sleeping capacity for more than two persons.

In the smaller cruisers which may lack full standing headroom, proper sitting headroom becomes even more important. Too often one cannot sit back and relax without one's head being brought up by a locker or coachroof side. Standing headroom is highly desirable provided it is not to be had at the cost of an absurdly high coachroof and consequent high windage. Better to settle for headroom in the hatchway and to fit a folding pram hood above the hatch which can, with a little ingenuity, become part of a cockpit tent for harbour use.

Layout may include one berth in the cabin and a quarter berth extending aft under the cockpit seats. Sometimes there is a double-bunk arrangement in the cabin with a flap lifting on the side of a settee-berth to increase the width, or the layout may have the conventional settee berths opposite one another. A berth cannot afford to be shorter than 6 foot, and 6 foot 2 inches is only just comfortable for a tall man, although a lot depends upon its width. Twenty-two or twenty-three inches is usual, but a narrow bunk takes a lot of getting used to after a bed ashore.

Sometimes berths are built into the forepeak of the hull, but unless there is a fore-hatch or a good ventilation system, bunking up forward is bad in hot weather and apt to make one wake up with a thick head. This also goes for any berth which has its head tucked into a corner; stale air collects and the sleeper is starved of oxygen. The shape of a berth is dictated by the curve of the hull, and this invariably means that it narrows towards the foot. Open plan accommodation offers advantages of light and air but not when small children need to be bedded down early. Better then to suffer the confines of bulkheads and have a separate saloon, toilet and forecabin for the privacy these offer.

Locker space is always limited, and in a flat-floored hull, with very little space for bilge water, the lockers below the settees are liable to be unusable at sea when there is the least drop of water in the bilge. Double skin GRP takes care of this problem as a general rule. There will be shelves under the deckhead, perhaps, and a couple of lockers for personal belonging, as well as a galley locker. This is the essential minimum. In a seaway, all movable objects must be properly stowed; it is the only way to avert indescribable confusion below. Most owners get into the habit of jamming everything into a vacant berth, but this should never be the normal stowage.

The galley may be only a simple flap-table with room for a two-burner stove, but one that folds away and stows properly and a well laid-out locker for crockery and food take up very little room; and the boat with a layout of this sort will save a lot of muddle and trouble. Cooking at sea is very seldom more than warming up soup or making hot drinks, but here again anything which can be done to make this easier will encourage the crew to make the effort. A hinged table which can be pegged at any angle is invaluable for putting things down on when the cruiser is heeling.

By and large, accommodation should not be the selling-feature of a boat but, if she is to be used in sheltered water only, an owner may be justified in searching for a boat with below-deck comfort—and to hell with her shape. If he does this he must be content to settle for what he's got and not attempt serious open sea passages in her.


## Sail Plan

Mainsail area is often modest in the smaller cruisers and without a genoa or a ghoster they are poor performers in light airs especially by comparison with dinghies and larger cruisers. A smallish main is nevertheless an asset in a shorthanded boat when the wind strengthens suddenly. They are a compromise in every sense and as such their better qualities are spread over the whole range of normal sailing conditions.

As already discussed, there are snags to the sail plan which favours a large fore triangle. What is perhaps more important than the combined efficiency of headsail and mainsail, in cruising terms, is how well the cruiser will handle under mainsail only or headsail only, and this is less a matter of sail plan than of sail and hull balance. Many of the larger fore triangle rigs albeit hard on winch work have the advantage that they can be handled smoothly, tacked and gybed, under headsail only.

By the same token there are other rigs about which the same can be said of the mainsail—provided it is of sufficient size to drive in lighter airs. Any potential owner on a trial sail might remember to try out this facility for himself—provided there is a reasonable amount of breeze.

Most of the small cruisers of today are masthead sloops; a few of the 30 footers sport yawl or ketch rig and there are the occasional cutters, particularly the latter-day gaff cutters in GRP which have appeared. As a general rule, any two-mast rig which plants a mizzen slap in the way of the cockpit creates more problems than it solves which is why the yawl, with its small mizzen well aft, finds most favour in smaller craft of the 25–35 foot range. Apart from splitting up the sail area into small and easy to handle parcels and allowing a big reaching staysail to be set sometimes there are no real advantages; these come with much bigger boats.

Speed under sail when cruising should be considered in averages. On a particular passage a cruiser's speed may vary between an optimum $6\frac{1}{2}$ knots at best down to a 2-knot saunter and the average may be around 3–4 knots. Based upon the entire cruise the average may be even lower if the weather is calm and sunny as we'd like it to be. The masthead sloop allows a really big and very light ghoster to be set, so big that it will set clear outside the spreaders even when close hauled. The result will be that the crew will want to sail the boat rather than switching the engine on through sheer frustration whenever the breeze falls light.

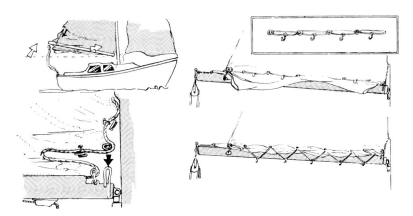

Fig. 8. The slab or jiffy reef is both fast and efficient. The boom end is first hauled up to the reef cringle by heaving on the reef pennant. Next, the halliard is eased allowing the luff cringle to be hooked on, the halliard is then set up taut and the reef is complete. The loose sailcloth can be tidied up later by means of the rubber cord rove through the sail eyelets and hooked below the boom.

The use of a spinnaker calls for prior training and experience, if for no other reason than that these sails are expensive and easily damaged; novice handling increases the likelihood of tearing it very considerably. There are those cruising folk who loathe this sail and others who wear it as readily as they'd wear their favourite jacket. It will move a boat across and downwind when nothing else will find a breeze but if it is going to become a standard part of the sail wardrobe its use must be learned, and not from a book. Remember this; other sails aboard are captive along one or two of their edges while the spinnaker is held at its three extreme tips and able, should it be allowed, to run amok. You cannot tame a spinnaker by luffing head to wind; all you are liable to do is wrap up the whole boat in it as effectively as a fly in a spider's web.

As mentioned earlier, the ability to reduce sail smartly and efficiently is all-important. The reefing system which is tricky, messy and time-consuming is dangerous to have aboard. Nowadays, slab reefing is rapidly overtaking even the better modern forms of roller reefing, not only for its speed but for the well set sail which results. In Fig. 8 it can be seen that the first stage lifts the boom end up to the sail, the second is to lower the luff and hook on while the third, hardening up the luff again, is all that is needed to reduce sail; the tidying up of loose canvas can come later if other matters are more pressing.

Reducing sail means reducing sail *while still retaining sail balance*. To set a storm jib with the whole mainsail or, alternatively, a working jib with a deeply reefed main can result in a boat so badly balanced that the helmsman can hardly hold her, let alone manoeuvre her. Thus it is that every offshore cruiser must have a storm jib and the means to sheet it correctly. A compact, well set and much reduced sail plan can see a boat comfortably through a gale which might otherwise have her blowing helplessly to leeward out of control.

## The Auxiliary Engine

The sail purist must be a man of leisure. To miss a tide by a few minutes and spend a night out in consequence is perhaps no hardship in a bigger yacht but it can be unpleasant in the smaller boat. The engine is, if not essential, very well worth having for any offshore small cruiser, but it should be looked upon as a second string and not an equal form of power to the sails.

If you decide to do without an engine, then invest in a good alarm-clock because in the tidal waters you will be rising at all hours to take advantage of a fair tide or to miss a foul one. On the other hand, if you do have an engine, get the usage of it into proper perspective. An auxiliary is an *aid* to seamanship in a vessel properly propelled by sail. It is not intended for use when the boat can as easily be handled under sail. A reliable engine that starts at once when needed can redeem many a basic error of judgement; this can become a vicious circle though. An inexperienced skipper attempts a manoeuvre under sail, loses confidence in the middle of it and starts his engine. He will never know whether the manoeuvre would have worked out or how well it came off. It is good seamanship to use every form of power available for the safe execution of any manoeuvre but, sadly, it also inhibits the learning of skills. Have an engine, start it and then see how far you dare go without engaging the gear. Some day—some day that engine will fail you.

Small diesels are the unquestioned favourites today and it is hard to find any argument in favour of a petrol engine. The more instantaneous acceleration of petrol has a bonus in terms of burst-power in short turning manoeuvres, a petrol four-stroke may be quieter too and it is usually a smaller and lighter unit but there isn't much else in its favour.

The power of the engine is worth thought. Any particular hull has its optimum speed and to push her above it means a wildly disproportionate amount of power required. It is a complex subject but in general it can be said that if the engine is to have a reserve of power it must be power that can be used. A fast-revving engine driving a small propeller is useless unless the hull can lift and fly the surface—otherwise it simply churns the same bit of water (cavitation). The same power in a slow turning large, coarse pitch propeller however gives solid thrust which can be used in a boat to drive her into the teeth of the wind and sea.

Such a propeller would need to be deeply immersed in solid water and unlikely to be exposed by the pitching or heeling of the boat. A motor-sailer needs this sort of power. Her engine will be used to back up her sail power, possibly while steeply heeled, or it may surplant sails altogether when the owner needs to get dead upwind in a hurry.

The true auxiliary though may be intended to push the boat through a calm or to manoeuvre her up-river and as such it is a modest little machine. Modest or not, an owner has to adopt an attitude to it. If it is absolutely reliable it is up to him to keep it that way; if it is a bit past its prime and he can't afford to replace it, he must build in an allowance, in all he does, for the fact that *it may* break down or *fail to start when needed*. In short, he never places his boat into such a situation that only the engine can get him out of it. He must always have an alternative, be it sails, anchor or a dinghy towing astern ready with kedge and warp. That is good seamanship.

It has been said that an owner should not worry too much about learning the ins and outs of his engine; his job is to keep it clean, fed with oil, fuel and cooling water and to make sure that the electrics are maintained as they should be. If it is running sweetly then *leave it alone*. One might qualify this by saying that an owner should know enough to recognise the simple causes of stoppage or non-startage. More important even than this is that the engine should be accessible from all sides, albeit maybe with a struggle. Grease caps, stern tube, pump, and sump drains should be easy to get at and therefore likely to receive their proper attention. It is failed electrics and dirty fuel that cause 90 per cent of failures and most of the lasting harm is attributable to lack of maintenance.

## Equipment

Earlier editions of this book dealt at some length with hull construction, considering plywood, planked and GRP methods of construction. Today, the GRP hull stands almost unchallenged and although the merits of timber, glass, steel and ferrocement make interesting study, it is perhaps the wealth of available equipment that puzzles most new owners. What is essential and what is by way of embellishment? The odds are anyway that the person who buys this book will have already bought or decided on his boat.

Equipment consists of those parts without which a boat will not sail (in the man, boat and sail context expressed in the simplest form, there is hardly any equipment needed) and items which make sailing easier or more efficient. This would include sheet winches, cooker and sleeping-bags because, after all, you could sail the boat without them. Such vital necessities as anchor and cable, warps and so on come into the first category. Thus a bare minimum is needed to simply sail the boat, a little more is needed to sail her in safety (anchor, storm jib, lifebuoys, etc.), more still is required to make sailing and living aboad easier and possible and whatever is added after that is for the most part either refinement or it is there to relieve the crew of some of their thinking or work. It is quite important to evaluate in this way otherwise the cheque-book is never at rest. There is a difference between equipping a boat sensibly and doing so lavishly. Better, for instance, for a man with a weak back to spend several hundred pounds on a hydraulic windlass than for him to install certain electronic wizardry that, at best, merely does some of his navigation for him.

On the above basis, the equipment for a 25-foot sailing auxiliary cruiser might look this way:

*Basic essentials:*
Anchor and kedge, plus cables
Storm canvas
Lifebuoys, safety harnesses, lifejackets, etc.
Distress signals
Navigation lights
Radio for forecasts
Charts and navigational instruments including compass and log,
    handlead or echo-sounder
Barometer
Radar reflector
Essential spares (reefing handle and the like)
Warps, heaving line, fenders and deck gear
Necessities for cooking and sleeping.

The above plus the host of such minor essentials as sail repair kit, spare shackles, first-aid kit and fire extinguishers really need no listing. The criterion is this: can the boat be sailed, lived aboard and faced with common emergencies without being found wanting?

Much of the equipment simply serves to cover up or remedy human error. If an engine installation was perfect and if rigorous safety rules for maintenance of engine and electrics, fuel and piping were enforced the need for an automatic fire extinguisher, a gas or fume detector or indeed even a fire extinguisher would cease to exist. Human error is a constant factor and so we must have at least the extinguisher. The man-overboard risk is similarly dependent upon human error and lack of precaution. The automatic devices for lifebuoy release, the throwing lines, automatic lights and dye markers, dan-buoys and harnesses, lifejackets and inflatable garments are all praiseworthy and all born of a need to remedy human error. The more rigorous the safety drill aboard the less need there is for such equipment, although it would be folly to dispense with it all. Additional to the first list then:

Light reflective materials for lifejackets
Water activated (or similar) light for lifebuoy
Boarding ladder to facilitate recovery of man in the water
Second fire extinguisher
Inflatable dinghy
Additional light weather sails
Radio direction finder
Echo-sounder
Second high power torch, etc.

Apart from the echo-sounder which is merely a more convenient device than the hand leadline, these items either improve the safety and performance or improve navigation. There are many other such items and each has a role. These two lists might be followed by a third and endless list of the things which gild the lily. With no disrespect to their efficiency, this third list would include the wind direction electronics, speed logs and plotters which, while vital to modern offshore racing and very useful in more sophisticated yachts, are not strictly necessary to the new owner who is trying to spread his money wisely. Radio telephone is a great aid to safety and so is radar—more so perhaps the inflatable liferaft but they are all very costly.

Again, much depends upon the *sort* of use an owner has in mind. The habitual weekender who seldom makes night passages can get by with one car-type 12-volt battery but a second battery is a wise buy for the owner who intends to make longer passages. Neither does the weekender need wind vane or automatic steering gear, unless he is a regular singlehander but the far-faring man and his crew will relieve much of the tedium of long hours at the helm by fitting one and therefore it has a full role to play. The difference lies between the things we need and the things we like to play with.

## Spars

The masting and rigging of this type of craft is very simple but nonetheless based upon carefully considered mechanics. Masts are struts under compression and subject to side and fore-and-aft strains. These are not even constant loads. Varying wind forces and the motion of the boat as well as flogging sails snatch and jerk at the spar from all angles. A degree of bend forwards from the middle of a mast helps to flatten the mainsail, but the main load is downwards, and if the bend is too pronounced the mast will buckle. The arrangement of the standing rigging has to be good enough to stay the mast efficiently, but it must also be easily set up by the amateur and not dependent upon expert adjustment.

The spreaders serve to hold the head of the mast straight athwartships and the lower shrouds keep the spar from sagging in the centre under the pressure of the mainsail. In the fore-and-aft direction, however, staying problems are more involved.

The masthead rig tends to pull the head of the mast forward and the normal forestay rig applies the load to the middle of the mast. The pull of the mainsail through the sheet and kicking strap pulls the spar aft in the middle. To offset these loads several alternative methods of rigging may be used.

The spreaders may be raked aft with the cap shrouds meeting the deck abaft the mast position, this means that the head of the mast is stayed aft by both cap shrouds and backstay against the pull of the jib; and the forward thrust of the spreaders against the mast combats the pull of the mainsail allowing the mast to take up an even curve. Alternatively both lower shroud and cap shroud can be sited a little way aft of the mast position and shackled to the same chainplate. This has a similar effect save that local strain on the hull and plate is greater and all one's eggs are in the same basket if anything fails there. As a variant on this method only the shrouds can be led aft. This isn't so clever as it means putting the full duty of staying the head of the mast against the jib and forestay on the single backstay, this results in a positive forward component at the masthead, and since that is more or less immovable the mast has to go somewhere—it bends aft in the centre, which is bad.

Larger yachts and offshore racers may have adjustable backstays

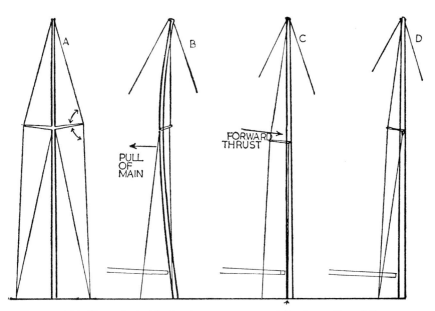

FIG. 9. 'A' Shrouds hold the lower mast straight laterally while cap shrouds passing over spreaders brace the head. 'B' As the main pulls the middle of the spar aft, the spreaders, if wrongly stayed, do nothing to counteract it. 'C' led abaft the mast by cap shrouds positioned well aft exert a forward thrust where it is needed. The main shrouds in this case are in line with the mast. 'D' Shrouds and cap shrouds may be led to the same chainplate position. While this is simple and effective, it tends to place an unfair load on one fitting.

which, by means of hydraulics, permit the mast to be bent in order to alter the flow of a mainsail. Older yachts may have running backstays to hold it straight; which are set up and released on each tack. The small cruiser with single- or twin-standing backstays leading to the stern has no such runners to worry about, which is a blessing when cockpit working space is limited. But it does mean that attention to the tuning of the standing rigging is important. Naturally this doesn't mean that the conscientious owner gives his turn-buckles an extra turn for luck every time he goes sailing. They should, in any case, have locking wire on them. Sooner or later overtuning means a parted shroud and lost mast or some distortion of the hull. In large offshore racers it is not uncommon for wooden boats to be overtuned to the extent that the heel of the mast, stepped on the keel, is simply shoving out the bottom of the hull against the upward drag of her shrouds—like trying to pull your pants up while standing on the turn-ups—the result is serious strain all round and (in the case of the boat) drastic leaking.

Most masts are stepped directly on the coachroof, which is specially braced below to take the load. Many are stepped in tabernacles, which allow them to be lowered easily for unstepping before loading the boat on a transporter, passing into a canal system where low bridges require it or indeed for an owner to lower or raise his own mast when laying up and fitting out.

Aluminium masts, although more expensive, save almost 50 per cent weight aloft and are usually stronger for a given size, and this is important to remember with small craft which need critical ballasting. Take a line to the masthead, and the ease with which a yacht can be heeled is proof enough of the mechanical advantage exerted by every extra pound of weight aloft.

*Additional Notes on Design and Construction: Points for Buyers*

Is the boat one of an existing popular class, designed by a reputable designer? Are the brochure claims of seaworthiness extravagant in comparison to similar boats? If the price is lower, on what points has the economy been made? Is the finish of the hull workmanlike (i.e. ply edges rounded or capped, sanded down before painting, butts between ply sheets invisible, general line of hull smooth and not showing dips or waves between frames. In the case of a glassfibre hull, is it to Lloyd's specification, properly supervised lay-up, laminate increased at stress points, gel-coat not crazed?

Is there adequate doubling in way of the bilge-keel bolts? Are the materials of a grade comparable with those of other similar boats? Is the mooring post anchored to the deck beams, or the mooring-cleat through-bolted to a pad?

Does the design cater for offshore passage making? If so is there a ballast-keel or keels of one-third of the displacement or not less than a quarter? Is the cockpit either self-draining or small enough to prohibit water entering if the boat is knocked down? Is the cockpit bulkhead above cockpit height to keep out water in an emergency? Are the bunks adequate? What ventilation is provided for the forepeak? Is there a forehatch? Is the bilge-pump (if one is fitted) placed conveniently? Will it serve the cabin as well as the cockpit? Is there sitting headroom below—too much headroom at the expense of windage?

Is the mast adequately stayed according to normal design requirements? Are the fittings standard? If the mast is stepped on the cabin top, is there proper reinforcement below? Reefing-gear adequate to roll down the deepest reef?

The Junior Offshore Group safety rules and recommendations form a criterion of guidance which can be studied with great advantage by any small cruiser owner. The following is a digest of these rules, repeated here with permission.

A yacht must be satisfactorily self-righting from ninety degrees—if it is a centreboard craft with plate or plates *up*. Hull, rigging, spars, upperworks and decks must be strong enough to withstand the weight of a heavy sea falling on her or the stresses set up by being rolled over on her side. It is recommended that the cockpit be watertight and of limited volume, lockers to count in this volume unless they are made watertight offshore. It is recommended that sufficient buoyancy be carried to support the keel, stores and crew with a reserve of 250 lb. The recommended area of the main- or fore-hatch in plan should not exceed 3 sq. ft in smaller craft, 4 sq. ft in larger ones. Adequate ventilators should be fitted and have water traps.

Rule VII I will quote in full as it is so eminently sensible as a code for all small cruisers offshore. 'Owners are reminded that they must anticipate spending longish periods at sea where there may be no harbour or refuge within easy reach and no means of obtaining assistance. Apart from assuring themselves of the soundness of the yacht and its gear, they should look to such matters as rudder hangings, chainplates, deck fittings, etc. They should make sure that glass in deck openings, etc., can be protected easily and secured if broken; that openings in the hull have seacocks on the flange of the opening; that propeller shafts are properly secured and cannot withdraw; that pumps are adequate and in good condition, can be worked at sea and can be cleared easily in the event of choking. And they must "then know the sea, know that they know it, and not forget that it was made to be sailed over".'

The recommendations for equipment are based upon wide experience:

(a) Two serviceable bunks not less than 6 feet long.
(b) Cooking stove capable of safe operation at sea.
(c) Adequate chart-table or plotting board.
(d) W.C. or fitted bucket.
(e) Anchor and suitable cable. When there is an anchor warp a short length of chain should be fitted between anchor and warp.
(f) An efficient compass.
(g) At least one fire extinguisher.
(h) First aid box and instructions.

(*i*) Suitable storm canvas. Alternatively the working canvas must be suitable for reducing in area and withstanding storm conditions.

(*j*) Internationally recognised distress signals (rockets, flares, smoke floats, etc.).

(*k*) Internationally prescribed navigation lights, and two powerful electric torches.

(*l*) A lifejacket for each member of the crew.

(*m*) Efficient personal lifelines for each member of the crew on deck with a line for properly securing to a strong point.

> *N.B.* These are regarded as being the most valuable single items of safety equipment and should be worn whenever risk of falling overboard exists.

(*n*) Adequate hand-holds about deck and cabin top.

(*o*) Taut and efficient grab wires or lifelines properly supported at a height of not less than two inches clear of the rail for the full effective length of the vessel, on each side.

> *N.B.* It is recommended that a proper guard rail be fitted at a height of twelve to fifteen inches.

(*p*) A lifebelt with a self-supporting light, or flare of approved type, carried on deck and able to be jettisoned readily.

# Chapter Three

# Family Cruising

THE financial state of most couples with young children is usually such that their cruiser has to be a small one, like it or not. In fact, I believe the smaller boats are a better bet. Their size means more modest local sailing, shorter passages, access to better shelter and a good deal more creek-crawling. Admittedly there is less room to move and small children more often get entangled in the sheets, but after all, the boat is small enough for father to handle with occasional help from mother and the little jobs which a child can be given to do 'to help' are usually within its strength in fine weather. It is all much more child-sized and the conception of fun is more strongly felt than it might be in a much bigger cruiser making long and rather serious passages at sea. The time to convince children that sailing is fun is when they are small. Sailing can bind a family together but it can as easily split it apart later on, as children get a little older.

The question of bringing the whole family into it still bothers a lot of people who are considering the cruising game. It poses a lot of questions, and the answers are not always so easy to find. Basically it is a question of whether a woman is able or prepared to cope with small children afloat. Assuming that father can handle the boat more or less unaided, any form of endurance test, the sort of thing resulting from a prolonged passage, is right out of the question. The very small child who can 'stay put' in a carry-cot is no trouble at all, apart from the inflexible feeding programme and a certain amount of laundry difficulty. An older child who is able to understand what it is all about and take an active part in things is an asset rather than otherwise, so long as he is absolutely obedient. The toddler poses very different problems.

Freedom to move around is as essential as the very breath of life to a three-year-old, and that includes climbing, of course. The woman who becomes alarmed, who never knows a moment of peace despite lifejackets and lifelines on the infant, is not a woman who is going to think very highly of a spirited beat down the estuary on a weathergoing ebb. One must be fair about this. It is any woman's right to worry about her children and every father's duty to give her no new reason for worry. In actual fact there is very little danger in taking small children afloat in the right sort of craft, far less than letting them wobble along the edge of the pavement on a tricycle, but there is no pleasure in a life afloat which moves from one alarm to another with all the attendant friction and recrimination.

The complete novice who buys a small cruiser and sets about learning to handle her with his family permanently enmeshed in the mainsheet can only hope for one of those utterly unperturbed women who accepts his wild-eyed dictatorship with well-hidden amusement and keeps her brood clear of his athletic seamanship. Quite obviously this is the wrong way to go about things. It is very important that a man should be sufficiently master of his art to be able to avoid all the basic disasters long before he takes his family afloat unaided. Whether a child knows what is going on, or whether he still finds it all rather strange and alarming, he must be able to feel an emanation of reassurance from the parents. The need to believe that 'my daddy is the best yachtsman in all the world' goes far beyond school playground line-shooting; and even though 'my daddy' may be the most ham-fisted yachtsman ever to sink his own dinghy, he must be able to convey the impression that it was the right and proper thing to do at the time, even if he doesn't say as much. Water, sails and boats are an alarming combination of noise and movement. A child may become terrified, and what should have been a child's idea of heaven becomes a dreaded weekend ordeal.

Children of an already well-established yachting family grow up in the atmosphere, and whatever they may do in later life, they accept and enjoy their holidays and weekends afloat as children. It is the already grown children who are pitched into yachting to the exclusion of their own long-enjoyed occupations who suffer. Worse still is the implication that sailing is in some way 'remedial', that it will 'make men of them'. The novelty of a family boat is quite enough to tide children over the first annoyance of having to miss out on Scout camp or stop hanging around a riding stable, but young enthusiasms are like a sky-rocket, they soar blazing and brilliant and then fizzle out from lack of fuel within a very short space of time. The only way to win them over wholeheartedly is by letting them take part wholeheartedly, even though this may often mean having the boat filled with 'my-very-best-friends' on more Saturday afternoons than you care to spare.

Possibly the best beginning is simply camping on the boat at the other end of the creek. The art of living in such a small space demands a lot of planning and family by-laws, so nothing is really lost in getting the sharp edges worn off first without the added complications of seagoing. To this end—that is, deciding whether the family idea is going to work—it is as well to remember that nowadays there are many charter firms which offer small sailing cruisers on weekly charter and a week in the Solent on a chartered boat is a safer bet than buying first and experimenting with human relationships second.

It is probably safe to say that for small children the duration of any sail should be in strict relationship to the child's age. A ten-year-old can obviously put up with a longer passage than ten hours but five hours for a five-year-old is plenty. It is of value in more ways than one to make a point of trying to land somewhere mid-way through an afternoon sail. A picnic from your own boat has far more attraction to the small child than any six-hour sail enlivened by being allowed to 'pull that rope when daddy tells you'.

Safety afloat is the greatest worry for parents who are newcomers to cruising. In truth there is very little danger beyond being trodden on, so long as the basic rules are observed. There is one all-ruling proviso however and it is one which, unhappily, will put a great many children outside the safety margin, it is a matter of instant *willing obedience*. Without doubt the habitually disobedient child afloat is in continual danger. Only the knowledge that in a sudden minor emergency a child will at once do exactly as it is told makes it possible to sail with an untroubled mind. A sudden need to gybe while the child is standing in the way for instance. If he can't be relied upon to 'Get below quickly!' without demanding to know why before obeying can mean trouble and possibly injury. For this reason alone wives should restrict their natural inclination to challenge father's authority. The one-ship one-skipper law was never more true than in the case of the family cruiser.

Far more important than a child being able to swim before going afloat is to know that he will instinctively put on his lifejacket, almost at the mention of the word 'boat'. Sooner or later a child will fall overboard and usually (fortunately) it will be at moorings when the rules governing use of the deck can be eased a little. There is no better way of instilling sea-sense and one might go so far as to say that parents of cocky youngsters might agree to watch unobtrusively for this very thing to happen. With a lifejacket on and a dinghy ready to hand no great harm can come of it. Naturally this drastic treatment is not for the nervous child.

It goes without saying that the cabin and the cockpit are the right and only places for children when under way, and for toddlers with climbing tendencies a rope's-end with a snap-hank on it is an added precaution well worth fitting. The cockpit isn't roomy enough to use as a play-pen and to consign a child to the cabin is to stand a chance of bringing on seasickness if there is the slightest motion.

Seasickness is another excellent reason why longish sea or coastal passages are something of a gamble with young children aboard. Naturally it is unwise to discuss it in front of them, but it is just as foolish to deny that there is any such thing.

Sleep is the one asset which a child brings into the sailing game to the benefit of all. A child can sleep soundly through most things and night is a good time to make a long and possibly boring passage.

Seasickness pills are of value, even if it is only that most of them produce drowsiness and enable a child to be tucked up in a bunk for a few hours—which is all the passage should be planned to take in any case. The pill habit should never be allowed to get out of hand or confined to the child alone.

Sense of proportion is more than ever important with small children aboard. Most men rather enjoy a spot of amateur dramatics at the helm. The 'how-can-I-cope-with-it-all-alone' pose is good rich stuff for a lone-wife audience but it has no place with children around. Taken by and large it may not matter in the very least if the boat has to be run up the mud rather than snatch the mainsheet from around a child's ankles, these things just happen and time suggests the cure. Calm and control are all-important, take care of the 'tone' and the tune will take care of itself—in time.

# Chapter Four

# Living Small

THE surest indication of a yachtsman's experience of small craft is the way he moves himself around in the cabin. He adapts his movements instinctively. A beginner, in the same position, seems to fill the whole space.

The essentials are proper sitting headroom (when leaning back), light and air, dryness and a carefully thought out system of stowage. Ideally one might add: a place where one may stand upright to dress and stretch. This last requirement becomes more and more essential as one grows older.

The basic layout of lockers is usually sound enough, but there was never a yachtsman born who would stay content for long with someone else's ideas. Generally speaking, though, lockers should be a feature of careful design instead of their size and shape being merely that of any odd corners not already in use.

Method, orderliness and habit are the secret of living small. Accessible lockers should contain things in frequent use and stowage in the tricky places listed on a plan. A lesson can be learned from blind yachtsmen who *must* know exactly where things are and who replace them exactly where they found them even when day sailing as a guest with someone else. A lot can be done to make the best use of locker space by converting the interiors for better stowage. At the start of a cruise an owner stows with care, fitting everything into place with jig-saw neatness, this state of affairs can't last. After about twenty-four hours every locker is in turmoil. By equipping lockers with pull-out trays, spring wire fiddles to prevent things from sliding around, and by using plastic containers chosen to fit the space, probably twenty per cent more stowage is possible.

Shelves are really more useful than lockers for personal gear, but for clothing I maintain (at the risk of being considered a rank heretic) that the despised weekend suitcase, shared between two people, is probably better in a very small boat. It can be left fully packed and stowed wherever it happens to be out of the way at the time; it will tuck away into a quarter-berth by day and stand on the cabin-sole by night; it also keeps a shirt from looking like a newly-hatched moth. Clothes in lockers, or hung up, should be in plastic bags. This not only keeps them dry but also protects them against the ceaseless rub, rub, rub. Laundrettes sell large and very strong plastic bags, which are ideal.

The whole concept of cooking in a very small cruiser is based upon the Saturday evening meal during a weekend cruise. Passage meals may be cold, nutritious snacks, but the Saturday 'dinner' is a challenge and one of the highlights of the whole weekend. It is a good deal more important than one realises. One must therefore be able to work in the galley without blocking access to the cockpit, because the meal is likely to take quite a while to prepare. Miniature gas-bottle cookers are light and clean to use, but paraffin pressure-stoves are a little safer, although the man who is careless with bottled gas can still be in trouble with a flaring paraffin stove. Two burners are essential if one is to cook any but the simplest one-course meal in a reasonable space of time.

A cook's first need is somewhere to put things down. Flap-tables across bunks can be improvised. He must also have a gash-bucket of some sort, even if it is only a large jam tin. A bucket with a disposable plastic bin liner is good if there is room for it, or alternatively our old friend the plastic bag clipped in a needle-work ring and fixed close at hand. (Plastic bags have unlimited uses: bedding, bread, flares and in fact any perishables can be preserved in them.) Fresh water is easily supplied from a container with a plastic pump, but make sure when you buy it, that the pump works smoothly, for some of them are sticky. When cruising you should reckon on carrying a gallon per head per day, though if you use it only for drinking and cooking you will get by with less. A miniature sink scarcely larger than a cooking bowl can be fitted to larger types of small cruiser, and this, though an infuriating thing to wash in, is a blessing to the cook for getting rid of waste water. Lift-out shelves, transparent containers, and so on, must replace the ubiquitous little screws of lard and butter. A drawer or tray for cutlery, and a really convenient size of bowl for washing up—no matter how hard it is to stow—are all-important.

One of the most useful of all additions to a small cruiser inventory is a pressure cooker. The advantages are most marked when a meal is to be prepared at sea, since the thing can be filled in the cockpit and lashed to the stove and left to get on with it.

It is difficult to plan an interior without first living in it. For this reason the owner who completes a hull later is better placed, for he can 'camp' in his boat for the first part of the season and learn how he wants things arranged. This is really the designer's job, of course. Keep an eye open for anything at all which constitutes a small annoyance. A series of small irritations add up to a big nuisance after a few days of living small.

In very small cruisers of 18–22 feet in length a good cockpit awning is important. A wet day in an anchorage can be a misery without one. Not only does it permit more freedom of movement, but it also stops dampness from spreading below. Oilies can be left in the cockpit, and driving rain is kept out. Its size depends on the size and shape of the cockpit, but ideally it should extend forward over the open companion hatch, secure to the mast, and give standing room under it. The usual cockpit cover, used to close up the boat when she is left on the mooring, is only suitable to rig as a fly-sheet over the boom and cannot be expected to keep out much weather if there is wind with it. A cockpit tent, on the lines of the Norfolk Broads cruiser tent, which has walling and windows, would be the ideal, of course, and many small cruisers have had them specially made. It need only be of lightweight canvas, since it is only in use occasionally, and press-fasteners can form the attachment to the coamings and coachroof. On a really windy night, though, it is unsafe to leave it rigged—and the billowing noise doesn't make for peaceful sleep.

Personal belongings are the bane of life afloat. The eternal groping and burrowing for cigarette lighters, films, toilet gear, and so on, are a major annoyance. A ditty-bag per head is one solution. It should be as wide as it is deep, and with a drawcord at the top, and can hold everything from loose change to toothbrush. An acrylic-fronted shelf along the bulkhead can be fixed to hold loose ship's gear, such as torch, spare shackles, vital reef pennants and so on.

Cabin lighting can vary between a pressure lantern, which is really rather large for such a small space, to electric lighting from car batteries. The gimballed oil lamps, although they are decorative and give a fair light, are neither bright enough to read by in comfort nor really safe. Bottled gas lanterns are simple and bright, but add just one more risk of getting the heavier-than-air gas into the bilge if they are not properly handled.

The pressure lantern has the advantage that it also acts as a heater on chilly evenings, but all forms of light that depend on a flame consume oxygen and must have proper ventilation. People have gone to sleep and suffocated before now. This is a very real and a very insidious danger. The only warning of peril is a feeling of drowsiness, and what is more natural than to lie back on a comfortable bunk and just fall asleep? It must be a rule that there is good fore-and-aft ventilation the whole time that gas or paraffin stoves or lamps are alight.

A very simple alternative is to use a flat battery lantern (Fig. 10) fixed to the deckhead by a tightly stretched strand of rubber shock-cord. But you will need a plentiful supply of batteries.

The worst bogey on small boats is the lavatory. The basic bucket in a box has much to recommend it, but if you are going to cruise constantly in crowded water you will have to get used to rising from the main hatch and producing a bucket at the same time. If you are not stiff-necked enough for this you will have to try another alternative, such as the small mechanical lavatories with plastic bowls. They are becoming less and less expensive and are almost essential in crowded waters. Living as they do at the heart of the family, like a pet St Bernard in a service flat, they must be kept serviced, polished, perfumed and generally pampered if their presence is not to become intolerable. The old argument that it is bad to cut holes in the hull doesn't worry people much these days. See that the installation is professionally perfect and that the sea-cocks are easy to shut off when not in use. To ensure this, the lever of the sea-cock can often be mounted so that in the 'open position' it is impossible to replace the lid over the machine.

On some inland waterways, chemical cans are the rule and any small cruiser owner venturing inland should remember this. One final point concerning pump toilets is that they can be an embarrassment if the boat is dried out.

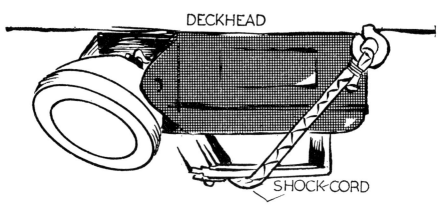

Fig. 10

# Chapter Five

# Handling

THERE is a difference between the ability to sail a boat and the ability to handle one. A slick gybe or a neatly executed tack is good sailing. The barge-master who furls his sails and lets his barge blow down to leeward beam-on until she falls into a berth is handling her.

I have seen a successful offshore racing man, with a stack of cups to his name and a fine reputation in bad weather, who went to pieces when faced by having to sail into a berth alongside—she had to be towed in. To handle a boat means that you must be able to gauge just what she is likely to do when she is drifting, as well as knowing how she'll respond to her rudder under varying combinations of sail, wind and current. The cruiser motoring back to her moorings against wind and tide may suddenly be put into a tricky position by the engine stopping (they do it on you sooner or later). The handler takes a look at the forces and assesses the situation. He will try to judge whether his craft, without the aid of sails, is going to drift into trouble or whether she is safe to leave while he tinkers with the engine. This is the fisherman's way. All too often the yachtsman is sparked into frenzied and often unnecessary activity with anchor or sail.

Handling is another way of enjoying a boat, particularly one so small that long-distance passages and marine touring of the more-days-more-ports sort is out of the question. It takes the panic out of congested rivers, and it is something to take pride in.

Take a half-brick, a length of fish-line and a bottle. Go offshore a short way, lay the bottle-buoy and start learning about your boat. Let her drift without sail and then under jib alone and main alone. Luff her, make sternboards, try seeing how close you can bring up at anchor and try sailing it out. Gybe round the bottle, heave to under various combinations of sail and carry out man-overboard drill. The object of that buoy (a toy balloon is better than a bottle) is that it serves as a 'watch buoy', a marker to help gauge your distances and speed—if you keep on hitting it, it doesn't matter, and there are no anchored craft to spoil your manoeuvres.

A boat sails into trouble far faster than she is likely to drift into it. Pressed hard in a squall an owner tends to hang on like grim death and sail into all kinds of nasty situations when, quite often, the boat with her sails down would probably fare far better and lose less ground.

When the wind's against the tide they rarely balance each other so well that a boat will stay in one spot if she breaks down when under power. Her probable direction of drift will be somewhere between the direction in which the current is bearing her and a point either side of the wind's eye. It is usually far better, if no sail is set at the moment when things go wrong, to turn her a hundred and eighty degrees with the last of the steerage way (if she was going in on the flood) and stem the tide with a following wind.

When wind and tide are together you must either anchor in the first clear space or get a sail set—whichever is the quickest—or there'll be a chance of damage done. On a flood, never discount the idea of running hard ashore on the first sign of trouble—this is in smooth water of course. Be sure too that it is mud and not a rocky lee shore. It sounds drastic but it can save money.

## Sail Handling

Since sails drive, and because the angle of heel and the wind strength are never constant, sail area must be altered constantly.

The foredeck of a small cruiser is a very tiny working area, and without a forehatch where one may stand and work, one may get into the habit of never changing a headsail unless one is driven to it. This is well enough for an afternoon sail, but bad policy offshore. The cruiser must always be under a balanced combination of sails large enough to drive her, but not so great that she has to be sat out or 'held up' by the helmsman. To start out under a small jib and whole main, griping up like a stuck pig to every puff, is *not* good sailing. She may be under-canvased with four rolls in the main, but at least she'll balance.

Reluctance to shift headsails results in people driving dangerously hard in a rising wind, and hoping to get back before the awful task is forced upon them. Yet the job can be made safe and simple just by slowing down the boat—by heaving to under the main and with the tiller lashed up a shade or just by keeping her aflutter until the job is over.

Sitting down is the only safe position on the foredeck of a small yacht. This way one is safe from overbalancing, and the sails can be trapped between the knees while both hands are free for working.

Synthetic cloth in the lighter weights is damnable stuff to control in a smart breeze. It must be bundled up tight for as long as possible, kept in the bag if practicable and kept low on the deck. Never get to leeward of a sail when handling it, especially the synthetics, as they are apt to explode into violent action as soon as the wind has the least chance of getting into the folds. Not only may the sail put you overboard, but flogging hanks can also do serious damage to an eye.

Foredeck work is far easier with a pulpit, no matter how tiny. Rubber shock-cord stretched flat across the deck also makes a good temporary stowage for a sail, and if there is a forehatch to stand in, so much the better. The amount of water that gets below during a sail-change with the hatch open depends largely on the man at the helm, but I have seen at least one boat which had a canvas 'skirt' fitted to the under-side of the hatch so that any water which came aboard only streamed straight down to the cabin sole instead of deluging the forward bunk. In the 22–24-foot cruisers pulpits and proper rails simplify things.

Fig. 11.

The answer to quick hanking is to have well-oiled triggers and no shackles to deal with. Bowlines are preferable for attaching sheets to headsails as they are less likely to part or to injure crew on the foredeck.

When you are transferring the halliard from one sail to another is the critical moment, one jerk and you've lost it. A short rubber becket attached to the pulpit or deck with a spring-hank to snap on to the halliard is worth fitting.

You should rarely need a torch for handling sails in the dark, particularly if the deck and sails are light in colour. As long as the hanks are not snapped on with a twist in them no harm can be done. The halliard can be made fast at its bitter end to a swivel at the foot of the mast (Fig. 11), this is a safeguard against losing the end. Barring the hated miniature shackle pin, there is nothing about the job that a blind man should not be able to do—at least if the layout is correct.

A few small cruisers carry spinnakers and an owner familiar with dinghy spinnakers will have no trouble in handling what is only a slightly larger one. Setting from the bag can be improved upon by setting straight from the forehatch; and the down-haul on the pole can be a simple tent-guy leading to the foredeck and mooring-cleat. Most small cruisers are rather under-canvased in light weather, so spinnakers and big, light genoas are worth their cost over and over again, providing that the owner is wise enough to know when to get back to his snug all-inboard rig. A small cruiser caught in a thunder-squall with a spinnaker aloft is easily over-driven. In such an emergency, the extra weight of a man on the foredeck can cause the boat to gripe up hard and broach to. It might be better (depending upon the circumstances) to abandon the standard procedure and let fly the sheet to empty the spinnaker instead of trying to crawl right forward to get at the tack, but such decisions can only be made on the spot. But *don't* attempt to luff. A spinnaker plastered over the entire fore-triangle will knock her down at once, and it will be well-nigh impossible to take in.

The ex-dinghy sailor will seldom get under way with *too little* sail set on a breezy day. The tendency is always to roll down two or three reefs, set the working jib and battle to hold her up. Small cruisers are short-hulled craft, and if they are sailed on their ear they immerse a great hunk of chine and topsides, which often means that one has to battle with the tiller to keep them from luffing. At the same time they expose the other chine and present a massive area of wind-resistance which has to be shoved bodily to windward somehow. Anyone who has tried to carry a sheet of plywood on a windy day will have some idea of the slowing effect which this is going to have. Reef deeply and sail upright. There will be the 'holes in the wind' when she will be grossly under-canvased, but these are not the moments when things go wrong. Remember, too, that the area of sail which a boat can carry in smooth water is a good deal larger than she can manage outside in a seaway, where waves are both stopping her and lurching her over to leeward. An 18 footer with her twenty-five-square-foot storm-jib may find this plenty big enough in even a moderate blow, but it must be cut as low as possible, too, and the mainsail must still be a good shape when it has five or six rolls in it. It is better to be able to lace down a deep reef. The row of eyelets and the luff and leech cringle mean that a smooth reef can be put in in a hurry when a deep-rolled reef might turn out badly (Fig. 12). It is difficult for an inexperienced owner to imagine the weight of wind in a blow. Even the tiniest scrap of canvas taxes most

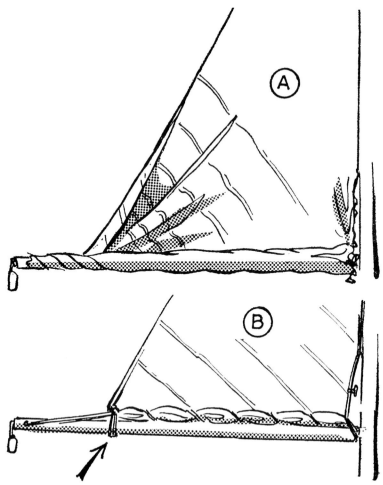

Fig. 12. A deep reef hastily rolled down in the dark can easily be bungled and the result might be something like 'A'. A row of lacing eyelets and tack and clew cringles enable a neater reef to be taken down, 'B'. Note the lashing indicated by the arrow. Without this the sail cannot be properly held down to the boom and the strain will be on the lacing. Booms fitted with a groove for the bolt rope must be laced round the spar instead of under the sail which is the correct method shown above.

men's muscles. Reefing is not an emergency measure to be resorted to only when things begin to get out of hand; it is to the sailing man what a throttle is in a power boat, and it must be easy and often practised.

## Leaving the Mooring

Getting away from a mooring is just basic sailing practice. One must decide in advance which tack is the most favourable and, depending

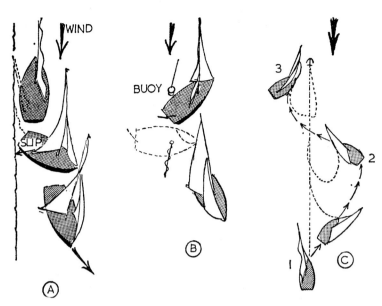

Fig. 13. In sailing away from a quay 'A' the cruiser lies head to wind and all the lines except a slip leading to the stern are cast off. Dropping down-wind from a mooring 'B'. If the buoy is taken aft and the jib is held aback with the mainsail paid right off, the vessel can be turned on her heel. Sailing out an anchor 'C' is often worth trying in a strong breeze when the lack of a winch is felt. Get the boat sailing on one tack by backing the jib and then homing it smartly as she begins to move. The mainsheet must not be pinned in and helm should be up a shade. As she reaches the limit of the tack (2) it will be possible to gather in slack chain and a second short tack usually takes care of the remainder. It is better to leave enough scope of chain out for her to sail over her anchor on the final tack and this enables the crew to take a quick turn and snub it out.

upon tide, of course, be prepared to haul her head off by taking the mooring aft along the weather side and/or backing the jib (Fig. 13b). It is important to see that the cruiser doesn't sail over her own moorings as the bilge keels, or even the rudder, can easily be snagged on underwater lines.

On a breezy day and with an inexperienced person as mate it is better to take the foredeck job and be sure that the mooring pick-up rope is going to be dropped clear, that the buoy isn't going to get hung up around a stanchion and that it is let go at the precise moment when she is filling on the chosen tack. It's easy enough to yell helm orders from forward, but hard to explain how to avert a mooring mix-up when you are aft.

In breezy weather a small cruiser will go away like a greyhound and if the headsail is aback to turn her it may force her over hard before you can reach the tiller. There is always a critical fifty yards or so after leaving a mooring. The yacht is not in trim, she has steerage way, but perhaps not in the direction of the open water, and with a novice at the helm things can go wrong fast. Aim to have the mainsheet either slack or made fast with one single turn, thus if it is necessary to bear away hard the mainsheet can be allowed to run in an instant—which it certainly can't if the sheet is made up with half a dozen turns. Decide on the plan before letting go the mooring and see that the crew knows

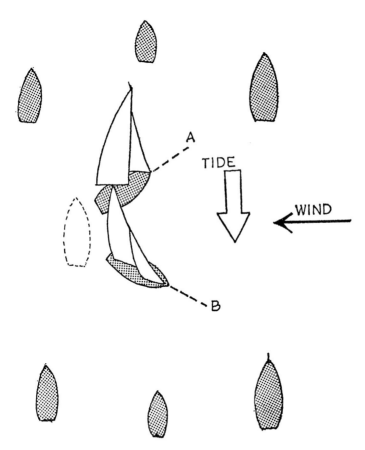

Fig. 14. Although tack 'B' appears to offer more room for clearing the outside line of moored yachts the tide will set her down and she may foul. Tack 'A' offers a choice of luffing a little. Bearing away hard is an alternative, but not always possible in congested moorings.

what to expect (Fig. 14). Remember too that the runaway cruiser, hot from her mooring and aimed at a neighbouring moored craft, will do less damage all round if, when it is a question of either bearing off or luffing up, she is put head to wind. Bearing away in a confined space depends upon three things, getting the mainsheet to run right out at once, having room to move the tiller and possibly getting the jib a-weather. A sharp luff needs only a movement of the tiller. Bearing away means picking up speed, but luffing means losing speed, and the fact that she may not have way enough to go about is less serious.

Most small cruisers respond instantly to the helm as soon as they begin to fall astern. By reversing the tiller (pointing the tiller in the direction that you would like the bows to pay off) the abortive attempt at an emergency tack can more often than not be saved, but the action must be quick or she may pause, fall astern, and then carry on sailing on the same trouble-hunting tack which all the fuss was about.

With wind against tide the cruiser will be lying half wind-rode and half tide-rode and probably rolling like mad. It is inadvisable ever to try setting the mainsail until clear of the mooring or the cruiser will begin to sail wildly to and fro. Set the jib, back it to cast her head in the desired direction, and then let go the mooring. If it is important to turn down wind immediately, hang on to the mooring and walk it back aft on the windward side during which time she will be rapidly spinning her bows down-wind. Let it go as soon as it leads right astern, and then sail clear of the moorings before rounding up to set the main.

## Picking up a Mooring

Picking up a mooring is the beginner's first nightmare, and it's not as simple as the diagrams make it out to be. Success depends upon planning and knowing just what the yacht will do. The small cruiser carries very little way and a long shot at the buoy rarely comes off. The weight of the wind will affect the issue as will a popple or a tide to be contended with.

Practice is the only answer, though many owners shirk it and start the motor as a matter of habit; this is crazy and bad policy. The yacht is primarily a sailing craft and handles best under sail. On the other hand, for a beginner to go at a mooring bald-headed from the first is bad seamanship, let him use his engine (in neutral) and regard it as an insurance. To become really competent practise somewhere else in clear water. Buy some toy balloons, anchor them with string to half-bricks, and keep on practising.

You can approach from leeward and then luff head to wind to take her up to the buoy; or you can come in on a close reach, easing the sheets to slow her as the buoy comes closer (Fig. 15). Then if she appears to be under-shooting, the sheets can be hardened a shade to give her more way. Getting on to the buoy against a fierce tide can be made simple by this trick for the cruiser can be 'crabbed' across the current.

Although a smart luff for the buoy which brings the cruiser up quietly head to wind with the buoy just under her bow is the dream of

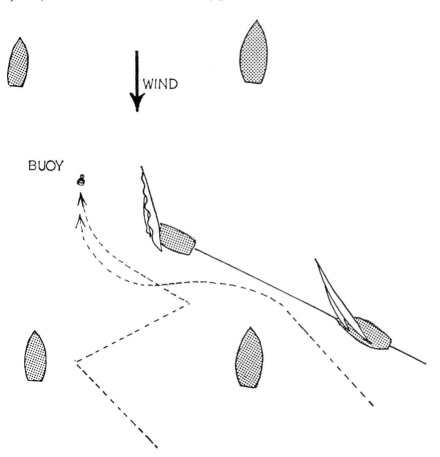

WIND

BUOY

FIG. 15. Dotted lines show two probable attempts to pick up a mooring by approaching closehauled and 'shooting' for it. In each case the approach is spoiled by having to negotiate other moored craft. The alternative is to approach on a close reach and, by playing the sheets and spilling wind, gradually slowing the boat. The advantage of this method is that a dud shot can be rectified by hardening sheets to keep steerageway on the boat.

every yacht-handler, the small light-displacement cruiser carries so little way that this manoeuvre often comes unstuck. Hitting the least popple will stop her almost dead in her tracks, and with way off her there will be some moments of uncertainty when the helmsman is trying to get her to cast off on to a safe tack and gather headway again. The over-estimated luff is less likely to go wrong providing the buoy is brought smartly aboard and the foredeckhand gets a quick turn on a cleat to check headway. It need hardly be pointed out that not only is it unwise to try grabbing the buoy from the cockpit, but having grabbed it, the antics of a boat moored by her tail with all sail set will be more rewarding for the watchers ashore than for the yachtsman on board. If the luff for the buoy looks like failing, pay off at once and sail past with dignity.

It is a good plan to make use of shore marks when making for a mooring across the tide. With both wind and tide together it is easy to misjudge the last few hundred yards to the moorings and end up to leeward and down-tide of it, sometimes within a yard or two of the buoy but fated to miss it despite a last-minute frenzy of short tacking. Take a sight on your own mooring buoy, and watch the shore behind it. As long as your buoy stays fixed against the background you can be sure of making it, but if it begins to cover the shore as though it was under way, then it is time to harden up a bit. In any case sail for your buoy as if aiming to get to windward of it, you can always fall off a bit when you get nearer.

With the wind against the tide there is only one rule. Sail up wind, lower the main (or both in a strong breeze) and run down against the tide. The only time this rule can be disregarded is when the wind is strong and the tide weak or the other way round.

## Handling and Anchoring

Getting away from an anchorage calls for dexterity in handling under various combinations of circumstances. It may be that the shore is close astern, and very little time is left for manoeuvring once the anchor is off the bottom. A jib is a handicap to the man on the foredeck, and if it is possible to leave it lashed up clear of the deck, so much the better.

Once the mainsail is set and the jib hanked on and lashed up clear of the deck by one tier, the anchor should be hauled up fairly smartly to give the helmsman a chance to cast the cruiser's head in the direction of the best tack. This must not be done too soon or the chain or warp will be leading at a wide angle to the weather bow, thus making life harder for the anchor man and probably hauling the bows around on

10. Man overboard. A wife left alone on board to effect a pick up *and* handle the boat is under great strain both physically and emotionally. Before she attempts tricky manoeuvres her first thought must be to put a lifebuoy right into the person's hands.

(*Photo: Yachting Monthly*)

. If a half deflated dinghy is carried on ·ck while on passage, it offers one of the siest and surest ways of getting a man back oard. Even if exhausted he can drag himf into its safety. (*Photo: Yachting Monthly*)

12. Even in the smaller cruisers wind vane self-steering gear has a valuable part to play —more valuable perhaps than in bigger boats with larger crews and therefore more helmsmen to choose from.

(*Photo: Yachting Monthly*)

to the wrong tack just as she breaks out. If this should happen and if there is precious little room to sail clear on that tack, it is far safer to let go the chain again at once, anchoring once more and snubbing her around on to the proper tack.

The man forward is going to be busy getting the anchor aboard, clearing it of mud, lashing it and setting the job. This should never be a two-man job with a three-man crew if the cruiser is so small that weight forward affects steering. The helmsman, as soon as the anchor is off the bottom, must concentrate on getting proper steerageway even at the cost of easing the mainsheet and running a little inshore. Under main alone it is unlikely that a tight windward course can be laid, and if it is vital that the boat is brought hard on the wind from the very start, then, of course, the jib will have to be set before the anchor is broken out. In this case you must control the jib just enough to save the anchor man from being slapped about and snatch it in hard the moment the anchor comes clear of the bottom. Then get her moving and jog her along as slowly as possible until the anchor is on deck otherwise it will be streamed aft under the hull and may damage the skin or foul the twin keels.

With more sea-room astern there is no need to worry about any particular drill, the main is set, the anchor is hauled in and, with the cruiser dropping astern, it is only a matter of putting the helm over to cause her to fall aslant the wind and begin to sail. The helm must then be reversed at once, of course. It sometimes happens that the yacht is lying head to wind and tide with very little room at either side for turning. The usual solution to this problem is to start the motor—the best thing for the beginner to do, perhaps, but not for the man who takes pride in his seamanship. Depending upon the strength of the wind and the behaviour of the cruiser—whether she'll turn fast enough, that is—it may be feasible to haul up and down, set the jib, back it, break out, and, by putting the tiller across *opposite* to the jib as she begins falling astern, pin-wheel on her heel until she is running before the wind. This is something to practise, as it is pretty to watch.

Alternatively she may be 'drudged' clear. Quite simply this is a matter of shortening the anchor until she is dragging it. The tide will be flowing past faster than she is dropping astern so that the rudder can be used to sheer her as needed and keep straight as she falls back into clear waters. The big snag is that this trick rather invites a fouled anchor. If (as it should be) a tripping line is on the anchor, bringing it aboard and using it to tug the anchor out gives the same effect. These tricks may be very big ship stuff and are quite unnecessary with power to hand, but they are fun.

Most small cruisers can be handled reasonably well under mainsail alone—though not sailed to windward, nor too well on a reach until they have full steerageway, but all owners should try sailing under main to get some idea of behaviour. The same goes for handling under the jib.

One of the simplest of all manoeuvres in a sailing craft, and one of the most useful, is heaving to. Most people associate this with bad weather and critical situations. Whether you want breathing space for chart-work or quieter going for a while to prepare food, it is handy to know how to heave to. Basically you have merely to come on the wind with the headsail sheeted to windward. It may be necessary to ease the mainsheet a shade, and in a few cases to lash the tiller slightly a-lee. It is also possible to heave to in some craft under mainsail alone or foresail

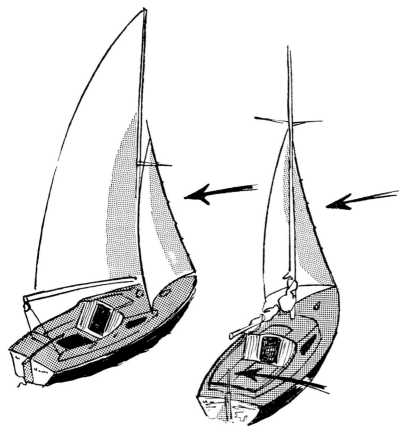

FIG. 16. The cruiser may still sail too fast even with the jib aback when hove-to. Easing the mainsheet and lashing the tiller a shade to leeward might slow her. She may lie-to more quietly under jib alone with the tiller lashed hard to leeward.

alone, lashing the tiller in each case to oppose the thrust of the sail from turning the yacht (Fig. 16). In fact, heaving to in a small cruiser through force of bad weather isn't entirely advisable unless the sail areas are very small and only then if you have experimented beforehand to get some idea of how she'll behave. Lying close-hauled and without appreciable headway, small, light craft are knocked over easily by sudden heavy squalls and with a sea running they cannot be prevented from alternately paying off and luffing up. Bad-weather handling is dealt with more fully in another chapter.

## Working to Windward

Sailing to windward in a fresh breeze demands a well balanced boat. As she heels down in a squall she may gripe hard up into the wind and temporarily get out of control. Then it is far better to hold the mainsheet dinghy fashion, less from any need to avert a capsize than to be able to check away (i.e. pay out) an inch and restore control if she begins to gripe. Working up through a crowded anchorage this is something to watch carefully. Moreover, if it should become necessary to bear away in a hurry to avoid some other craft, checking off the mainsheet is the only way this can be done.

When going about it is bad policy for the helmsman to make a rapid tack. The crew working the sheets is having to balance to the altering direction of heel and get in his lee sheet with a winch of limited power. Watch him and give him time to do his job. Without a winch he is severely handicapped, but even with one he needs help.

Cockpits are of necessity small and crews are bulky, and the less experienced they are the more room they need. Some sort of going-about drill is important. For the man and wife team this may be just a matter of letting the less experienced of the two take care of the sheets, but in a fresh breeze even the small headsails of the eighteen footer are a struggle to sheet home hard, and a woman may lack the strength to do it properly. One simple drill is for her to let go the lee sheet as the boat comes around, taking the tiller as the helmsman leaves it and begins hauling in the new lee sheet. He then moves back, lifting the tiller and taking over again as she moves back to her perch to windward. The hinged tiller which can be lifted is essential unless the rudder is hung on the transom so that a long tiller won't project into the cockpit space.

With a crew of three the sheet handling is a simple matter and the helmsman has only to move himself from side to side.

Nothing is more important than the helmsman's job when working uphill. Offshore, navigation must go on, but only to the extent that the navigator records position and gives warning of possible danger. He must never cripple the helmsman by tying him to a course line.

In anything of a breeze and with a lumpish little sea raised by wind against tide, it won't be possible to sail so close to the wind. Each sea will stop her dead in her tracks so she has to fall off to pick up way and make another slow luff. In such conditions a free full-and-by course which keeps the boat moving is better. These little craft cannot be pushed hard. If you hang on to sail they will stagger and lurch, with undue rudder work and a large, exposed area of bilge to windward.

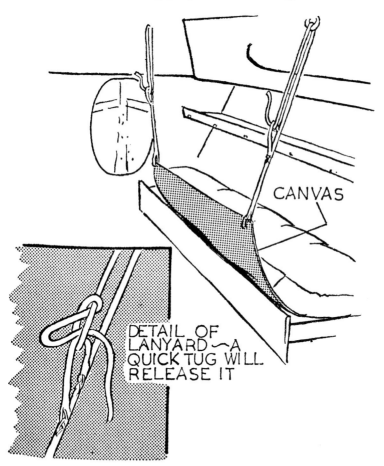

FIG. 17. Canvas weather screens can be fitted to bunks, making them usable at sea and safer for keeping bedding away from a wet cabin sole. The bottom edge of the screen is fastened with screws and a batten to the outboard edge of the bunk.

71

13. The inflatable boat while being absolutely safe is a problem to tow in a smart breeze and often becomes completely airborne. It is important to keep the painter as short as possible.

14. For weekend creek-cruising a sailing tender such as this GRP lugsail dinghy built by E.C. Landamore of Wroxham offers the added fun of exploring still further and more remote reaches.

15. Conventional pram dinghies allow better weight carrying size for size with a stem-type dinghy, but they may cause considerable drag.

When a boat falls into a trough or hits a sea she loses a lot of way, and an instant later the thrust of her sails will make her try to luff. The good windward helmsman senses this before it happens and pulls her off a shade just in time. This isn't to say that she should be allowed to lose ground, but she must be kept tramping the whole time. It is useless to point high and get nowhere.

The crew's weight must be kept to windward down below. Hence before any offshore passage is attempted, which will involve rest periods below, the berths may need to be equipped with leeboards of some kind so that only the weather berths are in use going to windward. Canvas lace-up bunk sides are adequate, but however they are arranged they must be possible to detach instantly by one tug at a slip-knot (Fig. 17).

In hard going, it may be difficult to persuade anyone of a nervous disposition to stay below. The noise and motion suggest that the cruiser is on the point of capsize and it will be a very weary man who can sleep through them.

## On the Mud

There cannot be a yachtsman living who hasn't run his ship aground at some time. The small cruiser spending most of her time in creeks and rivers is constantly doing it.

If you run on a sandbank of unknown shape and extent, possibly in some estuary, you will usually have to try to get off in the same direction as you went on. If the bottom shelves very gradually and the ebb is running fast the case is pretty hopeless and the only thing to do with a small craft is to turn the whole crew overboard to lighten her at once and walk her back.

Will the wind help or hinder? This is the first consideration. If you run slap up a bank with a following wind it quite obviously won't help. Get sail off her right away, push her round, and either motor off or take out the kedge in the dinghy, if you have one, and haul her into water deep enough for you to make sail again.

Most strandings occur during a beat up a channel when one tack is held for a shade too long. If the bank is fairly steep it is easy enough to push the bows through the eye of the wind and get the jib aback. This, of course, tends to drive her heel harder aground and if the crew were all forward pushing, their weight back in the cockpit may glue her so firmly to the bank that she still refuses to sail off. Let draw the jib and send them forward again.

Quite often a boat can be skimmed over the shallows after touching by heeling her so far over that her draft is lessened, but this trick

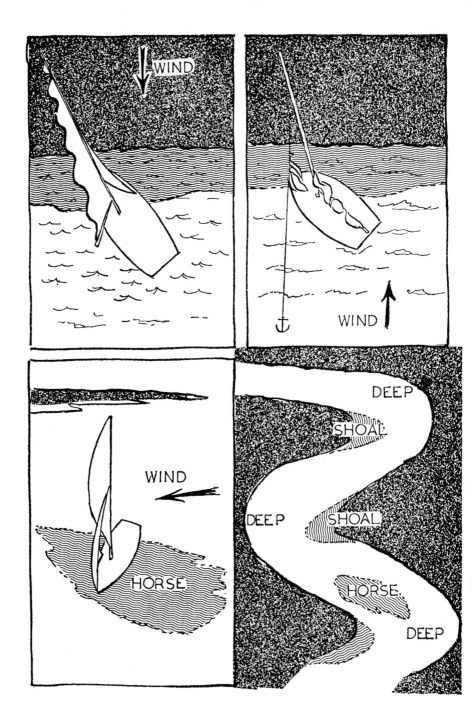

doesn't work with the twin-keeler which increases the draft of her leeward keel as she heels, the opposite is true in this case, the more upright the better.

Larger yachts are compelled to follow a more involved drill: using kedges, rocking (sugging) to loosen the hold of the mud around the keel, and so on. For the very small cruiser in danger of sticking on a falling tide as she makes her way up some creek it is far better to have one member of the crew all ready in a lifejacket and ready to push off than it is to follow any big-ship routine—better still to use a leadline.

## Man-overboard Drill

'Gybe at once' is the expected reaction of every seasoned—or even unseasoned—yachtsman to 'Man overboard'. It is a good thing to have an instinctive reaction in a crisis, and gybing is often the right and always a reasonable thing to do, even if, in certain circumstances, it is not the best.

With the yacht on a broad reach or close-hauled the gybe is the right action to take, *but* if it is to succeed in bringing the cruiser back to the point where the man went overboard, you must gybe *at once*. The object of any manoeuvre to pick something up is to go down-wind so that you can luff up.

With a man in the water there are two problems. One, how long can he stay afloat? Two, how soon can you pick him up? The point I want to make most urgently here is that any inexpert boat-handler who cannot pick up his mooring without a good deal of moustache chewing, *must* get some sort of lifebuoy, lifejacket or other form of buoyancy into

---

FIG. 18. A boat should blow off if she touches a weather shore but if the tide is ebbing she may need some pushing. Trim weight to conform with the deepest part of the hull, i.e. weight aft if the forward ends of the keels are on and weight forward if a single fin-keel is touching further aft. Aground on a lee shore, either an anchor must be taken off or the bows turned manually and the boat motored off. Running an engine astern may be effective in moderate or light weather, but the small auxiliary may lack power astern in a fresh onshore wind. All sail must be off and ready to hoist again quickly. On a falling tide quick action—getting the crew over the side—is usually the only certain means of getting off, especially if the bank is a gradual slope. Running aground on a mid-stream bank a boat may be lucky and bump over, but if she sticks it is better to try and get her off the same way she went on unless the shape of the bank is known. Shallow water in a winding creek is usually found on bends as shown in the sketch. Deep water is most likely to be on the outer side of the bend.

the hands of the man in the water *before* he begins a series of attempted rescues. This may be a simple matter of sailing past close and dropping it to him, or even putting it into his hands.

The sad fact about most life-rings or kapok horse-shoes is that if you throw them and miss, the wind whisks them out of the person's reach at once. A small drogue (like a miniature parachute) attached to the buoy will guard against this.

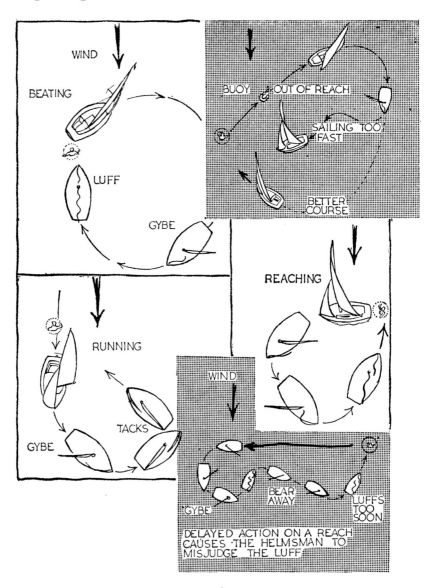

So much depends upon the nature of the person in the water, the time of year and whether he can swim strongly, and, oddly enough, upon the relationship between him (or her) and the helmsman. A man may be so horrified to see his wife in the water that his judgement is badly impaired, but a casual acquaintance, although in as much danger, may leave him emotionally calmer and better able to cope.

This all boils down to making a split-second decision during that first instinctive gybe: whether to gamble on a shoot or divert the attention in getting a lifebelt ready. Ideally, of course, a lifebelt should have been thrown as the man went over, but more often than not he will be well astern before the penny drops, and it is well nigh impossible for a helmsman to struggle to his feet, pull the buoy free from its (rubber cord) lashing and manage to shy it accurately around the backstay. There *should* be a second buoy ready to hand, but how many yachts are so equipped?

It is debatable whether a lifeline should be attached to the buoy that is thrown. Personally, I think not. Anything which interferes with throwing is bad. Seconds mean yards when you are sailing fast, and a half-dozen yards might as well be as many miles to a dazed man in the water. Another risk is that the line will drag the buoy out of the man's grasp before the yacht can be slowed. Ideally the buoy should be outboard and held by one peg, and there should be another buoy ready for a second shot as soon as there is a second chance.

Two people, one of them in the water, are dependent upon each other for calmness. If there is a third hand he must be given the sole job of keeping his eye upon the man in the water, since a head among

---

FIG. 19. To bring the cruiser back to the man in the water a gybe must be carried out immediately if she was close-hauled. Upper shaded inset: the approximate delay in thinking time if the lifebuoy is to be thrown before moving the tiller. Note that the first attempt at luffing after the gybe is made too soon and that the buoy is beyond the man's reach.

On a run, each second puts the boat further to leeward and it is immaterial whether she gybes or hardens sheets since she must make a tack to get back to her man in any case. With a spinnaker set she will sail some distance before she can get it down and beat back, but this must be done. It will be vital to keep a close watch on the man if he's not to be lost to sight.

A little delay on a reach also makes the gybe and luff technique impossible. Carried out instantly the boat may arrive back at the man in the water, but depends more upon speed at the time and condition of sea since these small craft lose way rapidly. Long delay in gybing may cause the helmsman to make a false luff.

77

white crests is only visible for a quarter of the time and is soon lost to view and a flag marker buoy might then save a life.

The manoeuvres shown in Fig. 19 show the basic action in handling the ship. In every case the object is to stop the yacht. It is often argued that it is dangerous to come up to windward of a man because a hull lurching down to leeward can force him underneath it. If the yacht cannot be brought head to wind alongside, and time is short, it is probably better to make a grab rather than try for the copy-book shot. It is extremely hard to haul a man inboard from the water, especially if he is exhausted, and if he is on the low leeward side the job is a great deal easier. The yacht may well begin sailing with no hand on the tiller (remember to cast off the sheets) and it may be necessary to simply hang on and wait until she luffs of her own accord.

At night, the risk is more than twice as serious. The safety-line is the first rule, more important even than wearing a lifejacket since the stable-door adage holds true enough. More important than having them aboard is to have them actually and permanently in the cockpit lockers where they can be found, and then insisting that nobody, not even the skipper, shall leave the cabin even for a moment at night without wearing one and hanking himself to the ship. Lifejackets may be enough by day, but the man overboard at night has to be found before he can be rescued. Use lifejackets as well by all means, since they double the chance of survival, and give one time to handle the yacht but lifelines must come first and foremost, particularly when you leave the cockpit to crawl along the deck.

Fine nights are no safer than uncomfortable ones. This is because bad weather makes men cautious and smooth water lulls them into carelessness. Like being run down and other accidents, falling over- board is one of those things which it is easier to imagine happening to someone else. For this reason one is apt to fear for the man at work on the foredeck while quite nonchalantly standing on the cockpit locker to reach the boom outhaul. We are *all* vulnerable. The fine night at sea is a sneak, for it robs the situation of any hint of danger.

Quite apart from risks of working on deck there are other more treacherous situations which rarely appear so dangerous. The person who has clung to the lee-side of the cockpit for an hour or more attend- ing to a mutinous stomach tends to be ignored in the dark. He grows feeble and ceases to care—it only needs a sudden lurch to coincide with his latest unhappy convulsion and the thing has happened. I make no excuse for mentioning another natural risk—one peculiar to men when indulging a comfortable though unconventional male ritual. The only safe alternative is an old jam-tin reserved for the night watch, who must have strict injunctions to use it when needed. If a man *must* relieve himself over the side, he should wrap an arm around a shroud or the standing backstay if there is one.

I have also seen a man go over the side while emptying the gash bucket—he let go his grip in order to capsize the empty bucket to wash it out, the yacht lurched, and he was over. It was daylight, but rough weather, and it took three attempts to pick him up.

No small yacht should sail offshore at night without a lifebuoy which is equipped with an automatic light and which can be seized and thrown *instantly*. One sees lifebuoys lashed to the backstay or held firmly on the coachroof, far too firmly to be released without a struggle. The water-activated light float calcium flares, too, are often lashed in such a way that the tangle of lines and lashings guarantees that they would foul up at night. Electric battery lights are safer, although not visible by day like calcium flares. On the other hand one ought not to have to give a hearty tug to tear the container free from its tab.

The chances of being picked up in the dark are often slim. Even by day it is hard to see a man's head in the water in any sort of sea. A light on the buoy will mean that it will be seen whenever the yacht and the buoy are both on the tops of waves at the same instant—a large flare can be seen better, of course, but it burns for a comparatively short time while an electric type may last for as long as twenty hours or even more. Very costly American makes such as the Guest Light have a high-power flashing light, which lasts a very long time.

Provided that the buoy is got away quickly and the night is clear with a calm sea, normal day-time man-overboard drill is possible. In a seaway and with only one man left in the cockpit it may be necessary to follow a different and seemingly hazardous drill. First it is vital to continue to steer straight ahead on the same course until the yacht can be properly put about under full control. Simply to chuck her about in a panic may mean that you lose all sense of direction at once, and find yourself sailing to and fro, staring and shouting in a nightmare of incompetence. By sailing straight ahead and then going about and sailing straight back on the reciprocal course the chances of finding your man are increased. There was one instance of a man lost overboard at night and not missed until two hours later, the ship returned exactly on her course and picked him up. He was extremely lucky.

A yacht which is running is in a more difficult position. She will have to beat back, and if the regulation gybe cannot be made at once then she too will have to try working back along a reciprocal *average* course. If a man can be spared to keep his eyes fixed on the spot, so much the better, but on such small cruisers it's very unlikely that he can. As soon as the yacht comes on the wind she must begin to beat back making

16. *Above*. The gently shelving shore may take a sharp plunge towards low water mark, particularly on the outside of a bend in a river. Anchoring close to such a spot might result in either a dragged anchor or going aground at a precarious angle.

17. *Below*. A quiet creek and a sheltered anchorage? High tide appearances are deceptive. Before choosing a berth it is essential to check the nature of the bottom. 18. The same creek at low water. Steep banks, stumps and soft mud. A sounding stick consisting of a cheap, jointed bamboo fishing pole is ideal for prodding around for a level berth.

short tacks of equal length—even if you have to time them by stop-watch.

If you arrive at the place where the man was lost, or as near to it as you can judge, the fact that you cannot see or hear anything need not mean you are too late. If you heave to and take all the way off the yacht, there will be less noise from the water and a better chance of hearing a cry. For this reason it is probably unwise to down sail and immediately start the engine. This certainly gives you better manoeuvrability but it prevents you from using the sense of hearing so valuable at night and increases the risk to the man in the water if by accident you should pass too close to him. It is sound sense to fasten a whistle to the lifebuoy.

Don't use torches any more than you can help. The natural reaction is to begin flashing in all directions thereby completely ruining your night vision.

## The Dinghy

No matter how much a small cruiser is scaled down in her fittings and design, two things defy reduction: the size of bunks and the size of the dinghy.

Contact with the shore calls for either beaching or boatwork. Thirty stone of crew demands a boat big enough to carry it in safety, no matter how large or small the parent ship. Since towing at sea is not a wise general policy and a conventional dinghy cannot be carried on so small a deck, you can only choose between inflatable or collapsible dinghies.

Rubber dinghies are absolutely safe. They are light and they take up very little room when deflated, but there are several disadvantages. They are rather expensive—and it is important that you buy the best and not a toy. They cannot be inflated quickly unless you use an air bottle each time, and they are too light to tow in a breeze since they are apt to take off and, with the wind aft, can come aboard on top of the helmsman. One of the worst disadvantages is that they are almost impossible to row against a fresh breeze; but let me stress again that they are wonderfully safe.

A folding dinghy can be used safely if it is large enough. The very small sizes, some of them under six and even little more than four feet long are only suitable in safe conditions. To use one as a tender for all kinds of running around in all weather is apt to be very dangerous. They are easily swamped and very difficult to row in even the slightest chop. On the other hand they are so obviously unsafe that people automatically take more precautions.

When a three-man crew goes ashore for the evening, an overloaded dinghy seems rather a lark. But when they come back late at night across a choppy stretch of water and with no help at hand it is quite another matter. One is apt to set off to 'see how we get on'. No one likes a shuttle-service late at night especially if it involves a half-hour row. We all make this gamble at some time or other. We can only provide ourselves with a reasonable size of dinghy and try not to be too foolish.

Folding boats can be towed in moderate weather, but they, too, tend to take to the air in a breeze and in a seaway. On the other hand they are quicker to erect and can be got aboard under way quite easily.

It is in any case rare to find a good folding dinghy on the market today and towing any dinghy of any type is to be avoided except for very short passages in settled weather. Conditions can deteriorate quickly and the antics of a dinghy astern can become an added burden at a time when other matters are becoming pressing. Light dinghies tend to flip and heavier ones not only squat deep as speed increases with the wind but they cause heavy drag. In a steep following sea a dinghy should be towed on twin painters, one from either quarter but even if the time honoured trick of streaming a warp from the stern of the dinghy, to check its wave crest rushes, is resorted to it is almost certain to give trouble.

## Learning to Sail

For a new owner who is starting completely from scratch it is better to master the basics of sailing by learning in a dinghy. Like driving or riding a bicycle, 80 per cent of the art must become instinctive; the wind shifts momentarily and the helmsman reacts and moves the tiller accordingly, without even being aware that he has done so.

To learn from scratch in the cruiser is easier in some respects because the novice doesn't have to worry about balancing the boat, moreover, the cruiser responds more slowly than a dinghy and this gives him time to think and act. On the other hand, mistakes can be costly. A badly judged tack can result in collision perhaps with some moored craft, whereas in a dinghy it would merely be a matter of fending off with one hand.

Learning from scratch in a cruiser usually means a much greater dependence on the engine. The cautious novice motors clear of everything before hoisting his sails and he stows them again long before he would otherwise need.

In the UK there is a network of teaching establishments unified by the Royal Yachting Association certificate scheme, which covers all types of sailing. Accordingly a beginner can graduate from basics to the Yachtmaster Coastal certificate or the Yachtmaster Ocean if so minded.

Most owners will read, attend night school classes and a basic sailing course, thereafter going it alone in their own boat or as crew in a friend's boat until they feel ready to take more advanced steps.

What is of most importance is to realise from the start that there will never come a time when everything has been learned and that there is no such thing as 'just learning enough for what I want to do'. A boat on the open sea takes whatever the elements have in mind to hand out and it matters not whether her skipper is an Extra Master or a first-time-afloater, the demands have to be met.

## Skippers Only

Trouble-free sailing is largely achieved by thinking ahead as a matter of habit. Things rarely seem to go wrong singly: an accidental gybe, a jam in the mainsheet, a wild luff which loses a sail-bag overside—and in the ensuing fracas to pick it up the ship is run ashore. A chapter of accidents like that is no exaggeration, and yet most of it was due to bad management.

Embark upon no manoeuvre without first looking ahead for possible snags. Plan ahead the whole time. If the motor misses a beat and then resumes running smoothly, cast off a couple of sail-tyers, coil a heaving line up again, or check that the anchor is easy to clear away. It is a habit of mind, and one which eliminates half the scrambles of sailing. Orderliness, too, pays off handsomely: one warp always coiled, stopped with breaking stuff and easy to get at; the boat hook ready to grab, at least one fender handy if not the rest—and so on.

Besides planning and order, cultivate calm. Most men on their own stay reasonably controlled in a spot of bother, but give them a wife or a crew and they feel that a performance is called for. The old saying, 'If in danger or in doubt, shout and scream and rush about,' is too true to be really funny. No matter how small the vessel a hysterical skipper is a crime. One order repeated only if it hasn't been heard, no sarcasm and no heroics. The quiet of an anchorage broken by the yelps of a big man in a tiny boat makes one shudder. Keep the voice down and stay cool, then, if something really merits a bellow you have an unexpected shot in your locker. Don't try to do everything yourself, even if you could do it better and faster, or your crew will let you get on with it and stay half-trained. Explain what you plan to do and then do just that thing—if a change of plan is forced upon you then say so at once. Make

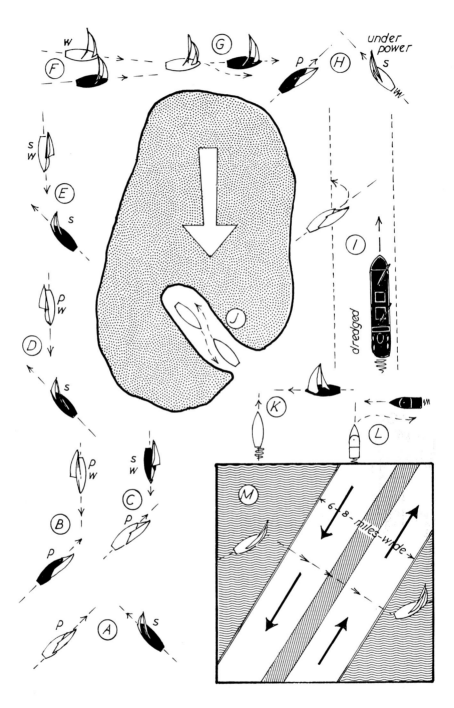

decisions and stick to them as closely as possible and then, if the hunch doesn't pay off don't embark upon a course of humble apology—even a two-man crew must have trust in the skipper's judgement. Be distinct and logical. Don't say 'To starboard' meaning put the tiller to port, either point, or say 'Port your helm' if you want it that way, and finally, learn to trust the crew when they're in charge and you are below or else don't blame them if they do something wrong, ultimately it's the skipper's fault.

### Additional Notes on Handling

*Avoiding Collision:* It is assumed that the basic rules are known. Remember that starting an auxiliary engine is to assume the role of a power vessel, and thus the rules of behaviour for power in relation to sail or other power craft will apply. Yachts racing are by courtesy given right of way by other yachts not racing except where this is unreasonable or likely to create a confusing situation. Remember that, no matter what actual rights a vessel may have, avoiding collision is the aim. A rigid adherence to a right of way may have to go by the board as a last resort if the giving way vessel is under difficulty in complying. Right of sail over power is limited by common sense. Furthermore, and this is very important, in confined waters or buoyed channels a large powered vessel may have sovereign right of way according to area rulings, as for example Southampton Water and its approaches come under the Southampton Harbour Board by-laws.

Unfortunately the rule that power gives way to sail is one of the few things which the beginner seems to remember and many seek to enforce it without realising their danger. A large ship cannot stop suddenly even with her engine going full astern, nor can she alter course as quickly as a small yacht. She is forced to keep up a speed which gives her proper steerage-way and this alone carries her onward at a rate which makes it impossible to pin-wheel in and out of a fleet of small craft. At close quarters vision is very limited ahead from a

---

Fig. 20. A. Starboard tack (black) has right of way. B. Black on port has R.O.W. over white, to windward, on port. C. Black on starboard has R.O.W. over white on port tack. D. Black on starboard has R.O.W. over white on port. E. Both on starboard but white is windward boat and must give way. F. White is the windward boat and must give way. G. White is the overtaking vessel and must give way. H. White is on starboard but because she has her engine running (driving) she becomes a powered vessel and must give way. I. Yacht must give way to a vessel restricted by her draft in a dredged channel. J. Both alter course to starboard. K. Black is under sail and has R.O.W. over white which is under power. L. White has the other vessel on *her* own starboard bow and must give way. M. Separation lanes; yacht must cross at right angles or as nearly so as possible and give way to big ship traffic.

position on the bridge, and last-minute alterations of course by some yacht tacking across her bows may not be seen.

Buoyage of dredged channels leading to big ports indicate where the deep water lies and small craft seldom need to stick to the deep water channels. Even when local by-laws do not enforce right of way for big ships it is in the interests of the yachtsman's safety to shape a course under the stern of the large vessel.

Alterations in course must be made in good time and with clear decision where necessary. There is nothing more confusing to the pilot of a big ship than tacking under her bows.

*Handling:* Sail a small cruiser like a dinghy but navigate her like a ship. On moorings, a shallow-draft boat will lie to the wind as the tide slacks, sooner than a deep-draft hull. Don't set sail on the mooring when the wind and tide are against each other, or at right angles. Never carry lee helm, i.e. small main and big jib causing the yacht to bear away if the tiller is released. Don't boom out the jib when running if she is rolling badly in a following sea, she may become unmanageable. A foreguy from boom to bow may avert a gybe, but never use a line which won't break at a pinch should you gybe. On the wind don't pin in the sheets racing fashion, pointing high is less important than sailing a little free but faster in a sea. 'Luff in a puff, keep her full in a lull.' Don't be a slave to the burgee, you can't see it in the dark. Use the rudder as little as possible and use it slowly. If the yacht gets in stays and begins to fall astern, reverse the helm, i.e. point the tiller in the direction you wish the bows to fall off.

Never tack close to a lee shore. Sail around twice and anchor once. Notice how other yachts are lying before you sail to pick up the mooring. Never try to grab it over the stern. Pick it up and take a turn at once, haul in the slack afterwards. Wind and tide at right angles; down sails the moment the buoy is aboard and fast. At sea, never let go with both hands unless you are sitting on the deck. Never get 'in a mess' with halliards, coil, clear away and stow as you go. Don't send an inexperienced hand to the foredeck sailing fast to windward, run her off and give him a quiet sail.

*Dinghies:* No small dinghy of conventional type can be regarded as a lifeboat. A round-bilge dinghy with sharp bow must be eight feet long to carry three persons in choppy water. With pram bow and flat bottom it can be six to six and a half feet long.

All hard construction dinghies must have sufficient permanently fixed buoyancy in them to support the full passenger load in the water should the boat be swamped. There should also be a bailer, permanently secured, with which the boat, aided by her buoyancy, can be bailed sufficiently to allow one man aboard to complete the job. At night there should also be an anchor and line, also an electric torch. These requirements are based upon the very alarmingly high rate of dinghy-tender accidents, most of which are due to the lack of such precautions.

*Chapter Six*

# Anchoring, Beaching, Mooring, Reduction to Soundings

SMALL cruisers fall betwixt and between when it comes to anchoring. Many main yacht anchorages are too deep and too exposed for really little craft. The slightest breeze starts them jumping around, and passing motor-boats can make life hell. There is also the critical business of getting ashore. The small dinghy carried by these yachts is not to be relied on for a long row in any but calm conditions. Any chance of a fouled anchor becomes more troublesome, too, if there is no anchor winch nor enough deck space for heaving and 'hanging off' (to be dealt with later).

A suitable anchorage must therefore have a maximum of three or, at the outside, four fathoms of water at high tide, reasonable shelter, a pitch well clear of power traffic, and within close reach of the shore or a landing of some sort. This all boils down to a position just outside the low-water mark in most waters, and choice of ground means care with chart and leadline. Big tidal ranges are a separate problem.

It is something of a guide to note the types of craft already moored there. Big, deep-draft yachts along the edge of the fairway and small keel boats and cruisers edging the shallows. The leadline is still important, because the inshore line of craft may well be on drying moorings or the soundings may rise abruptly from three or four fathoms to a drying bank. With a large-scale chart or harbour plan, a fair idea of where to lie can be planned in advance. It may not be possible to use the chosen spot when you get there, but at least there is something to aim for. The soundings (which may be shown tinted) show whether the shore is steep-to and the underlined figures give drying heights (Fig. 21). Charts always tend to make the space seem smaller than it really is, and the creek which looks impossibly narrow is apt to grow into a wide sheet of water by the time you arrive. This is a common snare. If you arrive at dead low water on a big spring tide the scene might be very different again.

If you aim to lie afloat at low water you must first calculate the level to which the tide on the day concerned is likely to fall—chart datum figures deal with low water ordinary springs and this means that there will be times at neaps when there is more water at low tide than the

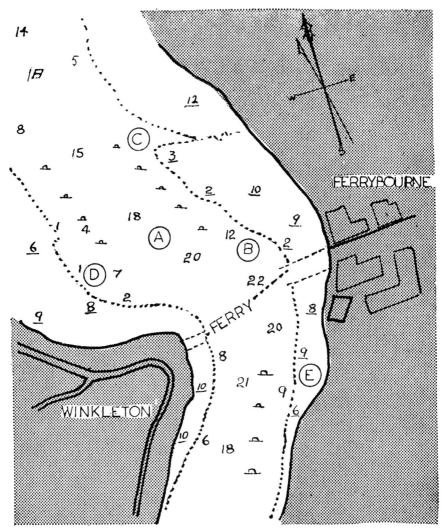

FIG. 21. Anchoring at 'A' puts the cruiser right in the fairway in the main tidal streams where there will be uneasy movement when wind is over tide. 'B' will also be in a choppy position due to the direction of the stream following the outside of the bend. At 'C' she will be a long way from the landing if the foreshore is mud and exposed to a wide 'fetch' of sea in a sou'westerly breeze. 'D' is better on some counts except that the drying bank is steep (note the change from seven feet to drying eight in a comparatively short distance) and she will have to be watched lest she swing ashore and ground at an awkward angle. There will also be a tidal back-eddy, and it would be risky to use a Fisherman-type anchor which might be fouled up here. Position 'E' is on an even steeper bank where she would dry out completely and pound in anything of a breeze.

chart shows, and other times—such as at equinoctial springs—when there may be even less.

If it is dead low water you obviously know whether there is enough water there for you to lie afloat—you'll go aground if there isn't. If it is dead high water, a cast of the lead will show how much scope of chain to let go. If there is, say, four fathoms, and the tide-table shows a height for that day of only two fathoms above chart datum, then obviously there will be enough water and to spare, but since we are trying to tuck into a snug shallow-water berth we must work to rather finer limits. This means understanding how the tides work and how to establish just what depth of water there will be in any particular spot and at any particular time. This matter is dealt with under the heading 'Reductions to Soundings' later in this chapter.

Without a large scale chart and some idea of the sea-bed contour, you may find your chosen spot fine for your ship, but only if she can stay in that precise spot, which isn't likely. Having let go the anchor and settled back on the scope, the yacht may be in very shallow water, or again the spot where the sounding was taken may be on the side of a steep underwater hillside, so that by the time the anchor is let go you may have drifted back into very deep water. The moral is always to take an approach line of soundings, three at least, and anchor where the bottom is reasonably flat and the scope of the swing embraces a circle of water deep enough to float the yacht.

If you make a mistake, and as a consequence are dried out for an hour or two, it will be no hardship in such a small boat, particularly if she is a twin-keeler, but it might delay a start or mean a muddy business getting back aboard in the dark. There are more sinister pit-falls dealt with under 'Beaching'.

The scope of chain or anchor-line is traditionally supposed to be 'depth of water at high water multiplied by three'. This scope was for the heavy fisherman's anchor and it was the *minimum* scope under normal conditions. Most patent anchors such as the C.Q.R. and Danforth should be given a shade more scope, about four times the depth and there should be enough chain in the locker to allow for veering twice the accepted minimum if the weather is bad. Some larger yachts have laid to a ten to one scope and still dragged, so the very small cruiser, which cannot carry much chain, has all the more reason to stick to shallow water.

As a guide to anchor weight, the size for a 25 footer for example will be about 25 lb for a C.Q.R. or 30 lb for a Fisherman type, with around fifteen fathoms of $\frac{1}{4}$-in. or $\frac{5}{16}$-in. (thickness of link metal) short link galvanised chain. Many craft stick to a terylene warp which has two fathoms of $\frac{5}{16}$-in. chain on the anchor end to add weight and protect it

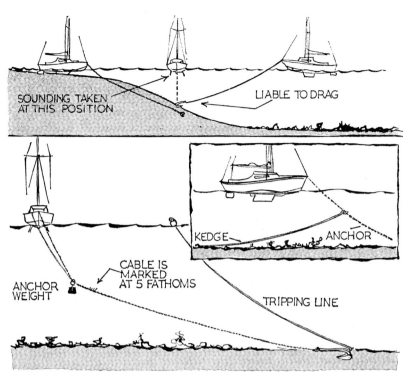

Fig. 22. Take care not to anchor on a steep-to bank if there is the least likelihood of the yacht lying offshore. She may drag her anchor into deeper water and fail to hold. Mooring with the aid of a kedge: make the kedge warp fast to the main cable and then pay out sufficient extra scope to take the kedge warp well below the keel. The lower sketch shows a cruiser at anchor with a tripping line bent on to the crown of the anchor and an anchor weight lowered one third of the way down the cable. Use of the weight minimises sharp snubbing in a seaway and permits lying to the minimum scope. The tripping line enables the anchor to be freed if it fouls a mooring or obstruction on the seabed. But be warned, a tripping line can also foul your rudder.

against sharp rocks. This has a lot in its favour: it is light and more of it can be carried, but in a blow it is harder to haul in because synthetic fibres are so slippery. By choosing plaited terylene you will partly overcome this trouble. The length can well be more than fifteen fathoms. This only permits three to one anchoring in five fathoms, with no reserve for hard weather. While it is always better to anchor in shallower water, there are plenty of times when you may have no choice about it. Therefore for cruising, especially on the South and West Coasts, twenty fathoms should be the minimum. There should also be a lighter kedge two-thirds the weight of the main anchor, and another twenty fathoms of say 1½-in. yacht-grade sisal. If you choose synthetic fibre instead of sisal, don't decide on the size because of its equivalent breaking-strain, for it will be so thin that it will be almost impossible to haul in against any weight of wind or tide.

One of the finest guarantees of a good night's rest is an anchor-weight. This is simply a weight which can be lowered down the anchor-warp or chain to a position well below the hull. It greatly increases the holding power of the anchor by directing the pull at a lower angle, and it reduces the tendency to snub and sheer a vessel in a tideway lying to

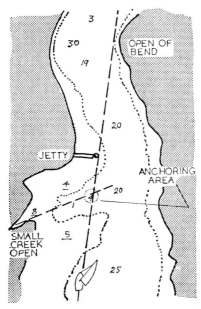

FIG. 23.

her full scope. The 'Chum' anchor-weight traveller marketed by Gibson (534 Gorgie Road, Edinburgh) is a ready-made bit of gear which anyone planning to cruise in unknown waters would be well advised to take along. For a pocket cruiser I should advise a 14-lb weight and a Chum traveller, lowered about two and a half fathoms down the cable.

Handling at the time of letting go naturally varies according to circumstances. You should plan your approach to a crowded anchor-age before you reach it. When you have studied the chart and chosen your anchorage, rough transits will give a guide to the selected spot. They might, for instance, be: A jetty open of the next bend in the river, sail until the small creek to port opens up. This will be the spot to begin looking for a space and taking soundings (Fig. 23).

Although it seems foolish to prescribe a course of action more befitting a twenty-tonner, the broad principles hold good for any size of craft, and in practice amount only to a long, careful sizing up of the situation as you approach. For instance, sail in and have a look, then sail around and come in ready to let go. This simple habit saves a lot of trouble. It may be high water with the ebb just beginning. The moored yachts will have swung, but all their slack cable will still be ranged out along the bottom *down tide*. To anchor too close astern of one of them

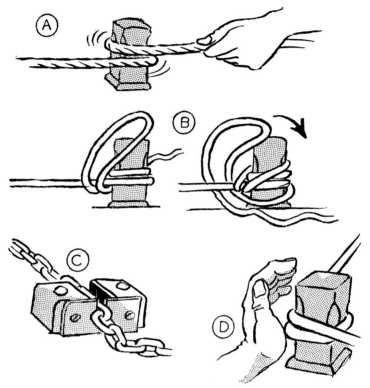

Fig. 24. While an anchor winch is considered unnecessary on small cruisers, in a strong wind and sea, getting in the anchor can become a tricky matter. The warp will be alternately slack and then bar taut as the cruiser sheers. Taking a turn 'A' must be done quickly and with the fingers well clear, especially with Terylene warps which may surge around the post. 'B' shows a method of making fast which, unlike many knots, never becomes difficult to release. On a windy day, handling chain without a winch is even more difficult and dangerous to fingers. A simple snubber shown at 'C' is worth fitting. The correct safe method of holding the turns while making fast or doubling up is shown at 'D'. The heel of the hand and not the fingers should be used.

may mean that she'll be on top of you when the strengthening ebb causes her to lie back on her mooring. Again, at slack water there may be fine wide gaps in the ranks due to the yachts lying at different angles to each other, as the stream begins the gaps may close. Make allowances for shallow-hulled power-boats which skate around in a wind and deep-keeled hulls liable to sheer when the wind is against the tide. Note that a yacht with a kedge out as well may mean that her swinging circle is going to be small. Suspiciously vacant areas where submerged wreckage or oyster-beds may lie should be regarded with caution.

Possible future shifts of wind should be taken into consideration, especially if the anchor lies on the side of a steep-to bed, as a strong offshore wind may drag it into deep water. In such cases it is better to let go the main anchor in the shallows and lay a kedge to keep you from swinging inshore. This is done by taking the kedge well off in the opposite direction to a scope of maybe five to one (the kedge is much lighter and needs extra scope) then making it fast to the main cable and veering a fathom or so to take it below the hull depth. (See Fig. 22, page 90.)

A tripping line and buoy are most essential if you are anchoring where there is a risk of fouling moorings or rocky ground. The line goes to the crown of the anchor and need be no more than five fathoms in length since it is unlikely that there will be more water than this at high water. If your anchor fouls, the buoy will be visible at slack water, even if it tows under in the current the rest of the time. By means of this line the anchor can usually be pulled free from the opposite direction. Be wary at slack water low tide however; a tripping-line buoy can foul your rudder and later trip the anchor.

If your anchor is badly fouled you may well need help from a shipyard, or even lose both anchor and some chain. The normal method of clearing an anchor that has fouled a mooring-chain is to haul it up as far as possible at dead low water, lifting the mooring-chain off the bottom until you can reach it. A line is then passed under the mooring-chain and secured on deck. If you pay out your anchor-chain, the anchor, with luck, will fall clear, and you can then slip the mooring-chain by letting go one end of the line. It is a back-breaking job at the best of times, and may be impossible. See end of chapter note on the use of the chain collar.

## Anchor Noises

After a while one learns to interpret the sounds made by a small yacht at anchor, but at first every rumble is hailed as a sign of a dragging anchor. Chain will rumble loudly each time the tidal stream changes and the yacht swings and begins dragging slack lengths of chain one across the other. On stony ground the noise is even louder. The true dragging sound is very little different. Like the slack chain noise it is spasmodic, but more likely to occur as the vessel snatches at her chain or snubs to a sea. A cruiser sheering to and fro when the wind is against the tide produces a similar sound.

To check whether an anchor is holding, line up marks or lights ashore and watch them for some minutes on end. In squalls the yacht will lie back on her anchor and then move ahead under the pull of the weight of the bight of chain in the lulls, and this will tend to make marks in line shift a little. Only by watching steadily can a real drag be detected—unless, of course, the anchor is hardly holding at all. If you put your hand on the chain or rope you can feel the anchor grumbling as it jerks from hold to hold on the bottom, but do not mistake the rhythmic throbbing of the tide against the cable for a dragging hook.

If she is taking up slack cable on the turn of the tide (often the tide is flowing strongly before the yacht decides to lie back) the chain may sometimes be seen to lead taut ahead, fall slack, lead ahead again and so on. The important moment is when she finally brings up on her full scope. The chain will then lead straight out and go bar taut as it takes the load.

If the anchor is going to drag then that is the moment to notice it. The chain should sink quietly back into its catenary instead of suddenly jerking and tightening again.

More and more scope will be needed in bad weather, but the chain may have to be shortened in when wind and tide are in opposition as the yacht may begin to sheer wildly around the anchorage. It is then that it is best to lie between two anchors in order to limit the range of sheering.

## Beaching

One of the great advantages of most twin keelers is that they can be beached. Twin keels offer a chance of sitting upright, and make it possible to have a safe berth ashore with the least amount of dinghy work. But it isn't safe to assume that any shore will be suitable for drying out, especially in strange water.

The ideal is a gently sloping shore which is level and firm, preferably the weather shore if she is to lie quietly afloat at high water. If the cruiser has made her port in the evening, her crew will want to be able to go ashore for the ritual drink and get back safely in the dark. If they put her where she'll take the ground this will either mean rowing the few yards to dry land and carrying the boat back dry-shod later on, or the other way about.

With an evening high water, it is sensible to arrange the programme ashore so that the cruiser is beached with a couple of hours still to flood. This means that she'll still be afloat roughly the same amount of time after high water, but her anchor must be taken off and dropped so that she can't wash in as the tide rises. Knowing just when you can get away from a dry berth is important for an owner cruising to a plan. It isn't much use sticking the cruiser up among the bullrushes on the top of a mid-afternoon tide if you have a passage to make next day, since she won't float until some time in the early afternoon, and the alternative is to start before dawn—not always popular with a weary crew.

Knowing height of tide and rate of rise and fall, the owner can decide how much water he'll need beneath him at high water if he is to have time enough for a later departure. Since rise and fall is slower towards the top and bottom of the tide, his boat may remain afloat in a few feet of water for perhaps three or four hours just before and just after high water. After that the level begins to fall rapidly and the boat must be moved well out if she is to remain afloat for a longer spell; merely anchoring a few yards further offshore will mean grounding again within an hour or less.

Suspiciously vacant plots along an otherwise crowded shore must be investigated. There may be an underwater groyne or row of piles, a hardway or landing, or the bottom there may be intersected with gullies into which one of the twin keels might fall with dire results. The bottom may be dotted with large chunks of masonry, or there may be a by-law forbidding anchorage there. A steep, or even moderately steep, shore has two main disadvantages. If there is a stiff onshore breeze the waves will roll straight ashore and may be eighteen inches or so in height which will mean gross discomfort afloat and some bad banging as the tide ebbs. A gently shelving shore causes the height of such waves to diminish safely before the keels begin to ground. The second snag is domestic. Most bunks are tapered to one end so that they can only be used lying with the head forward. To beach a cruiser on a steepish shore means passing the night at an odd angle if she grounds up and down. The alternative of beaching her to lie beam-on is easier for sleeping, but a constant nuisance for cooking and general moving around.

If bad weather is forecast any beach other than a flat one should be avoided, unless it is almost certain to remain a weather shore. Most blows are likely to come from south-east to sou'west, and veer around through west to north-west, which means that beaching on a shore

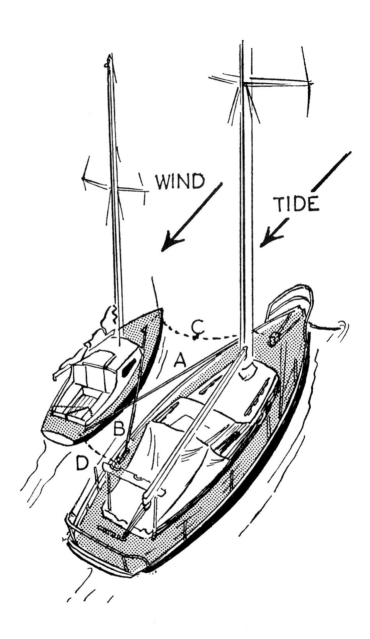

Fig. 25. Rafting alongside: 'A' is a long spring upon which the small cruiser will lie back. 'B' is a check spring. 'C' and 'D' are breast-ropes which may or may not be needed.

sheltered from those quarters is usually safe. But if the bad weather is due to a depression shaping to pass to the south there's no guarantee of peace.

There is one final point to remember. A house ashore may own the foreshore rights. This means that while you may beach there below the mean low water level, you have no claim of access to the dry land. You may beach in an emergency and get ashore, of course, but be careful you don't trespass. A good many waterside house-owners spend their lives trying to defend their privacy against picnic parties which have no respect for private property. This means that you will need to use a little tact. But most of them are yachtsmen and this will open a lot of doors, for their objections are usually to noise and litter and damage to their property.

You may resort to lying alongside a larger yacht or 'rafting' if you have permission to do so. But try to make sure you will have quiet water and not too many passing power boats. A motor inner-tube inside a sail-bag makes a good and silent fender for light craft, but only if it is up against smooth topsides.

For a short stay, to go shopping for instance, a small boat can be rafted alongside a larger craft in such a way that she lies clear by a foot or more, provided that there is a fairly smart tidal stream and the wind in the same direction. A line is taken from the inside quarter of the smaller craft to the bow of the moored yacht. Bow and stern breast-ropes and a short spring amidships (see Fig. 25) are also needed. With a little rudder to induce a sheer the smaller boat will lie clear on her long spring.

## Moorings

It is a common enough practice to pick up any old mooring in a strange anchorage. This is usually quite permissible as long as one or two things are borne in mind. The mooring is private property borrowed without permission. It may have been put down to hold a light dinghy, or, if it is a yacht mooring, the owner may return in the middle of the night and even if you rouse out quickly and get off it there will be a lot of fuss all round. Ocean-racing yachts in particular are likely to return at any time of the night, and, what is more, they have to moor and get the crews back to their jobs in time. A dinghy left on a mooring 'to save his place' usually means that the owner is returning shortly. It is therefore unwise to pick up a mooring without first finding out from a neighbouring yachtsman or boatman whether it is likely to be wanted.

By law, a mooring is a permanent anchor and the owner has no right to more room than the swinging space of the boat using it. Morally, there is little difference between putting your boat on somebody else's mooring or putting your car into somebody else's garage, but legally the owner of a mooring is in a weaker position. However, sea-lawyering among yachtsmen is abominable. Keep it friendly if you can; and better still be independent and lie to your own anchor.

The rate of damage to boats at their moorings is ridiculously high. One rarely hears of them lifting their moorings, since most are either laid by professionals or made far heavier than necessary. The damage arises from failure due to lack of inspection (how often is a private mooring lifted?), carelessness in making it fast aboard, inadequate mooring cleats and the inevitable risk of other boats getting out of control when trying to pick up their own buoys—and not much can be done about that.

Any deep-water mooring laid in sandy waters should be inspected at least every other year as the constant scouring of sand grains between the links wears away the metal at a fantastic rate— a good reason for choosing chain a bit oversize. It should go without saying that no mixture of metals, such as copper wire to seize a shackle-pin, should be allowed, for electrolysis can ruin a mooring in a single season. Screw shackles should be avoided in any case, and the oval-pinned cable joining shackle used instead.

Permission to lay a mooring is almost always needed, and this may be the business of a local harbour board or yacht club. In deep water, where the yacht is to lie constantly afloat, a concrete 'clump' is often used. This can be a cast concrete block, flat in shape and concave on the bottom and weighing about 50 lb for each ton by Thames Measurement. This would give a block of around 250 lb for an average 25 footer but much depends upon locality. This should be increased in small sizes, particularly if the bottom is hard sand.

The chain is made up of a ground length (which may be heavy stuff, $\frac{7}{16}$ in. or so) one third of the depth of water, and the riding chain, which is a size larger than the normal anchor cable, and three times the depth of water. Extra length should be allowed for making fast on deck. A synthetic riding line may be substituted as long as it can be fully protected from chafe. Between the ground chain and riding chain comes a swivel, large enough to match the general breaking strains. If chain is used all the way, the buoy should be made fast to a pick-up rope one and a half times the depth of the water. This rope should be strong enough for the yacht to lie to until the yacht is properly moored. Alternatively the riding chain may be supported by a large buoy with a short length of chain left hanging to be taken aboard. In some cases the yacht may be secured direct to a strong ring on the buoy itself.

Two clump moorings may be used where space is limited. Here the weights are laid, usually up and down tide, six depths apart with the riding chain coming from a swivel in the middle of the ground chain or bridle. Old anchors may be used so long as the yacht cannot sit on them at low tide. These should be about twice the weight normally used on the yacht.

The dug mooring which dries out at low tide conforms to the same rule regarding size of chain and scope, except that the ground chain goes to a 'root' chain which in turn is secured to the sinker. The experts have a fine time stipulating the best type of sinker, but the truth is that almost anything buried to a depth of about four feet will do whether it's an old gas cooker or half a railway sleeper. On the East Coast of England, a 3-foot cross made from $4 \times 4$ in. or $4 \times 6$ in. timber is a favourite. These can last up to twenty years buried in the mud, witness the ancient ship finds. The chain is usually the vulnerable part of it, particularly 'black' chain (ungalvanised). Railway sleepers are especially good because, of course, the timber has been pickled to preserve it. One argument against a solid sinker such as an old fly-wheel deserves consideration. When beachcombers are looking for coins in the sand they look for small wet patches and beneath them, sometimes six inches down, is the coin—the moisture lies above it and the sand remains fluid. There was a case of an iron wheel which came to the surface time and time again, in the end a wooden baulk was substituted and that stayed put.

A final word about pick-up buoys. It is most important to paint on it the tonnage of the yacht for which the mooring was laid. A bigger visitor may lift it otherwise.

## Going Alongside

The way carried by a small cruiser when going alongside can usually be checked quite easily but there are still some basic rules to be followed.

Try for a longish approach. The straight-at-it-and-then-swing man-oeuvre is for experts only. The turning circle becomes harder to judge towards the middle of the turn, and it's then that nerve fails. Lower the sails and head into the tide, even if the wind is stiff. Only if the tide is nearly slack can this law be ignored. Get a stern line ashore to stop her and watch for her stern swinging in. Fenders should be ready and in position, but keep one loose on deck in case of a last minute change of plan.

Many wharves or quays have protruding vertical baulks of timber serving as rubbers for bigger craft. Avoid such walls if possible, since yacht-fenders are useless on them. If there is much current, use a back-spring as well as head and stern lines, otherwise the bow will hit the quay wall as she falls back.

If a boat is to be left alone, springs are essential or she will never stay on her fenders. The action of a spring is to prevent the yacht from ranging fore and aft on the swell or as the wind catches her rig. Head and stern lines moor her to the quay and breast-ropes (if used) hold her close against it, but the springs are the ropes which protect the topsides, they need only be of very light line but they cannot be dispensed with (Fig. 26).

If a fin-keel hull is to take the bottom at low water you must take steps to hold her upright. If she lies outwards from the foot of the quay

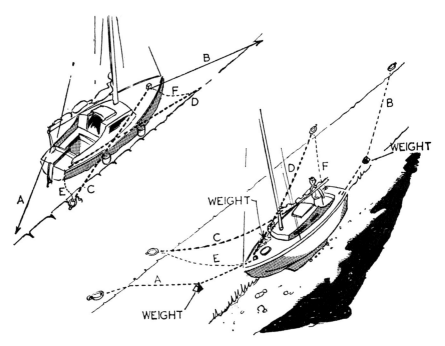

Fig. 26. Moored alongside big-yacht fashion. A B head and stern lines, C D head and back springs to check fore-and-aft movement, E F breast-ropes to hold her against the berth. Head and stern lines and springs, or at least one spring, are the minimum for a boat left alone for a number of hours. Drying out alongside (lower drawing). It is essential to hold her close to the wall with a small induced list inwards. Masthead line must be used as a safeguard if people are to move around on board a small ship standing on her keel.

she may be hard to get up on the next flood, and if she leans too sharply towards the wall, her spars may be damaged (Fig. 26).

There are two methods. One is to hold her at a list by means of a line from the mast to the shore (preferably no higher than the cross-trees), and the second is to give her a natural list by shifting ballast or chain, or just loose gear, on to the side-deck. If the tide has far to fall the second method is the only practical one, although, in such small craft, anyone moving around down below may cause her to fall the wrong way if there is no masthead line to the shore as an extra safeguard.

The shape of the fin-keel is important. Drying out alongside is quite impractical with some craft because of the angle of the bottom of the fin which makes them go down bow-heavy. It is also vital to know what the bottom of the wall is like, whether it is littered with rubble, smooth mud, or sand.

With a fair list inwards (five degrees or so) the hull must be kept in constant contact with the wall, otherwise if she dries out at some distance from it she will lean her mast against it. The first time she goes down the crew must obviously be in attendance, but if a proper list can be maintained and the hull kept close to the wall, there is no reason why she shouldn't be left to get on with it alone in future. To be certain of this it is far better to get her in trim and watch from the quay the first time, giving her no further help unless needed.

A simple dodge for holding the hull against the wall is to hang two good heavy weights to the middle of the bights of the head and stern lines. This keeps tension on them all the time. Another tip to remember, this time if the crew are living aboard and need to wake up just before she begins to touch down, is the bell and leadline trick. The lead should be a heavy one, which means that a rock from ashore will do the job better. Suspend it overboard on codline a little below keel level. Make a bowline on the inboard end, tuck the bight through a ventilator or crack in the door and peg the frying-pan (bell) handle into the bowline. When the rock takes the bottom the line goes slack and down falls the pan with a crash to wake the dead.

## Reduction to Soundings

Sounding with the leadline is, or should be, one of the mainstays of piloting a small cruiser. It is the means of correlating the tide-table with the soundings shown on the chart.

First you must understand how the tides behave. It would be easy to assume wrongly that the height of tide in the tide-table simply shows how high the level of the water will rise from the figures shown on the chart, that it will rise a long way at springs and not so far at neaps,

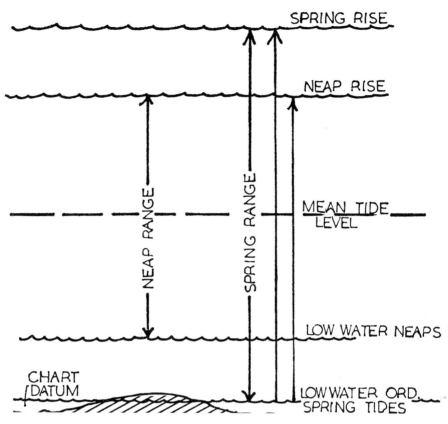

Fig. 27. The terms used in reference to tidal height calculations. While Chart Datum is usually taken as being Mean Low Water Spring, it should be noted that on certain charts (French charts for instance) the lowest possible tide is taken as Datum, thus there is usually a little more water at low tide than indicated by the chart. The present Chart Datum is gradually being replaced on British charts by L.A.T. (lowest astronomical tide). This is the lowest level predictable under average meteorological conditions and any combined astronomical conditions. L.A.T. is only occasionally reached and some years not at all. Always check the chart you are using; is it C.D. or L.A.T.?

sinking to chart datum at each low water. To explain what it really does calls for a little elaboration.

Imagine a tall building with eight floors and lift shaft up the middle. The lift leaves the ground floor slowly, picks up speed, and goes nonstop to the top floor losing speed at the same rate as it nears the top. This is the ordinary spring tide, ground floor is chart datum and the eighth floor is M.H.W.S. (mean high water springs). The fourth floor, exactly mid-way, is Mean Tide Level, and the lift never stops at it, only goes up and down an equal distance above and below it (and how well we know that floor!).

Now imagine the lift at say the second floor. It goes non-stop to the sixth, picking up speed and slowing as before but only travelling the shorter distance between those two floors either side of Mean Floor Level, this is an ordinary neap tide.

If our lift follows a schedule starting with the full non-stop run from ground to top floor and back, and each day shortens the run a little, working the intermediate floors until it is only plying the middle of the building we have a fair idea of how the spring tides gradually 'cut' to become neaps and then, as the lift service commences to range up and down a bit further each time, how the neaps pass into springs again. This cycle takes roughly a fortnight or one week neaps and one week springs.

At intervals throughout the year come the big springs when the lift starts from the basement (below floor at datum) and goes straight through to the roof garden. Also, at certain times come the dead neap periods when the lift merely calls at a floor either side of Mean Floor Level.

This analogy helps to define the terms used in tidal information. Chart Datum is the ground floor, it is generally taken as M.L.W.S. (mean low water springs); therefore M.H.W.S. (mean high water springs) is the eighth floor. Height of Tide refers to the height of the particular floor from ground or datum level, and the rise is this distance from ground floor to the height in question. Here is the critical part, however. Tide Range is the distance actually travelled by the lift and it may be the whole way from basement to roof-garden at extra high springs, or the shorter distance between intermediate floors at neaps. Thus the lift may rise to the seventh floor but it has only ranged between that and the first floor—an equal distance either side of that neglected Mean Floor (tide) Level.

Returning to salt water, the yacht which anchors at high water neaps on a fifteen-foot tide rise is not going to fall fifteen feet on the ebb, she is going to fall the distance which the tide is ranging that day, and it will be more like a distance of say twelve feet or three feet short of the ground floor or datum.*

To find out exactly what the tide is ranging that day and what depth of water will be available at low tide is a simple matter. First we must know the M.T.L. (mean tide level) for the locality and this varies enormously. This information is to be found in Reed's as 'Tidal

* In the interests of UK readers still struggling to think Metric the figures have been kept in feet and inches.

Differences on the port of . . .' (depending upon the nearest Standard port which will be the tide-table you are using). Having found M.T.L. double the figure and subtract the Height for the day. Thus: Mean Level 9 ft, Height of tide 15 ft, 9 × 2 = 18. 18 − 15 = 3 ft, or three feet above Chart Datum. Therefore if the chart shows soundings of 6 ft there will actually be 9 ft of water at low tide.

Now a yacht will most often approach her chosen anchorage at some stage during the rise or fall. It may not be possible to pin-point her position on the chart, so the navigator just doesn't know how much water there is likely to be at datum, for all he knows the place may dry out (above Chart Datum). By using the echo-sounder and the tide-table and knowing the Mean Level he can calculate this.

Using the same figures again, we will assume that he has arrived two hours after high water (15 ft height); he wants to know how many more feet the level will fall in order to judge whether the eleven feet he has found with his leadline will enable him to lie afloat with his draft of say 2 ft 6 in.

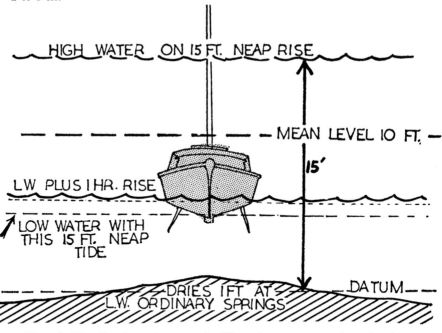

FIG. 28. We often hear the remark, 'There is more water than the chart shows . . .' The cruiser has arrived an hour after low tide and the navigator is surprised to find almost five feet of water where the chart indicates a drying patch. Rise from Chart Datum 15 ft. Mean Level 10 ft. 10 × 2 = 20 − 15 = 5 ft, or 5 ft above datum at this neap tide. One hour of rise or $\frac{1}{12}$th of the 10-ft range adds another 10 in. approx.

First he must find the Tide Range for the day. If he uses the formula given above he will establish the Low Tide Level, and since the Tide Height in his tables refers to its distance above datum, by subtracting Low Tide Level from Height he has the distance which the level of the water is ranging or: Height 15 ft, Low Water 3 ft above Datum, $15 - 3 = 12$ ft. Tide Range 12 ft.

Harking back to the lift analogy we saw that it started slowly, accelerated towards the middle of its passage and slowed down at the same rate towards its final stop. The rule of thumb method of estimating how far a tide rises or falls during any stage of its movement is known as the 'twelfths' rule. We reckon the tide will rise (or fall) $\frac{1}{12}$ in the first hour, $\frac{2}{12}$ in the second and $\frac{3}{12}$ in the third then another $\frac{3}{12}$ in the fourth hour, $\frac{2}{12}$ in the fifth and $\frac{1}{12}$ in the last hour, thus 1, 2, 3, 3, 2, 1.

Thus it can be seen that the tide will have fallen $\frac{3}{12}$ or one quarter of its 12 ft range by the time the cruiser arrived at the anchorage, two hours after high tide. It has another 9 ft to fall, and this will leave only 2 ft of water at low tide ($11 - 9 = 2$). She will therefore be just aground.

This whole matter, once understood, and reduced to these simple calculations (which are quickly made after a little practice) is in constant use whether you are seeking an anchorage or attempting to cross some shallow patch at an intermediate state of the tide.

## The Lead and How to Use It

Although the echo-sounder has replaced the hand leadline, it is good seamanship to know how to use a lead. Electronics can fail and a leadline should be carried aboard for just such an emergency as this. A lead must be heavy enough to reach the bottom quickly when you are sailing at speed, and the line strong enough to pull it out of the mud afterwards. A three-pound lead is about the lightest for depths up to five or six fathoms if it is to be used when sailing at four knots, and a thick codline is, when soft and fully stretched, none too heavy.

True leadline is laid up 'left-handed', or the opposite way to most rope and small stuff, and it seems less prone to stretch, but it is also difficult to find this type of cordage in sizes light enough for small cruisers.

The marks shown in Fig. 29 are simple to make up from odd scraps and far superior to the horrid little knots which so many people make in the line. There is one snag, however. Any new line is apt to stretch or shrink. Mark the line temporarily for a week or two, and then re-measure it before marking it for good.

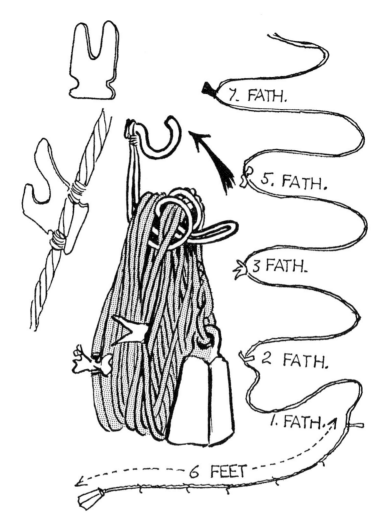

FIG. 29. Marks of the leadline. Standard marking is: 2 fathoms, leather with two tails; 3 fathoms, leather with three tails; 5 fathoms, white duck; 7 fathoms, red bunting. Longer than this the line becomes an encumbrance in a very small boat. It will be seen that only the 'marks' have tallies, the intermediate fathoms or 'deeps' are judged by eye. To modify the line for shoal use a 1-fathom mark is added and the line below it whipped at 1-foot intervals. Note that the coiled line is hung with the coil ready halved for use by means of a short bight of cord.

It isn't necessary to whizz the lead around the head when making a cast; in fact it is suicidal to do so on a small boat. Take the line, coil it small (about the size of a dinner plate), divide the coil in two, and holding the lead in one hand with half the coil, allow the lead to hang down a couple of feet and give it a good, sweeping under-arm swing, releasing it as it comes parallel with the waterline. Work from the lee side and aim to land the lead well ahead of the bows, so that as the yacht sails forward the lead, still sinking, reaches the bottom when the line is vertical. The feeling of slack shows when it has bottomed, and if a foot or so of line is quickly taken back and released again before the line is leading aft, the up-and-down depth can be noted.

So much for technique. It should be mentioned in passing that the old practice of 'arming' a lead can be of use to the small cruiser even though very few yachtsmen still do so. To arm a lead one presses tallow (or soap) into the cavity which *should* be found in the base of the lead.

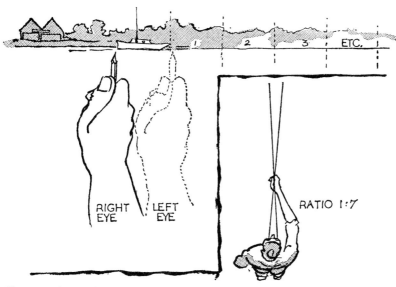

FIG. 30. A rough means of judging distance away from other moored craft or the shore when coming to anchor is to hold a pencil at full arm's length and look beyond it with the left eye closed. Line it against some object at the range required then close the right eye and open the left one. The pencil will jump to the right (dotted line). If the amount of the jump is then estimated seven times across the line of vision this distance will be roughly equivalent to distance off. The ratio of distance between eyes to length of arm is roughly 1:7. Check also by remembering that at 60 yards a man's features are visible and at 120 yards the eyes, nose and mouth are merely dots.

Upon hitting the sea-bed, samples of sand, gravel, shell, mud, and so on, stick to the arming and can be compared with sea-bed characteristics shown on the chart. Muddy rivers afford very little joy, but deep, rocky coastlines make the arming well worth while if you are trying to check your position in a fog.

### *Additional Notes on Anchoring, Beaching and Mooring*

The holding power of an anchor varies from 2–7 times its own weight for a Fisherman to 30–100 times the weight for Danforth or C.Q.R. The load which a boat can put on her anchor in a gale, but not plunging or sheering, is roughly her overall length × 2, × 10 (thus a 20 footer is 20 × 2 × 10 = 400 lb load) much less under normal conditions, possibly more in a seaway.

The weight of $\frac{1}{4}$-in. chain per 15-fathom length is 75 lb. Breaking strain 1·7 tons.

Paint the chain at leadline intervals in similar markings as a guide to the amount of chain you have let go or have still to haul in.

Never throw an anchor over the side—it might catch in your clothing and take you with it. A 'shackle' of chain is 15 fathoms. Anchors used with rope instead of chain should be one size heavier. When mooring alongside with *nylon* lines in average heights of tide, make the lines fast at half-tide and they'll stretch enough to be right at low water.

Always mark your mooring-buoy with the displacement or T.M. tonnage of your yacht.

*Drift Lead.* If dragging at anchor is suspected, lower the hand-lead to the sea-bed and allow it enough slack line so that the normal swing and surge of the boat will not disturb the lead. If the yacht begins to drag, the line will be found stretching taut.

*Chain Collar.* A fouled stockless anchor (C.Q.R., Meon, or Danforth) can often be cleared by the following method. Take a short length of chain and join the ends to make a 'collar' of about 12 inches diameter. Lowered down the taut up-and-down cable on a line, the collar will slide over the upright anchor shank, the cable is then slackened, simultaneously jerking upwards on the collar line. With a little luck the anchor will be tripped clear of the obstruction.

*Solent Tides.* Due to the phenomenon of the double high water which occurs at points in the Solent area, the method of finding the height of low water given in this chapter cannot be used between Swanage and the Nab Tower. In *Reed's Nautical Almanac* a Height of Tide table giving hourly heights above datum at a selection of positions is used instead. Due to the behaviour of the tidal stream there is either a high water period which stands for two hours or a definite ebb lasting about an hour before flooding again—the second high water being higher than the first. For this reason the whole flood period is longer than the ebb, a point to be borne in mind when calculating the fall.

To find tide range (without having the Mean Tide Level) the Spring range is virtually the same as Spring *rise*. The neap range is found by multiplying neap *rise* (height above Datum) by two and subtracting Spring *rise*.

*Chapter Seven*

# Sailing by Eye, Allowing for the Tide

THERE is nothing frighteningly technical about the sort of navigation, or coastal pilotage to give it a more exact name, required for small cruisers. The simpler it can be made the better. Without the big chart-table and steadier working surface on bigger craft, the small boat man will get on better by sticking to a very few rules than by trying to work to fine limits.

The ancient Norse pilots worked by studying headlands. They had no instruments, but they had a keen eye for the shape of the land. The small cruiser man has the advantages of charts, compasses and tide-tables, but he is attempting much the same type of navigation.

Above all things he must be a map reader. This is no heresy, and it does not mean that he should use a map in lieu of a chart. But he will have very little time in which to practise chart work at sea, and map-reading from a one-inch Ordnance Survey before he goes will teach him to look at the flat sheet and visualise it as a landscape or coastline which has height and depth.

Most navigational trouble arises from losing one's sense of orienta-tion. One can get lost while in full view of a clearly recognisable stretch of coastline, merely because one has failed to 'look' at the coast in the bustle of laying courses, reading logs and taking innumerable bearings on buoys. It needs but one or two of these fixes to go wrong and one begins to get anxious. So the first thing to do in a small coasting cruiser is to keep a constant watch on the coastline as it unfolds, at the same time studying the chart.

Plotting is often a labour in a bit of a sea. Watching the coast calls for no instruments, and fixes upon buoys and shore-marks are only for confirmation. The compass course may be used when there is risk of suddenly losing visibility or it may be a simple matter of convenience for steering straight. At other times it is really only important if there are offlying dangers athwart the course, which have to be given a known safe berth, or in verifying a transit when there is doubt about the identification of one of the objects.

It is possible to navigate clear along a coastline without looking at the instruments, simply by noting the natural transits provided by headlands, piers, rocks and so on. By laying a ruler on the chart, for instance, the yachtsman may notice a headland which, at a certain point, becomes obscured behind a bulge in the coast. By watching for it he gets a position line which is indisputable and, if at the same time, a glance ashore shows a small bay or group of rocks coming abeam he has his second line—rough, of course, but a succession of such transit fixes takes him safely down the coast without him once becoming involved in the complexity of chart work which seems to be considered so vital.

I mention this habit of studying the coast first for an important reason. There are times when a man has his hands far too full sailing the boat to indulge in lengthy sessions on the chart. If he can 'see' his way along it will stand him in good stead. But first he must learn to see the coast as a chart and the chart as a coast. This chapter deals with pilotage by eye and the look of the land from seaward. In the next chapter the use of compass, calculation of tidal effect, laying a course offshore and so on will be dealt with stage by stage.

## Looking at the Land

Each coastal region has its own typical features. The East Coast man is often terrified of West Coast rockiness and the deep-water man, accustomed to rock-fringed coasts, is nervous of navigating among the shallows of the Thames Estuary. Nowadays the owner of a small cruiser may trail it from one coast to the other in the course of a day, and so he must be a versatile navigator.

The low-lying coastline is particularly difficult to identify. The shape of the sea-bed usually continues the run of the flat shore, and it is therefore shallow for a long way out to sea. This means that the cruiser is forced to stay well out, and details on shore become harder to identify. The absence of pronounced headlands, cliffs, distinctive bays and rocky outcrops complicates things further. Headlands run out to sea so gradually that the exact point where the land finishes and sea begins is hard to decide. On this kind of coast the navigator becomes a buoy-hopper. He concentrates entirely on buoys and ignores the land, and he can easily lose his sense of position if he makes a mistake in a compass course between buoys.

The low coastline rises and falls in hazy undulations and it's difficult to decide whether a gradual fading away into the sea is due to the height of the land diminishing or the coastline receding. The only clues are such objects as houses, trees and people ashore. Compare them constantly through the binoculars and note their relative sizes at different spots along the coastline.

The direction of natural light must be reckoned with. If the sun is low and behind the land there will be a featureless monotony of bluish shadow in which a block of flats may look no different from a church-tower, or a clump of trees may masquerade as a prominent spur of ground shown on the chart. On the other hand the sunlight shining full onshore can pick out a strip of wet road and make it appear to be a white tower, while the actual tower is muted by the shadow of a cloud. You must therefore never accept the obvious without due thought.

A hilly coast is far easier to correlate to the chart. The yacht is usually closer inshore and bays and headlands are more distinct, also villages and small towns do not straggle, each is contained more compactly in its valley. There is only the risk of one headland looking much like another, especially with the effect of sunshine and cloud shadow to alter the apparent contours.

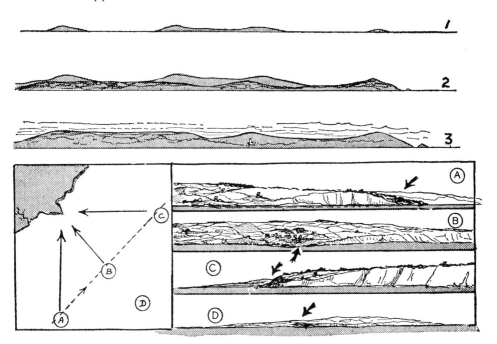

FIG. 31. Approaching the coast in clear visibility, distant hills may be seen as a row of islands (1). Nearer inshore (2) the foreground is still overshadowed by the inland contour, but close inshore the inland hills are hidden and the skyline shape of the coast is quite changed (3).

The small headland seen from positions A, B and C may be hard to distinguish against the rest of the coastline although from the chart it would promise to be easily identified. At position D, well offshore, only a slight sharpening of detail indicates its position.

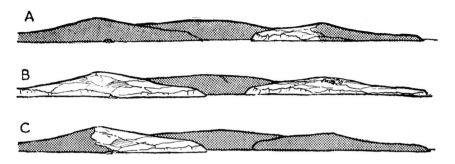

FIG. 32. Sunlight striking a hilly coast can alter the importance of prominent features. 'A' highlights the right-hand headland, but 'B' gives an impression of a deep inlet, while 'C' from a distance might cause the right-hand headland to look like a receding coastline.

FIG. 33. Leading marks and transits. Plan shows the difference between the headlands 'closed', or the nearer one covering the more distant headland, and 'open', when the distant headland can be seen projecting beyond the nearer one. In this case the headlands are being kept open as an indication that the cruiser is clearing Black Rock which lies on the transit of the headlands.

Leading marks (*bottom*) may be man-made beacons for entering a river, the vessel steering to keep the back one in line with the front mark. In this case there are two sets of leaders, an inner pair guiding the vessel into the river. The leaders may be lit by night.

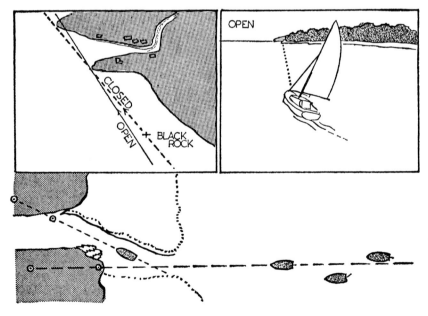

Seen from far at sea the contours of a coastline can be very deceptive if there are ranges of inland hills. The switchback effect of more distant hills may be quite different from the actual coastline profile, and only as the yacht gets closer are the background hills hidden by the coastline. It must be remembered that bays and headlands seen from offshore are foreshortened. Often it is only low-slanting sunlight, casting shadow, which reveals the position of a headland at all. The navigator may sail straight past it only to find it, as he thinks, some miles further on when a lesser headland is exaggerated by tricks of light (Fig. 32).

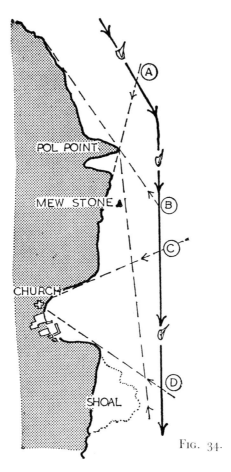

Fig. 34.

It is easy to con a cruiser by identifying prominent features as they come into line ashore once you have mastered the symbols on the chart and learnt to match land and paper in this way. In tricky waters, infested with rocks or sand-bars, it is no substitute for careful plotting with compass and parallel rules, but it dispenses with 80 per cent of it in straightforward waters, while the safe transit method of keeping an offing from inshore dangers is better than any mechanical plot.

Many transits (objects in line) are marked on the chart for the guidance of the navigator approaching a river or passage between dangers, and most of these are man-made beacons, towers and so forth. The coastline furnishes many, many more which are there for the finding.

In Fig. 34 the cruiser is coasting offshore along the unbroken arrowed line. At 'A' headlands are in transit, and at 'B' a headland hides the bulge in the coastline astern. Yet another transit of sorts comes up as the bay opens up from 'C', and at 'D' the navigator finds a safe transit to see him past the shoal. By glancing at the church-tower he knows that he will not be in the danger area until it is lost to view behind the land, while by keeping the Mew Stone astern *inside* Pol point he can stay outside the danger area.

There will be buoys to aid him, naturally, but it isn't always so easy for the inexperienced navigator to be certain of the identity of a buoy until he is close. The buoy which appears where he would *like* to see it may not be the one he is hoping to find, and, of course, there is no excuse for not checking the compass bearings between buoys as they are passed. Many of them form useful transits in their own right, but it must be borne in mind that at close hand the swinging room of a

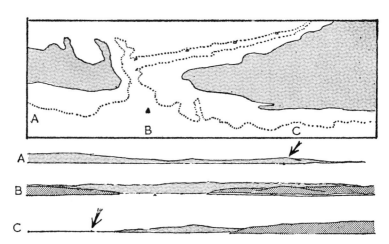

FIG. 35. The chart indicates that the buoy will be found close inshore, but from positions A and C it may be missed since it will appear to be lost against the background in the one case and further offshore in the other. At B it becomes plain to find if the yacht has made a proper approach.

moored buoy upsets the angles a lot, especially if it should be a little out of position. Both buoys and lightships rarely get out of position, but occasionally they do so and they ought not to be relied upon implicitly.

The chart usually gives a picture of compactness with the buoys in cosy proximity to each other. In reality the details are unexpectedly distant, and the whole picture greatly extended. An observer takes in the whole chart-coast at a glance, but the land is seen as a mass which tapers in perspective on either hand. The buoys marked on the chart would need to be engraved as pin-pricks to approximate to their correct scale, and it is important to think of them as pin-pricks. At a distance of three miles a really large buoy can just about be seen, though probably not identified, and the smaller buoys without top-marks are not visible until within one and a half miles. The navigator studying his chart may expect to see half a dozen buoys all within a small area and he may get worried because they don't show up. In coasting, it is a common mistake to look too close inshore for an expected buoy probably marking an offlying spit. In fact, it may be visible as a tiny black peppercorn apparently far out to sea. But once you reach it, the coastline behind it appears close again due to the effect of foreshortening. Practice with the ordinary Ordnance Survey map ashore helps a lot by giving you a feeling of distance away from land. Coasting and keeping a safe distance offshore are largely a matter of judgement. The navigator may cover his chart with fixes, but when the shore is featureless and barren of seamarks it is judgement which counts.

## Distance by Eye

It is deceptive to attempt to judge distance through binoculars. Distance blurs detail even though the object may be visible for a long way. A large tree at between one and a half and two miles can be seen in crisp detail in a good light, but if a pencil is held at arm's length, the tree will be no taller than the lead. At four miles the tree is seen with rounded outlines, and shadows are blue, with the foliage masses appearing to have been dabbed on roughly, though the shapes of trees are still quite individual. At eight miles trees are simply blue humps and can easily be confused with, say, a water tower or a row of houses.

A small building with a white or pale facing wall becomes blurred and loses sharp edges at a mile and a half although darker windows and doors are still recognisable. At four miles these details have gone and the shape is almost lost. At six miles it has become a dab of colour without shape. Caravan parks at five miles are scattered chips of white, cars can be seen if they are moving and hedgerows are about the size of a pencil line.

The effect of lighting is again very important. A coastline under the full blaze of early morning sunshine is crisp in detail and appears closer than it does with the detail lost in shadow. At dusk, with the light behind the land making it a flat silhouette and the reflection of high ground extending across the water, it is often hard to form any true estimate. This is especially true at night and many a cruiser has navigated inshore to find an anchorage, and finally anchored at what seems to be a perilously close distance from the shore; but daylight finds her stuck out in the open a mile from land. The black land mass and its reflection seem to loom far higher than it really is.

Weather also affects one's judgement of distance. The vivid clarity which often comes in advance of rain and wind can mess up the estimates; the pearly haze of a hot day, which so often accompanies easterly weather, or the refraction which seems to jack up the whole coastline, must all be reckoned with. Refraction, extending the height of shore buildings to a grotesque proportion, can fool the navigator into thinking that a row of particularly nasty bungalows are actually oil storage tanks. The beach also becomes a prominent feature, to be searched for anxiously on the chart, though it is really just a narrow strip of shingle.

The effect of the earth's curvature when one is looking for shore-marks also comes into the picture when visibility is very clear. A harbour wall, sole clue to a small port perhaps, may be 'dipped' just below the horizon when the town behind it is vividly seen in detail, and at night whole rows of shore lights can be seen jauntily nipping up and down with a disturbing ripple effect.


## The Look of the Water


Without a certain knowledge of position, a passage down the coast becomes rather frightening. Every wind ripple or tidal swirl becomes, in the imagination, an 'uncharted' rock. The look of the water is a necessary study.

In rocky coastal districts the colour of the water is significant. Blue-black for the deeps, paler blue and then green for shoal patches, with black shadows marking underwater rocks covered with weed—in sunshine the pilot can get plenty of warning of shoaling water. On the east coast of England, however, it is rare to find clear water, and a two-foot patch is often the same colour as a ten-fathom channel. In fact the swirl of a fast tide may bring sand to the surface and imitate a shoal where none exists. The movement of the water is another matter altogether.

In Fig. 36 some of the many faces of the sea are shown. At 'A' unbalanced breaking crests give warning of rocks beneath. This is familiar deep-water rocky coast stuff and there may be ample water above the rocks, but they must still be avoided. The sheen on the water above a sandbank 'B' is often imitated by a 'hole' in the wind on a quiet day, but with the least breeze there will be a subtle change in the surface of the water which is unmistakable. 'C' shows how a tidal overfall may look very similar to a shoal or reef. At 'D' a calm sea allows the tidal stream running through the deeper water of the channel to reveal its whereabouts by a rippling of the surface. Note how the awash shoal by the beacon is barely distinguishable from the water around it. The same channel in a light breeze 'E' may be marked by a slick of smooth water if the stream is flowing, with the wind, fast enough to prevent the formation of wavelets. At 'F', however, wind against tide has raised a steep sea in the deep water, while the regular wave-formation indicates shallower water where the fast tide is not felt. 'G' shows the same channel when the stream is running with the wind and the higher waves are seen over the shallower water. Open-sea waves of a trochoidal type of swell (H) may be left-overs from a distant storm, they may be high but they are usually harmless. In shoaling water the crests may spill forward, and again not necessarily be troublesome. The cycloidal wind-driven wave, which increases in size according to 'fetch' or distance unimpeded by land, frequently becomes a plunger in shoal water and must be avoided. The shallow bar 'I' seen from seaward is deceptive because only the backs of the breaking waves are seen. Overfalls are often caused by an abrupt rise in the sea-bed 'J' which forces the tidal current on the surface, but an isolated rocky outcrop may also be the cause. It is dangerous to venture close to any overfall unless the exact depth of water is known. To skirt it in order to stay on a making tack, for instance, is risky since the actual water disturbance takes place at various distances from the rock itself. A fast tide in deep water creates 'smooths' or slicks which may be frightening, suggesting as they do some unseen rock 'K'. The yacht may be spun completely around in a slick, but the real danger comes if there is a sea running, when a 'race' may develop which can overpower a small boat. The ripple above an underwater obstruction 'L' is a good guide close inshore when the outer mark may have passed unnoticed further out to seaward. At 'M' is a section of shore showing the difference between shoal and steep-to coasts. Note how the diminishing size of wave in shallow water, due to the slacker tidal stream, is a guide to the nature of the bottom.

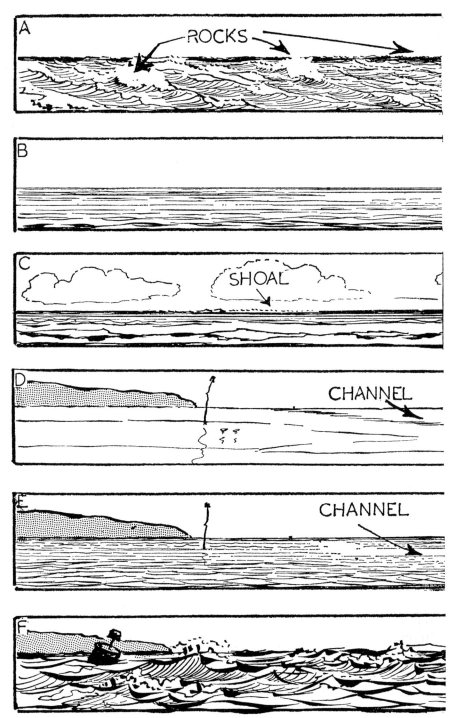

Fig. 36.

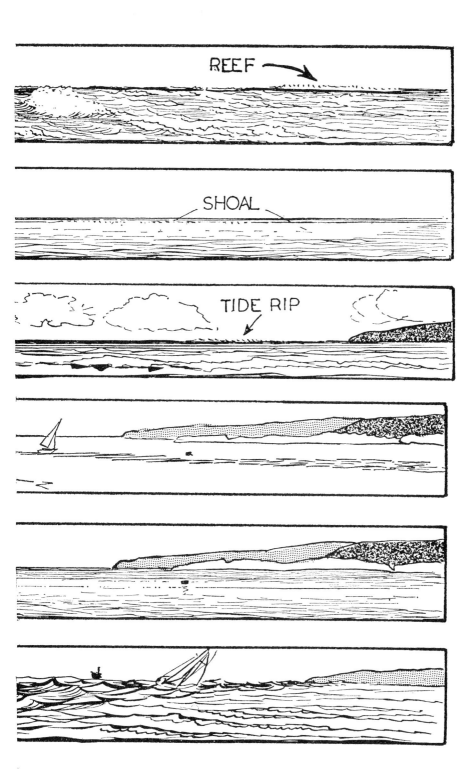

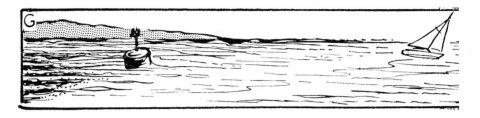

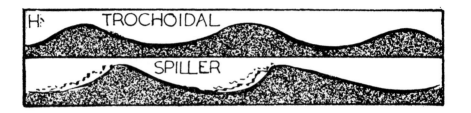

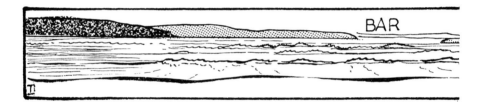

Fig. 36 (continued).

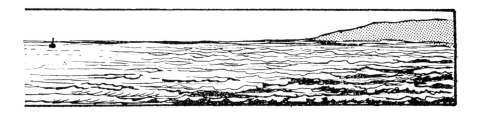

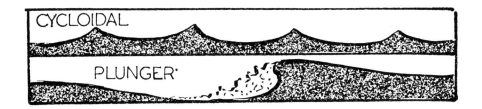

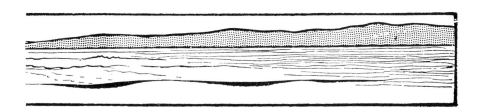

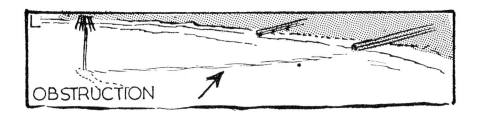

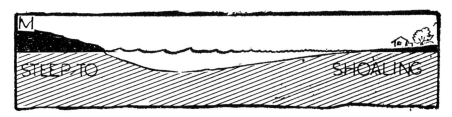

Fig. 36 (continued).

## Working the Tides Offshore

A small cruiser on a coasting passage is in much the same position as a sailing barge. For both, working the tides and taking full advantage of a fair wind are the most important considerations. When she is contending with head winds the tides are more important than ever, and when the tide serves, day or night (weather permitting), she must be out there using it. Since most of the small cruiser's passages are made fairly close to the land, the tidal streams are likely to be stronger, and a breeze which, well out to sea, might allow her to sail 'full and by' is often bent by the shape of the land mass and forces her to make a dead flog along the coast.

Faced with a passage along the coast and dead to windward she will have about eight hours of usable sailing time on each tide. Of this perhaps six hours will be actually fair and the other two consisting of relatively slack water at the beginning and end. If the tide is seen on the atlas to be turning fair at 10 a.m., the yacht must be mustered under way by 8 a.m. so that she can be on the spot by 9 a.m. or thereabouts and fighting the last weak trickle of foul tide. If she can manage to struggle on over the next foul tide so much the better, but it is far wiser to anchor in shelter, if it can be found, for six hours rather than exhaust the crew and make no more than a half-mile or so to windward. It is up to the individual skipper to decide whether to adopt the alternative of using the engine, but if it is to shove a boat against wind and sea it will have to be a good big one. There are plenty of times when an anchorage is out of the question, of course. In calm weather there is the alternative of lying to a kedge, leaving the mainsail set to keep her from rolling, and just waiting it out.

A long beat to windward is a sharp test of a crew in any size of sailing yacht, but it is more than ever so in the small cruiser. Discomfort, sea-sickness and wet going are not conducive to careful navigation. It is very easy to over-tax one's strength. Ten miles won at a cost of a whole day of flogging to and fro are not to be lightly thrown away, for the sake of running back for a night's shelter and the temptation is to press on beyond the limit of ordinary endurance. It is better to be content with sailing carefully through the seas and letting the tide give you most of your progress. The whole fair tide may give you twelve miles plus the five or six you make good to windward, a total of seventeen or eighteen miles. By dint of motoring against the foul tide in the smoother conditions this may be stepped up into the twenties perhaps, but it will have amounted to a good day's work and the time will have come to seek shelter and a rest.

Bigger boats can keep going on a long beat, but small craft with

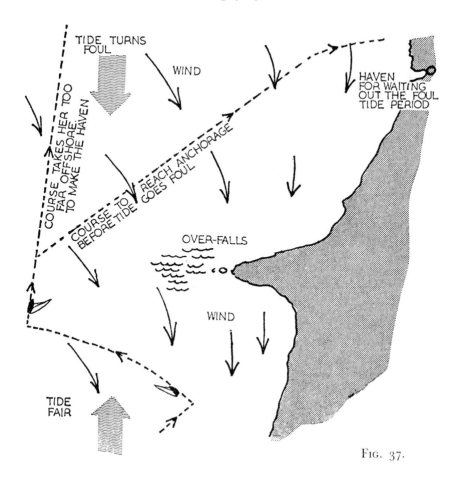

TIDE TURNS
FOUL

WIND

HAVEN
FOR WAITING
OUT THE FOUL
TIDE PERIOD

COURSE TAKES HER TOO
FAR OFFSHORE.
TO MAKE THE HAVEN

REACH ANCHORAGE

COURSE TO
BEFORE TIDE
GOES FOUL

OVER-FALLS

WIND

TIDE
FAIR

FIG. 37.

small crews must be content with shorter hops. It is very seldom, though, that the wind stays dead on the nose for long. It may shift a few degrees, enough to make a fair slant of it, so if you keep close watch on the weather so that you don't miss these shifts you will have won more than half the battle. A few hours of fair wind and a whole day of fruitless flogging is saved.

There are times when it pays to forsake the inshore course and stand well out to sea on one leg and back again on the next. With a headland to round this is often the wiser course for small craft. When the wind and tide are in opposition, headlands invariably produce bad tide-rips and overfalls. These are marked on the chart in many cases, but quite small tide-rips can be unpleasant in a small cruiser. The wind direction may alter offshore, possibly freeing off the land. This tempts one to stand on further and further to take advantage of it, but it must not be forgotten that the next inshore tack may well waste all the ground made good if the tidal stream changes in the meanwhile (Fig. 37).

## Plotting a Course, the Compass

In recommending a type of compass to suit a particular craft it is difficult to do more than generalise. The compass must be large enough to be seen without strain (at least 4 in. diameter), clearly marked and have a card (never a needle) which moves resolutely. By this I mean that if you tilt the compass so that the card jams and then turn smartly on your heel and level the compass to unjam the card, the north point should swing gently back into orientation, carrying on past magnetic North, stopping, and then swinging back across North a short way before finally centring itself. A sleepy card which takes too long to centre again will spin like a top if the yacht is pounding to windward and a compass which is too 'dead beat' is jerky. Any well-recommended make can be relied upon, but be canny about the cheap all-purpose instruments. They are seldom really suitable.

Dinghy compasses are better than nothing, but for navigational purposes the sparsity of markings on the card limits their use. Some compasses are designed like an inverted pie-dish with points and degrees marked around both rim and top surface. These can be used as bearing compasses by reading the rim and staring across the top at the distant object. The ship's course is steered by looking at the top face. This type may sometimes be equipped to be illuminated at night; but here there is a snag. By daylight one reads the top, but by night the rim; and this means reversing the tiller movement each time you change day to night. This may not be disastrous perhaps, but it is a great annoyance.

On a very small cruiser the steering compass is seldom a fixture, and this means that it can rarely be properly lit. Obviously it must be positioned where it can be seen without effort from wherever the helmsman may be sitting. If he has to crane his neck or bend too close, then it is obviously badly mounted. Although it is important that the compass should be well away from any metal work which might cause deviation, it quite often happens that in the interests of avoiding magnetic interference it is placed in a position where it is impossible to read. Within sensible limits it is probably better to have two alternative mountings so that it can be seen on either tack. By sighting on the mast with a hand-bearing compass and steering until the bearing reads 'on' for the course required and by noting what the steering compass reads at the time, it is possible to ignore mild deviation on the steering compass. The two instruments may not agree, but you will be navigating by the hand compass and simply using the other to steer a straight course. Any subsequent alterations, of course, will mean repeating the operation, but the advantage of having the steering compass where it can be seen far outweighs the trouble of checking one against the other in this way. The compass mounted as far away as possible from steel fittings, stowed outboards, and radios and so on, will still show a few degrees of error here and there. The error can be properly plotted on a deviation card if the owner wants to go to the expense of having a compass-adjuster aboard. For coasting passages a rough check can be made while under way simply by steering between distant buoys or a series of chosen shore transits (identifiable marks in line) and checking the compass course against the magnetic bearing indicated on the chart. Alternatively a borrowed and accurate hand-bearing compass held from a standing position on the stern and sighted on the mast can be tallied against the suspect instrument—don't put one beside the other though or they'll go mad. A simple method of 'swinging' a compass is given on page 138.

The great bogy of the fledgling navigator is converting True North bearings and courses to Magnetic and vice versa. A dozen or so couplets have been composed to elucidate this matter and they serve only to add complication to confusion. True North, to all intents and purposes the lines of longitude on the chart, remains constant, but the compass North aligns with an ever-shifting magnetic field, and the amount of variation between the two differs year by year and from place to place. The short (though heretical) answer from the knee-cap navigator's point of view is to forget all about True North, buy an up-to-date chart and plot straight from the compass rose to the compass card. On most charts the compass rose consists of a True North circle and a Magnetic North rose. The compass rose referred to is the magnetic one. This matter is dealt with more fully in the next chapter. Let him do this and steer straight and he will make his landfalls—later he can reason out the conversion of True to Magnetic and back. Many Pilot Books refer to True bearings, which means converting them, but most yachtsman's charts deal in Magnetic to the extent that many compass roses don't even show a True North rose, only a True North line.

Taking the case of a cruiser faced with a long drag across a wide bay or plotting a course, in thick weather perhaps, from one buoy to another several miles away. She has a known point of departure. The navigator lays his parallel rules on the chart joining his two points, he walks them across the chart to the nearest compass rose and reads off the bearing which he plans to steer (we'll assume, just for once, that his compass is accurate on this particular bearing). He now has a course to steer and, so long as nothing deflects his ship from her course, it is only a matter of time before she makes her destination.

## Plotting Tidal Set

A stream which is either dead against her or dead astern obviously only affects the yacht's time of arrival, but if it sets across the course the navigator will have to make due allowance for it. The simple instance of a boat sailing across a river to reach a point on the far bank will show that the helmsman gauges the extent to which he must head into the current entirely by eye, and he may have to head up 45 degrees off course to get there. When he reaches the slacker stream near the bank he adjusts his angle again, and so on. The navigator who cannot see his destination must calculate the angle by means of tide-table and tidal atlas. Hour by hour the tidal stream alters in strength and direction, and hour by hour the sailing boat may alter her speed and direction according to the dictates of the wind.

The navigator notes his time of departure. He turns to his *Reed's Nautical Almanac* and looks up the tidal atlas appropriate to his part of the coast. These atlases consist of a series of chartlets showing, by means of arrows, the direction of the stream hour by hour, and, by means of figures, the rate of the stream for both neap tides and spring tides.

Perhaps he is crossing the mouth of the Thames Estuary and it is ten o'clock in the morning. The atlas is based on the Dover tide times (in this case also upon Sheerness) so that a check shows it to be let's say two hours after high water at Dover. Turning to the appropriate chart-let he sees that a weak stream is setting across his course from west to east—maybe half a knot. In the next three hours, however, the stream

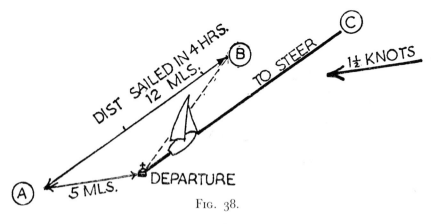

Fig. 38.

| N° | LOCATION | LAT | LONG | N° | LOCATION | LAT | LONG |
|----|----------|-----|------|----|----------|-----|------|
| 01 | | | | 11 | | | |
| 02 | | | | 12 | | | |
| 03 | | | | 13 | | | |
| 04 | | | | 14 | | | |
| 05 | | | | 15 | | | |
| 06 | | | | 16 | | | |
| 07 | | | | 17 | | | |
| 08 | | | | 18 | | | |
| 09 | | | | 19 | | | |
| 10 | | | | 20 | | | |

© Yachting Monthly and Northern Star Insurance Co Ltd, a member company of the worldwide Generali Group

## Instructions

1) This Waypoint programme can be used in conjunction with any position fixing system - Decca, Loran or GPS.

2) The form is self-adhesive and can be placed close to your position fixing unit for instant reference. Remove the backing paper carefully and attach to a smooth surface.

3) Enter the Waypoint name and Lat/Long co-ordinates using a 2B lead pencil; entries can be erased using a soft rubber. Only use a ballpoint pen for permanent entries.

4) By listing all waypoints anticipated for the passage or cruising area, Lat/Long co-ordinates can be inputted, without reference to listings in the yacht's log or nautical almanac.

5) The numbered self adhesive chart indicators can be directly superimposed on the chart (or charts) for quick refer...

will increase to $1-1\frac{1}{2}$ knots (first figure neaps, second figure spring tides). At the speed he is sailing—three knots perhaps—it may take him four hours to reach his destination and saying, just for the hell of it, that the tides are at springs, it means he will be set to the east about five miles during that time. Later, the stream will slacken and then begin running from the opposite direction, and if, during his passage, his speed falls so low that the whole thing takes him twice as long, he might expect to get pushed back again that five miles. Meanwhile (see Fig. 38) he lays off a course to steer which will keep him on the straight and narrow. Setting off the five miles down tide from his starting-point and then setting the dividers at the distance he expects to sail during the four-hour span—twelve miles in this case—he places one point at the five-mile down-tide position and swings the other point to cut the course line. He rules in the line between the two points of the dividers, and this gives the direction in which he must steer to keep his ship proceeding in the direction in which he wants to go. The point where the dividers have cut the course line will be his position in four hours' time.

Four hours is a long time ahead to forecast the sailing speed of a small boat. A motor boat, counting on keeping up an exact speed the whole time, can be navigated the whole way in one go. We know how long she'll take to cover the distance and can set off the tidal effect in one step. Under sail it is often safer to take it hour by hour, adjusting the course steered according to the increase or decrease in speed of boat and rate of tide.

It may so happen that the route across the estuary is a buoy-hopping one, zigzagging, sometimes up-tide, sometimes down. In thick weather the compass courses will have to be worked out for every change. In normal weather, when each buoy can be seen from the preceding one, it is the best practice possible to plot every fresh change just as if the visibility were poor, the disparity, if any, between course steered by eye and course plotted will reveal any inaccuracies in your allowances for tide.

Since tidal streams rarely set exactly up and down but tend to deviate towards the beginning and end of each run, you must allow for this if plotting is to be accurate. If you make a plot hourly or half-hourly—and in a thickly buoyed area this isn't too frequent—some account of this deviation from the straight stream will be taken, but on a long hop across open water, with a steady breeze and some hope of a steady speed, a four-hour plot may be ample. In this case the whole tide effect, both rate by the hour and direction, can be plotted in advance and the resultant course steered. But it is important to remember that the yacht is not going to travel along a straight line. As the tide effect strengthens and slackens she will go forward along her sailed course but will be carried down and then back in a long curve. As destination may be the first concern of the navigator, where the yacht goes in the process may not seem so important. However, should there be a shoal or a danger of some sort along this curve, the vessel may be in trouble, despite the fact that the straight line rules on the chart skirts it safely (Fig. 40).

A sailing cruiser meandering quietly to her destination across a relatively large expanse of open water and taking long enough about it to allow several tides to elapse is a rather different case. She may plot

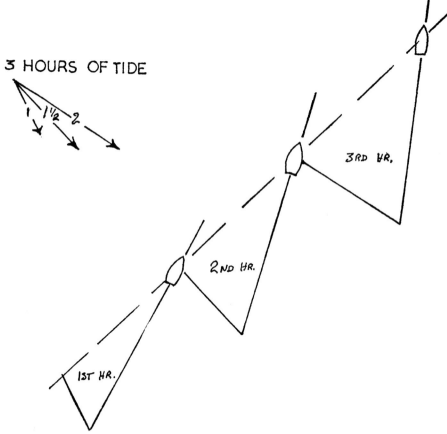

3 HOURS OF TIDE

3RD HR.

2ND HR.

1ST HR.

FIG. 39. The tidal streams have been computed and a separate change of course to offset them has been made for each of the three hours of the passage. The yacht is sailing at 3 knots. In fluky winds or on short passages between buoys in thick weather this alternative to the method shown in Fig. 38 may be necessary.

and allow for tide at regular periods, in the manner described or, since her time of arrival under sail alone cannot be estimated with certainty, she can sail the direct course from A to B and simply plot her tidal wanderings either side of the course line. Ultimately she will be near enough to her goal for a prediction to be made and a tidal stream allowance worked out. For a crew of two or three men, of whom only one is navigating, this is the easier method. It wouldn't do for an offshore racer, but it is safe, it is easier in a small cruiser, and it places no strain upon the watchkeeping.

A study of the tidal atlases shows that the streams sweep along the coasts, filling the rivers and setting up eddies in bays, building up to very high levels in some places (study the various tide height tables) and

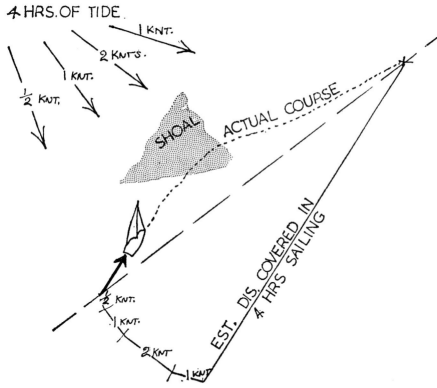

FIG. 40. In this case the navigator has taken four hours of tidal set and plotted it in advance, laying off his predicted speed during the next four hours. The fluctuations of the tidal stream will cause him to sail along the dotted line averaging out so that he will arrive at X as planned. It must be noted however that he has made no allowance for sailing so far above his intended course line and he skims the shoal by mistake.

only reaching modest heights at others. The French Channel coasts and the Bristol Channel have tides which range to the thirty-foot mark and over, while the English South Coast may have its highest levels of only half that figure. The rate of the tidal streams varies just as much. The fastest stream in some areas may not exceed three knots while speeds of seven and eight knots are not rare around the Brittany headlands. At times, the course to steer, plotted in advance, may seem quite mad. The coast may be distant and the sea calm, yet the tide has the cruiser in an iron grip, and only by carefully planning beforehand can one get her to port in reasonable time. So many carelessy navigated yachts can be seen shooting up and down the French coasts, aiming uncertainly at some harbour and never quite hitting it, that the lesson for the man in the very small cruiser, making a cross-Channel passage, is to study the tides with painstaking thoroughness. Half a mile down-tide on arrival can mean either frantic motoring to make up or six hours or so spent waiting for the turn of the tide and the risk of missing one's harbour if the wind goes light.

The atlases are as accurate as plain mathematics can make them, but the streams vary quite a lot depending upon prevailing wind and atmospheric pressure. Prolonged north to north-west winds in the North Sea can jam the tide up in the narrows and cause devastating flooding (the 1953 disaster is a case in point). At other times, tides may become erratic, with fierce ebbs, perhaps. Thus, a tongue in the cheek is not out of place. The tidal atlases published by the Admiralty have a graph which enables one to interpolate between Spring and Neap figures, and there is also a very handy tidal publication called the Ellis chart which shows rates by means of a colour code; it is very easy to read and very valuable to the little vessel, since dangerously fast tidal areas can be clearly seen and so avoided.

### The Making Tack

So far, the yacht has been considered as luckily blessed with a free wind and able to sail any course which is plotted. We can allow ourselves a bitter laugh at this presumption. Facts show that about half our time seems to be spent hard on the wind. Once the system of plotting and allowing for tidal set is understood, the added disadvantage of having to lay a course which can be sailed becomes just a matter of com-promise. The yacht beating along a track which cuts athwart the run of the tide must seek to lee-bow when she can. The wind rarely stays constant for long, and sooner or later the yacht will find one tack more advantageous than the other. Her final track may show an apparently haphazard stagger across the channel. The extent to which it diverges from the most direct line will depend entirely upon the navigator's skill at marrying the course sailed with the allowance for tide.

The simple example would be a yacht on a cross-Channel passage facing a head wind. If she tacks down-tide it will carry her many miles to leeward of her destination, but if she makes her tack a lee-bowed one, the end of the tide run will see her somewhere not so far from her

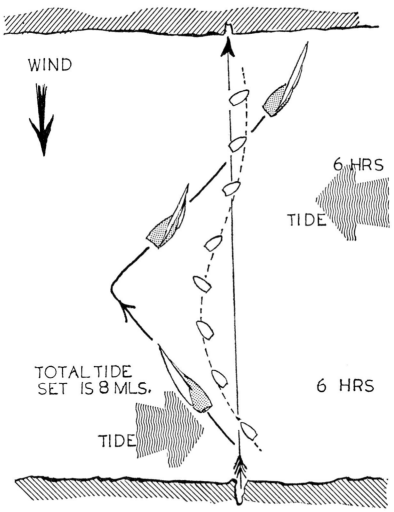

WIND

6 HRS

TIDE

TOTAL TIDE
SET IS 8 MLS.

6 HRS

TIDE

FIG. 41. By lee-bowing the tide each time it changes, the yacht will make good a course roughly shown along the dotted line as well as being pushed to windward.

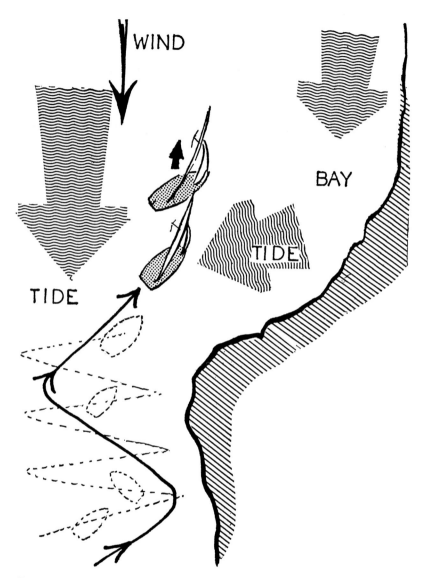

FIG. 42. Having flogged against wind and tide along the coast (dotted lines) the cruiser meets the tidal current flowing out from a bay. By holding the lee-bow course she has the benefit of a push to windward. This is purely a demonstrative situation. In actual fact it would be very doubtful if the small cruiser could work over a tide against a head-wind unless the tide was very weak.

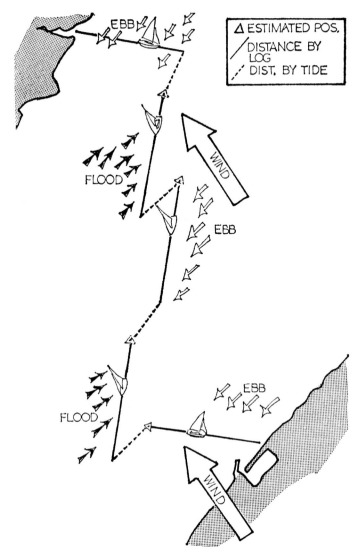

Fig. 43. Three ebbs and two floods are to elapse before the yacht has completed her cross-Channel passage. Obviously her speed cannot be predicted for this length of time in advance. She also has a head wind.

It will be noted that she lee-bows the tide, changing tacks at each turn or thereabouts. The dotted lines indicate the amount of tidal push to be plotted each time a reckoning of position is made (leeway, etc., has been omitted). She has been navigated to a point where she can stem the coastal current with an opportunity for freeing sheets should she need to do so. A power boat, knowing the duration of her passage with some certainty, could have assumed that two tides would cancel each other and simply lay off for the extra ebb. Naturally this assumes that the tidal rates would be fairly equal.

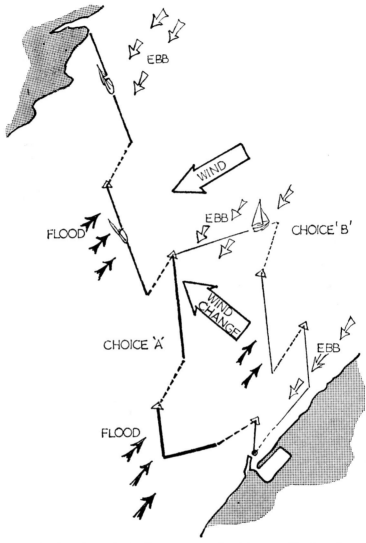

Fig. 44. A changing wind affects strategy in this case. She has dropped down Channel with the ebb and held the same reaching course when the flood began to lee-bow her. The wind comes ahead and she is faced with a choice of tack. Choice 'A' carries her well down the coast so that she can take the next flood up to her port. Choice 'B', a lee-bowing course, takes her longer in the end since she spends less time on the more direct making tack.

planned course. In a river she may even sheer straight across on one tack.

A long passage in which several tides may ebb and flow and which the yacht lee-bows, will see her far ahead of another which simply drifts up and down the Channel (Fig. 41). Lee-bowing has the effect of reducing the loss of ground from leeway and it enables the yacht to stay somewhere near her desired track even if the wind shifts its direction. Even if the direction of the wind allows her to lie almost directly on the bearing of her destination, a strong cross-tide may make the losing tack more profitable, although, of course, this would only apply to a short passage involving one tide. If the tide could be counted upon to turn and shove the yacht back on her track later, the making tack would certainly pay better.

## Other Deflections

The helmsman can make a farce of the finest course ever plotted. One cannot expect ocean racing accuracy from the helmsman of a small cruiser. He will make the best course he can consistent with the distractions of sunbathing, yarning, eating and drinking canned ale. This doesn't matter as long as all are enjoying themselves, but it is still important to have a shrewd idea on which side of the course line to expect the greatest errors. On the wind people may tend to eat up to windward a shade, sailing in a series of long luffs. If they are pinching, a good deal of leeway may also be expected. On a run, fear of a gybe shows in an error upwind or at least towards the direction opposite the boom. Without getting acid about it, the navigator must induce his companions to try noting their average course steered—the fact that their errors are so plain will in any case improve their steering. Leeway can be checked by taking a bearing of the wake while the ship is being sailed as straight as possible, the result, checked against the compass course, is a rough guide, but it cannot be applied to all on-the-wind courses for leeway will vary with the conditions.

## Distance and Speed

The modern yacht log may be anything from the towing rotator variety to the latest in electronics with through-hull impellers or inside-hull doppler type. It is as accurate an instrument as one might hope to find dealing with such erratic things as wind, water and sailing craft. It is a costly device for the small-boat man to buy if he is only likely to use it once or twice in the course of a season, but it is vital that he should have some idea of his speed through the water and hence distance travelled through the water if his navigation is to be anything but a series of guesses.

There is no equivalent substitute for a proper patent log, but there are rule of thumb speed-checks which can be made and which, with practice, can yield good results.

The original 'log', which consisted of a weighted wooden kite allowed to run astern on a vastly long line and checked at the turn of a minute glass to see how many 'knots' in the line had run out, was quite accurate enough. But it is impractical for small craft. A modification (which we'll call the drag-log) plus a stop-watch, is a scaled-down version that works quite well. A fifty-foot fishline with an old sock, stiffened at the mouth with wire and toe-less at the end, is thrown overboard as the stop-watch starts and the jerk of the line as the limit is reached marks the second when the watch should be stopped. A simple table of feet-per-second gives an approximation of speed. A check made every quarter or half hour intervals will keep a close tally of the speed and distance. But the short length of the line makes timing critical, and the brief moment when the line nears its limit and is straightening out should not be mistaken for the final tug. The table appears at the end of the chapter.

A check on sock-log timing should be made whenever there is an opportunity of a tideless run between buoys. The speed of small cruisers capable of about five knots and averaging about four can soon be judged quite accurately by eye, but on a long passage, when speed checks may be ignored for hours at a time due to the call of bunk and board, the temptation is to over-estimate at a later count. The result of this is that any landfall in thickish weather becomes a horror of suspense. Distance run may put you among the pastures, but there may still be many safe miles of water ahead. Without accurate direction and distance, the failure of a landfall to turn up on time leaves the navigator helpless to know which way to head. Transverse tidal sets will further bewilder him, as he will have no idea how far astray he has been carried.

It must be thoroughly understood that the speed sailed through the water is quite separate from the speed covered over the sea-bed or along the shore. Just as a beetle scuttling along a carpet towards a hole in the wall can be given a lot of extra exercise if the carpet is pulled away from the hole, so a foul tide cuts down the useful speed of the ship. Sailing five knots against a four-knot tide obviously means only one knot made good over the sea-bed and a nine-knot passage when the tides goes fair. It seems an elementary matter, but it is one which often trips up the inland owner venturing to sea. The moving carpet of the sea is a delight which takes all chance of monotony from sailing and makes the same little weekend cruise to the same old place a never-ending novelty.

## *Additional Notes: Navigation Inventory*

THE chart-table can be a sheet of hardboard which clips to the deckhead when not in use and is laid on a bunk for working. Size: minimum 12 in. × 18 in. but 2 ft 6 in. × 1 ft 9 in. is better if there is room. Fiddles or beading on one long edge to stop pencils rolling off, other edges plain so that parallel rules can be used more easily. More elaborate tables can be thought up to suit the cabin layout.

(*a*) Charts as required, corrected annually by chart dealers.
(*b*) Nautical Almanac.
(*c*) Local tide-table for convenience.
(*d*) Small parallel rules or Sestrel-Luard combined course setting and compass conversion protractor. (Many time-saving instruments are available which replace the parallel rules.)
(*e*) Pair of dividers.
(*f*) HB pencil, rubber. (Recommend at least three pencils.)
(*g*) Yachtsman's Pilot Books.
(*h*) Protractor.
(*i*) Ordnance one-inch survey map of coast. Optional extra but very useful for coastal recognition.
(*j*) Barometer with setting hand, and adjusted to sea-level readings.
(*k*) Log book (Exercise book). Jotting pad.
(*l*) Chart-table light, such as battery lamp to hang overhead or flat multi-battery lantern.
(*m*) Hand-bearing compass, or any simple substitute. Ex-army marching compasses can be used with practice.
(*n*) Patent log or substitute drag-log.
(*o*) Stop-watch (not essential but extremely useful for the beginner).
(*p*) Steering compass either luminous or lit by an accumulator. Torch batteries are too short-lived when used continually.

*Drag-Log:* 50-ft fishing line. Old nylon sock with wire-stiffened top attached by three short lines to end of fishing line. Method: Flake the line on deck for free running (don't coil it or it will snarl up). Drop the sock and start stop-watch. When the line begins to tighten stop the watch. (Line stretches and the final bringing up may add seconds, check at the first drag.)

| Line out in 30 sec. | Approx. speed 1 knot. |
|---|---|
| 15 | 2 knots. |
| 10 | 3 |
| $7\frac{1}{2}$ | 4 |
| 6 | 5 |
| 5 | 6 |
| $4\frac{1}{2}$ | 7 |
| $3\frac{1}{2}$ | 8 |

*Log Book:* Rule vertically as follows: Time, log, course to steer, barometer, notes (i.e. headlands abeam, fixes, weather, etc., etc.). It is important that all courses steered, positions estimated or checked, leeway and any information relevant to the plotting should be noted. Chart plots should be marked on the chart with time and log-reading. Thus, the workings can be gone over from the beginning of the passage in case of later uncertainty.

*Compass Deviation:* An outboard motor stowed close can cause 40 degrees of deviation. Simple check: Mount a second accurate borrowed compass on the coachroof or in any place where there is no possibility of deviation from metalwork. Align it with the lubber-line exactly fore and aft. When the boat is just afloat on the mooring have two people watching ship's and coachroof compasses and one man wading overboard to swing the cruiser right round her mooring, heading on each point of the compass. Note readings as in the following example. Coachroof compass N., Ship's compass 005; Coachroof N.E., Ship's 046; Coachroof E., Ship's 93, etc., etc. The deviation card would then read:

For N.   . . . steer 005<br>
N.E. . . . steer 046<br>
E.   . . . steer 093<br>
etc. around the compass and . . .<br>
W.   . . . steer 264 etc.

Get under way with the engine running and check by steering on each heading. Also under sail steeply heeled (sitting to leeward maybe). If there is much extra heeling error, a tip suggested by Robert Tucker is to make an inclinometer (small pendulum) marked with heeling error on each degree of heel.

A simple alternative way by which a steering compass can be checked for accuracy on all headings is to tow a man astern in the inflatable dinghy. By means of a carefully sighted hand-bearing compass he can align mast and backstay and call out when he is 'ON' for each heading. The yacht, meanwhile, is motored absolutely straight on each heading, the helmsman noting actual ship's head at the time of each 'ON' call.

*Chapter Eight*

# The Chart, Fixes and Drift

NEVER economise on charts. The belief that a single small-scale chart showing all the ports and rivers you plan to visit on a cruise is the most sensible buy soon leads to grey hairs. The small-scale passage charts covering large areas of coast are intended to be used by vessels following the sea-lanes around the coasts. They show all the principal lights and give all the relevant details of headlands, soundings, nature of bottom and so forth, but once the vessel, no matter how small, makes for a river or begins to coast close to the land she begins to need more detailed information. The small-scale chart may show an offlying shoal, but not all the small unlit buoys around it, and the cruiser, seeing a beacon pole far to seaward, may search his passage chart in vain.

The chart folder might include one general passage chart showing the whole cruising areas as well as many large-scale charts and river plans as are likely to be needed, also one or two which you may be forced to need. For instance on a long passage along an exposed coastline, it's wise to have a chart of available shelter. To back up this information, a yachtsman's pilot book is needed. Those compiled by Adlard Coles—*Creeks and Harbours of the Solent, Pilot to the South Coast Harbours*, and so on, are ideal—provided the reader realises that changes in lights, buoyage, and so on, are constantly taking place. *Reed's Nautical Almanac* is indispensable as it contains the tide-tables, lights lists (names of buoys, light characteristics and harbour signals) and a good deal else besides. Tidal atlases or tidal charts may not be necessary, for many yachtsmen's charts incorporate this information, and it is also to be found in *Reed's*.

To outline all the information to be found on any chart would take far more room than I have to spare here, but the details in regular use by yachtsmen can be noted.

Buoyage, soundings, coastal features, compass rose and scale of sea-miles claim first attention, but the wealth of additional detail given in symbol form must be learned by close study. The whorl which indicates a tidal eddy, the different types of pecked line denoting three-, five-, ten-fathom lines, and so on. The various ways of indicating whether a wreck is dangerous to surface navigation or quite harmless (save to

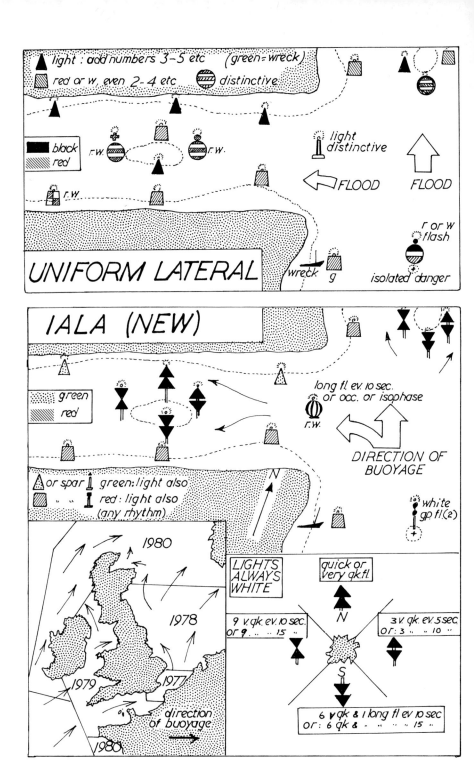

UNIFORM LATERAL

light : add numbers 3-5 etc    (green=wreck)
red or w, even 2-4 etc    distinctive

black
red

r.w.    r.w.

r.w.

light distinctive

FLOOD    FLOOD

r or w flash

wreck  g    isolated danger

IALA (NEW)

green
red

long fl. ev. 10 sec. or occ. or isophase

r.w.

DIRECTION OF BUOYAGE

or spar  green: light also
    red : light also
    (any rhythm)

N

white gp. fl.(2)

1980

1978

1979    1977

direction of buoyage

1980

LIGHTS ALWAYS WHITE

quick or very qk.fl.

9 v. qk. ev. 10 sec. or 9 „ „ 15 „

N

3 v. qk. ev. 5 sec. or: 3 „ „ 10 „

S

6 v qk & 1 long fl ev 10 sec or: 6 qk & „ „ „ 15 „

140

anchors), the nature of the sea-bed and types of rock and reef are all listed in *Reed's* so that you can recognise them on the charts.

The system of buoyage used on charts is shown in Fig. 45.* It is international in principle although the general design of the buoys may differ. Other systems, the French quadrantal system for instance, are easy to pick up. On the chart, buoys are shown in symbol and under-lined with a centre dot to show actual position—bearings plotted upon buoys should be taken from this point. Lit buoys have a tinted halo to distinguish them, and the light characteristic in abbreviation beside it (see Night Sailing, page 171. Colour tinting makes the *Yachtsman* chart easier to read at a glance, with drying banks and shoreline distinct from shoal water which doesn't quite dry out and deep soundings, while dry lands remains a uniform grey. Chart scale is all-important and before working on a new chart its scale should be noted. The change over to metric depths can also catch the careless and the unwary.

Drying heights are underlined, and the figure refers to the height of sea-bed exposed on mean low water spring tides, which is taken as the datum for most soundings. The adjustment of existing tide height to the figures shown on the chart as M.L.W.S. is a job for the navigator. (See page 103.)

The chart compass rose mentioned earlier can vary between a circle of 360 degrees with zero on the Magnetic North line and the principal points marked N, NNE, NE, ENE, E, etc. Or it can consist of concen-tric circles, the outer one orientated on True or chart north and the inner on Magnetic. It is important to remember that only the inner rose should be used unless the navigator is able and prepared to convert True to Magnetic and back again.

Compass 'points' bear no direct relationship to 'degree'. Points of the compass are the four cardinal markings north, south, east and west, divided and subdivided into a total of thirty-two points (each $11\frac{1}{4}$ degrees), and again by quarter-points. Thus a bearing by points compass might be 'north by east and a quarter east' or 'south-west by west three-quarters west'. *Reed's* contains a conversion table to render points notation into degrees, but beyond remembering this in case of

* Note: Substantial alterations to the International System are gradually being introduced at the time of going to press. Readers should be alert to possible changes.

FIG. 45. From 1977, IALA buoyage will be phased in to replace the uniform lateral system buoyage hitherto prevailing in UK waters. Inset shows the programme of changes. IALA combines lateral with quadran-tal systems and should prove simpler. In the main, the new buoyage simply calls for red to port and green to starboard when proceeding in the *direction of buoyage*. The direction will not necessarily be the direction of the flood tide stream as hitherto.

trouble the best plan is to forget the picturesque points system and its problems (Fig. 46).

Yet another method of marking the compass rose is the quadrantal system. This consists of a 360-degree circle, but instead of running from zero to 360, the rose is divided into four quadrants running north to east (0 degree to 90 degrees), north to west (0 degree to 90 degrees) and south to east, south to west in the same manner. Many yacht compasses are marked in this way, and there is no difficulty, once the thing is understood. A course plotted on the chart as, for instance, south-west or 225 degrees Magnetic would be given to the helmsman as 'south 45 degrees west'. With practice it is easy to remember that 135 degrees is S 45 degrees E, 180 degrees is south, 270 degrees is west, 280 degrees is N, 80 degrees W and so on. Quadrantal notation is easy to steer by, but there is the snag that a helmsman, especially a sleepy one, can quite easily wander off course and come back *on the wrong quadrant*.

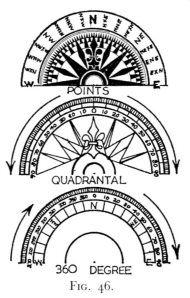

FIG. 46.

The charts mark coastal features according to their value as means of identification. Thus, if a church is marked it will be a prominent one. Cliffs are shown as a bird's-eye view, principal coastal roads are given and some charts give contours to indicate land heights. High hills have their height in feet above Mean High Water Springs. Gasometers, windmills, quarries, high chimneys, and so on, are all indicated by appropriate symbols. Most chart symbols are self-explanatory, but as there is no room to reproduce the whole lot in these pages, your only alternative is to settle down with chart and *Reed's* and study them.

Unlike those on a land map, which gives a separate scale of miles, the distances measured on a chart must be taken from the side-margins (latitude) (Fig. 47). A sea-mile is equal to 1 minute of latitude and 60 minutes make 1 degree of latitude. (A knot is purely a measurement of speed—sea-miles per hour. One cannot speak of being six knots away from land, nor is it correct to speak of six knots per hour, knots are just knots.) It must be emphasised that all references to 'miles' in this book are to sea and not to land miles.

Charts are always drawn on Mercator's Projection, which gives a true picture of angles and bearings, but only by distorting the scale, which becomes larger as it nears the poles. On small-scale charts this change in scale is quite noticeable. It is therefore usual to measure distance by using that part of the side margin which is on more or less the same line of latitude. The usual procedure is to set the dividers at the distance to be measured and then place one point on a convenient figure of the scale and read off above it. Alternatively, setting the

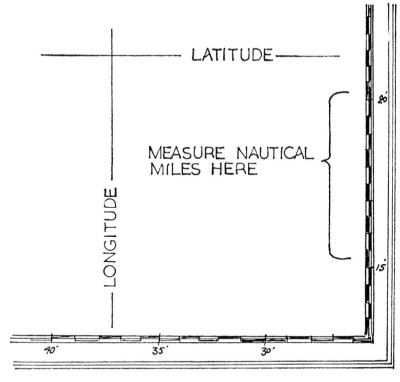

FIG. 47.

dividers to a five- or ten-mile span, they can then be 'walked' across the chart.

Large-scale charts or plans do sometimes give a separate scale of sea-miles in the title, divided into smaller distances of one cable for the purpose of estimating safe navigable distances from rocks, wharves and so on. A cable is one tenth of a sea-mile, and near enough to 200 yards for purposes of distance judging. It is worth remembering this as Pilot Books refer to safe offings from river-banks, cliffs and so on in terms of cable-lengths.

## Bearings and Fixes

There are few things so reassuring to the man in some doubt which side of safety his ship is lying as a set of bearings taken with an accurate hand-bearing compass on identified lights or landmarks. The procedure is simple. The bearing read on the compass-card is plotted on the chart from the identified mark. Several such bearings taken within an approximate right-angle will intersect: the intersection is the ship's position—or should be.

Two bearings only, taken inaccurately (Fig. 48), can yield a nice

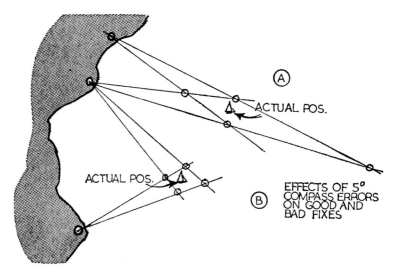

FIG. 48. Two-point fixes are liable to inaccuracy without the virtue of being able to detect the fault as in the case of three-point fixes. At 'A' the small circles show a number of 'positions' which could be obtained due to five-degree errors in reading the compass. At 'B' the angle is wider and the area fixed becomes smaller despite the five-degree error.

144

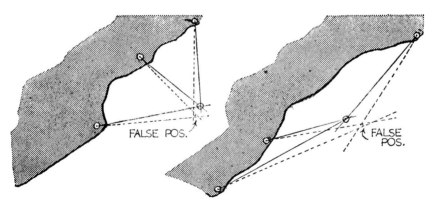

FIG. 49. Three-point bearings are also liable to error, but it is usually noticeable especially if only one bearing is taken or plotted wrongly. In the above case however there are errors on all bearings due perhaps to wild motion or carelessness. Dotted lines show how even these can fall into a small cocked hat, but that if the angles are suitably wide the area of error is far less than if the angles are narrow.

variety of possible positions, particularly if the marks are spaced at a narrow angle as shown at 'A'. The addition of a third bearing clinches the matter in the form of a 'cocked hat'. The relative size of this headgear largely determines the accuracy of the fix. It is, however, possible to produce a tidy little hat when the bearings are well adrift, but it is more likely to be wide and obvious to see. The important thing is that inaccuracy should be limited to small errors and be consistent (Fig. 49).

The bearing compass must be pretty dead-beat, that is to say it must return smartly to its true orientation after a wild swing caused by the cavorting cruiser. It will often be impossible to get the card to centre exactly on a bearing and the average of the swing must be taken. Thus, the navigator looking at the object over his compass sees it swooping around in the sights and the card swooping to and fro in the prism. Steady helmsmanship and patience are required. Never take a hasty bearing if it is an important one, and never tell an inexperienced crew to do it unless it is a routine check and not vital. When using a hand-bearing compass make sure you are holding it clear of iron stanchions, steel rigging or neighbouring iron.

Since accuracy is important it may be necessary to correct the chart bearing for change in Variation before plotting it. In general, a chart which is one or two years older than the date shown on the compass rose will be so little adrift that one can get away with plotting straight from it. For instance, the chart shows that Magnetic Variation at that position was 9 degrees and 45 minutes west of True North in 1961 and that it is decreasing by 8 minutes annually. In two years Magnetic North has crept nearer to True North by 16 minutes. There are 60 minutes to 1 degree so that the error is just over a quarter of a degree or the thickness of a very fine pencil line. Had the chart been ten years out of date (although corrected for other little anachronisms we hope) the error would have been 10 × 8 = 1 degree, 20 minutes. When one remembers that the bearing may be taken in rough weather giving another 2 degrees error and that the compass may have been nestling against the backstay at the time and been deviated by another couple of degrees, the possible total error of 5 degrees, 20 minutes is going to matter. All efforts towards accuracy should be made providing the results are plottable.

To correct the chart for, say, a 1½-degree decrease or *easterly* error, one must visualise holding the parallel rules (or whatever gadget is in use) steady on the bearing just taken with the compass and turning the

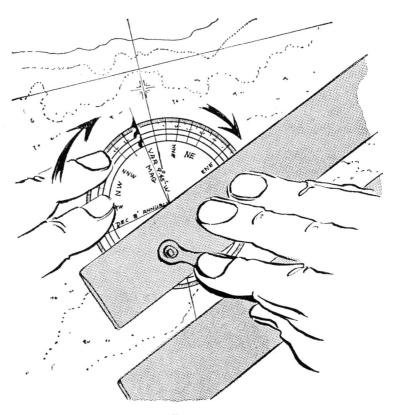

FIG. 50.

chart 1½ degrees clockwise or to the east (Fig. 50). If the bearing taken was 70 degrees, the swing to the east will decrease it to 68½ degrees.

If a bearing is to be read from the chart and then sought with the hand-bearing compass, the same rule must naturally be followed. The case of a yachtsman faced with lights in line or a line of safe bearing is one in point here. From the chart he notes that the bearing must be 120 degrees magnetic for a safe course. The chart is 2 degrees out of date, he would look for a bearing of 118 degrees with his compass. In point of fact, any really serious situation involving a yes or no of safety which rested on a matter of 2 degrees would be rather nasty.

Generally speaking, practically all the bearings taken in small yachts are confirmatory ones. Position is known within reasonable limits from dead-reckoning, the bearings confirm and implement. Among the most important are sets of bearings taken to give a fix at the end of a long passage offshore when D.R. is possibly a bit adrift. On this score, the temptation to trust in a fuzzy bearing taken on the distant 'loom' of a light, before the light itself has cleared the horizon, must be resisted mightily. Such bearings, taken at right-angles to the course as a check

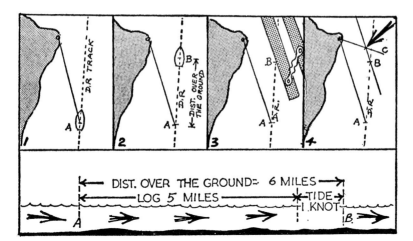

FIG. 51. The running fix. Stage 1. A bearing is taken of the headland from position 'A'. The log is read and time noted. Stage 2. Log read again at a convenient figure and the run adjusted for tidal effect. Position 'B' is marked on course line and a second bearing of the headland is taken. Stage 3. The first bearing is transferred to the logged position 'B' and, Stage 4, the second bearing plotted. It will be noticed that the fix has fallen some way inshore of the dead reckoned course line. (*Below.*) Distance by log must be corrected for tidal stream effect, the log reads 5 miles but the ship has moved her position a total of 6 miles along the coast from A to B.

on distance to the land ahead, can be wildly adrift. Take them by all means but don't rely on them simply because they 'confirm' D.R. position, for both can be out. Beware, too, the bearings taken on buoys. These can be, and quite often are, a little out of position after very hard weather. Moreover, if they are close at hand, the range of the buoy on its mooring can account for inaccuracy. Whenever buoys are the sole means of fixing, take a set of shots on every buoy which is in a position to give a cross. Four or five bearings in fact—that is if the result is of serious importance.

On a coastal run, and with a fast tide under the cruiser, you must take bearings in quick succession. To take one, plot it, and then take two more is bound to give a poor result as the yacht will have travelled a long way between the first and last bearings.

Our old die-hards, those monsters of possible inaccuracy, the running fix and the double-the-angle-on-the-bow must come into the picture here. Perhaps I am hard on them, but these fixes, being subject to failure because of the unknown speed of the cruiser over the ground, do produce an 'answer' which fairly screams reliability while remaining forever suspect.

The great advantage of the running fix is that only one object can be used for the bearings. In brief, the yacht takes a bearing, sails along her course for a while and takes another bearing of the same object. By marking off along her course the distance she sailed between the two bearings and then transferring the *first* bearing line to a point where it will cut the second at the limit of the distance sailed, we have our fix. Accuracy depends entirely upon knowing how far the cruiser has sailed. This means an accurate log and a very accurate estimation of the tidal stream effect—plus or minus.

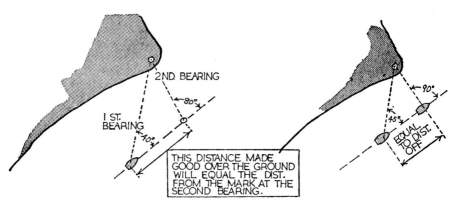

FIG. 52.

Doubling the angle, while being another one-object trick, also relies upon one's knowing the tide effect. In this case, though, a tidal stream which is either dead fair or dead foul does not matter so long as it can be calculated, but any cross-current or the effect of excessive leeway will ruin the fix. With the cruiser sailing a straight course past the object a bearing is taken—we will say that it is plotted and makes an angle of 40 degrees to the course-line (Fig. 52). If the yacht sails on until a bearing can be taken which will given an angle of 80 degrees to her course, the distance measured along the course-line between bearings will then be the same as her distance from the object at the time of the second bearing. What must be remembered is that it is the *angle to the course-line* which must be doubled and not the actual magnetic bearing. This means that when you have plotted the first bearing and used a protractor to measure the angle, you must use the protractor again to strike off a doubled angle which can then be read off against the compass-rose to determine its actual magnetic bearing. Armed with this knowledge the navigator waits, compass in hand, until the bearing comes 'on'.

Distance off by the four-point method is a good mental check for the man who is only able to leave the helm for short and hectic rushes to the chart. The object must be well ahead. He waits until it bears four points (45 degrees anyway) on his bow then he reads the log and notes the time. He sails on, waiting again until the object bears full on his beam or eight points (90 degrees). By reading his log again and mentally adjusting the result for tide effect he now has his distance from the object (Fig. 52). Again it can be seen that a difference of a knot of tide can mean a big error in a thirty-minute interval between bearings, but since, in darkness, the yachtsman may not know his distance off within two miles or more, the method is still of some comfort to him.

## Plotting Drift

Calculating position when out of sight of the shore in light, variable weather taxes the navigator to the utmost. The cruiser drifts along with barely steerage-way and the log-line turns dispiritedly every minute or so. Wind shifts mean repeated alterations of course, and flat calms punctuate the whole performance. Sooner or later, though, the breeze will harden and the cruiser will begin to move. It is then, from that moment, that the certainty of a good landfall rests upon the amount of care which has gone into plotting the drift. One tends to relax, potter with the gear, or swim over the side if the sun is hot, but the plotting is not to be neglected.

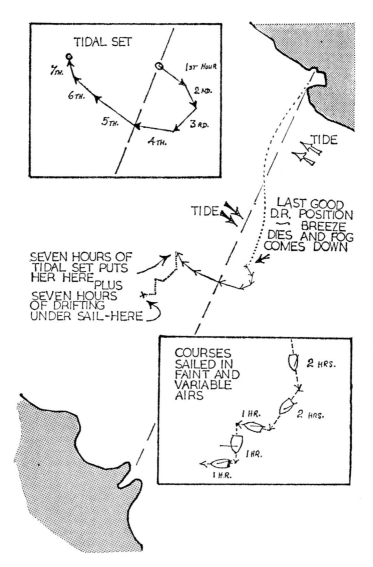

F<small>IG</small>. 53. Plotting drift. Note is taken of direction and rate of drift through the water in light airs and any courses actually sailed during the period of calm (*lower inset*). Note of tidal stream rate and direction during the same period is also made (*top inset*). The two are plotted one after the other and the final position taken as the point of departure when the cruiser ultimately begins sailing again.

As soon as the speed drops and all signs of calm are manifest—possibly the fog as well—the navigator must check log, time and tide and put his latest calculated position on the chart. As the speed falls still further he can amend the position hourly until the log-readings are no longer to be trusted, from then on he calculates drift (Fig. 53).

We'll suppose that the period of calm and light airs has lasted all day from 8 a.m. until 6 p.m. when the cruiser is sailing properly again. The navigator may not have put a position on the chart since early morning but he has filled the log-book with careful entries of every alteration of course made in the fluky airs and the estimated distance sailed on each course. Distrusting the almost vertical log-line (or maybe not having one at all), he will have done the best he can by calculating speed through water either with some sort of chip-log or drag-log or based his calculations on the fact that one knot is equivalent to (nearly) 100 feet per minute.

He begins, however, by plotting the tidal drift from the time of his last good D.R. position. It is to be noted here that the effect is not 'so much east' and 'so much west' (or north and south) but a gradual circling effect as the tidal stream has flowed, slackened, turned and ebbed again. With an Admiralty chart, he will have been able to plot his tide by finding the nearest code letter to his position on the chart and referring to the tidal stream table found elsewhere on the sheet. Thus in the last eight hours he may have been set south-east a mile, south half a mile, south-west half a mile, and then west for five, west-north-west a mile, and so on. This is all plotted, and when the final position is reached he begins to plot the actual sailing courses for the period. The ultimate result is (if he has taken due care and the tides have run according to plan) his departure point from thenceforward. While all this was being worked out he would, of course, have given the helmsman a snap course to steer, having noted time and log-reading at the onset.

### Additional Notes on Chart and Compass

(1) *True North* is a geographer's line taken from pole to pole. Broadly speaking, the top of a chart is North and the bottom is South and the chart is laid out to True North.

(2) *Magnetic North* is the ever-altering point, slightly off-centre, to which a magnetic compass points.

(3) *Variation* the difference in angle between True and Magnetic.

(4) *Deviation* the angle by which magnetic compass is pulled out of line by ironwork, etc., placed too near to it.

(5) If, for example, the chart is printed with its Magnetic compass-rose showing the exact variation and the compass is exactly accurate, courses

steered, and courses plotted using Magnetic North bearings would be identical.

(6) If all courses steered and bearings taken are to be plotted on the chart using *True North* they must be adjusted for variation. This might involve adding or subtracting large amounts (perhaps 9 degrees).

(7) By using the Magnetic rose on an up-to-date chart, figures dealt with will probably be no more than 2 degrees and mistakes less likely to be drastic.

*Just for the record: converting Magnetic to True, etc.:* When applying Magnetic variation and compass deviation, whether working from chart to compass or compass to chart the rule is: If it is west, the compass is 'best', if it is east the compass is 'least'. In other words, to convert a Magnetic bearing to True when the local Magnetic variation is, say, 8 degrees westerly, west being compass best, the 8 degrees would be subtracted. If there was also a 4-degree easterly compass deviation to allow for east being least the 4 degrees would be added. The resultant figure would be a True bearing, all the inaccuracies of the magnet having been ironed out. The crux of the matter lies in the references to the compass being 'best' and 'least'. If this is understood then working in reverse, i.e. converting True to Magnetic or compass, follows the same rule. A True bearing on the chart might be 130, and magnetic variation 9 degrees west 'west compass best'. In other words the True figure must be made 'better' if it is to become magnetic or compass and so the 9 degrees will be added to the True figure giving 139 degrees magnetic which will be steered. If there is a deviation figure this too must be applied.

With westerly variation common to the British Isles the word MUTS (magnet-unto-true-subtract) is a memory aid.

(8) Working on the chart Magnetic rose only the small differences of variation and deviation have to be accounted for. Compass-card pulled east or west of its source of attraction and chart rose showing variation as it was several years ago instead of at the present. Westerly variation which has 'decreased' or grown less is called 'easterly' error. Compass deviation when the card is pulled to the right (clockwise) by local interference is also easterly error. If the chart has 2 degrees E. error and the compass has 3 degrees E. error the total of 5 degrees east is applied. Again: 'To the east compass least.' Add working from chart to compass.

If chart variation has decreased during the age of the chart by say 3 degrees, giving a chart error of 3 degrees E., and there is a deviation of, say, 5 degrees W. on a particular course, the error to plot would be the difference or 2 degrees W.

*Timing drift, Duchman's log:* One knot equals roughly 100 feet per minute. Measure a handy length along the deck such as edge of forehatch to other end of cockpit—a distance perhaps of 16 feet. Throw overboard, ahead of the cruiser, a tightly rolled ball of paper (if wind is practically non-existent) or an empty bottle on a length of fine fishline for recovery. Start the stop-watch as it passes the first position and stop it as a watcher shouts 'NOW' at the aft position. If the time taken was, say, 3 seconds the sum is resolved quite simply $\frac{16 \times 60}{3 \times 100}$ or $3\frac{1}{5}$ knots.

*Dry-Swim Navigation:* For the purpose of getting to know the chart and finding tidal information quickly, fireside navigation on winter evenings is the next best thing to actual practice.

The 'dry-swimming' rules outlined here are not unlike some aspects of wartime instruction, save that the inclusion of dice and so forth makes more of a game of it.

You will need small-scale passage-charts—(one chart is enough so long as it deals with waters which are sufficiently littered with navigational hazards to make it interesting), a copy of *Reed's Nautical Almanac*, a pair of dice, navigator's dividers and parallel rules, plus a couple of small needles with sealing wax heads to represent the yachts.

Starting from an agreed port or river, the first player glances at his watch and looks up tidal information for that very moment. Whatever it may be he must start at once—and it may mean a foul tide out of the river for instance. The dice are then thrown, both together, and the combined reading taken as the 'log reading' and since it may be as much as twelve, this is reckoned as being the total of three hours sailing (a low number then simulates a lessening wind). He then checks tidal set for three hours from starting and plots his position. The second player may now start—plotting his tides as they would be three hours after the first player set out. Thus the two yachts sail on, making good three-hour runs and poor ones, being set into all manner of troubles by the tides, having to cross shoal water and checking tide-height for that hour, etc.

The introduction of a 'changes of wind direction', forfeits and extra throws can be engineered around the throwing of doubles as in an ordinary dice game. If all relevant information is looked up with each move (allowing 30 seconds to find a light characteristic in *Reed's* for instance), the value of this game is extremely high and it is also a fine way for a couple (or more) of sailing people to pass a winter evening. By using the charts of next year's proposed cruise there is even more advantage to be had.

Practice at plotting bearings can also be had without going to sea by making a winter weekend trip to the coast armed with a chart, a drawing-board for a chart-table and bearing-compass, rules, etc. Bearings taken of buoys, harbour lights, lightships, and so on, plotted from the land, will give a fix which is easy to check for accuracy. Using an Ordnance Survey map in the same manner, only inland, gives the same opportunity of pin-pointing mistakes but, of course, lacks the added benefit of working with sea-marks.

*Passage Plan* (before starting): Study chart and tidal atlas—tide-table for the standard port upon which the atlas is based (i.e. Dover, Cardiff, etc.). Study local tide-table for suitable time to leave river or harbour. Estimate distance to the next stage on passage, estimate average speed needed in order to carry a fair tide, estimate the effect of light head winds and foul-turning tide, is there alternative shelter *en route?* Study entry to ports or rivers in case of tidal difficulties. Listen to shipping forecasts to the latest possible hour before departure.

*On Passage:* Keep an up-to-date track. Avoid tide rips and overfalls, follow all shipping forecasts, watch the barometer, plot tidal streams even when it is possible to navigate visually (against those times when you will need your skill at working out an off-set). Plan to arrive up-tide of your destination whenever possible. Before entering but not too long before, work out the depth of water likely to be found in the charted anchorages. Check pilotage instructions for port entering signals likely to be displayed on signal masts, etc. If there is doubt about the weather don't hesitate to use the outboard in order to maintain average speed according to conditions. Know where you are all the time.

# Chapter Nine

# Planning a Port-to-Port Passage

IN a powerful motor cruiser a port-to-port passage is a simple matter. If the weather is fit to go you just go, and foul tides make very little difference. The man in the small sailing cruiser must use everything he knows about tidal streams, wind and strategy to make his arrival on time.

We will take the case of a cruiser at anchor well up some sheltered river (Fig. 54). We will assume that her power, if any, is so insignificant that it is a last resort rather than a first consideration. The intended passage consists of a three-mile run down river, a fifteen-mile sail along the coast and a five-mile plug up the next river to an anchorage, twenty-three miles in all. Tides are at Springs, and the high water is coming around mid-day and midnight. To get out of one river and to sail up the other one will mean catching the tidal stream fair in each case, an ebb and a flood respectively. Now the planning must begin.

The winds have been offshore for some days and show no signs of changing so that a fair wind out is a reasonable gamble. However, in any settled period of weather there is a good chance that the wind will fall light during the hours of darkness. With an early start in mind the navigator looks at the tidal atlas. High water is at 12.30 midnight, he has reasoned that a 04.30 start still gives him a couple of hours fair tide to reach the open sea but now he notes that if he does this, he will get out there to find the main tide stream beginning to go against him soon afterwards (at 08.00 hours in fact). He revises his plans.

The fair tide up the coast is important. It means that he must try to catch the whole of the ebb along the coast. This will also mean that with ordinary luck he will have the flood to take him up the next river, but he must try to avoid having too much of the flood against him while coasting. It is actually better to start out plugging the last of the foul tide.

With a moderate breeze aided a little by the engine if he is really forced to it, he reckons that he can average four knots over the ground—providing of course that the wind is still fair. Once outside then he has some four hours of sailing to put in before he reaches the next river mouth. On the face of it, it seems he can do the whole

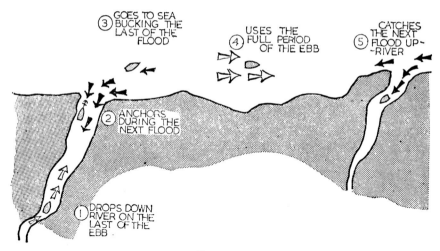

FIG. 54.

*Note:* Streams may not always conform to the simplified example shown here.

passage on one ebb, leaving at high water and arriving in time for the flood up to his anchorage, a choice, in fact, between making a midnight departure or a mid-day one.

With any doubt about his average speed, he might decide to drop down to his river mouth on the last of one ebb tide, anchor, and wait until the next flood has weakened sufficiently to let him get out and then have the advantage of some seven hours of sailing before the next flood gets him.

This is a typical case typically dealt with. The alternative is for him to go when he feels like it and arrive when he gets there. He may be lucky and hit a fine slant of breeze, but more often than not he will be yawning his way through his second 4 a.m. watch while wiser men are sailing abeam having just gone to sea.

Sometimes the whole aim of a planned passage is to arrive off some distant headland at a certain hour in order to catch the tide. It may be a matter of negotiating a shallow bar or swatchway between sand-banks, or it may be a simple passage with no other complications than getting the best out of wind and tide. The man with a twin-keel cruiser may be anxious to make his arrival when there is sufficient water to beach his boat on a hard; and, as we have already seen, the fact that he is high and dry before his start may mean that he slipped up badly in not being able to get away when the tidal stream was fair.

## Planning a Cruise

The tendency is to be over-ambitious in planning a cruise. To have a general objective is good, but one should be prepared to enjoy cruising for its own sake rather than as a form of transport to a particular place.

New owners who are short of experience are better advised to choose an area which has plenty of scope for day-sailing and short hops between fresh anchorages. The Solent is a classic example of a place where it is possible to sail every day for a fortnight and never anchor twice in the same place at night. Falmouth, the East Coast rivers and creeks, the Clyde and many more areas are to be found which are ideal training grounds. The man who takes his family to sea for the first time is well advised to choose short-hop cruising if he is not to risk putting them off for ever after.

In a very small cruiser, life can be cramped, especially with children aboard and in wet weather. A night or two ashore in an hotel is sensible, and he will certainly need a few days in port for excursions ashore. Sailing to a schedule can ruin a cruise for this one reason. The eternal pressing on is tiring and one loses the pleasure of being a vagrant. Plans should be elastic enough to allow a little dallying.

The answer to the eternal question 'How far can we get?' is like the length of the proverbial piece of string, but with settled weather, good sailing breezes, some fair and some foul, a small family cruiser might cover getting on for a couple of hundred miles in ten days, sailing during daylight and having the occasional day in. The same boat with a tougher crew who want to push harder, sail at night, and use every fair breeze could double this distance. We are presupposing of course, that the winds, if not always fair, are never so foul that the cruiser is weather-bound in port for days on end. Some cruisers never get further than a few miles down the coast, and there they stay until the weather lets up a bit. The Solent type of cruise which offers more sheltered sailing has a big advantage here.

With wind and weather permitting and an energetic crew, it is possible to make a twenty-four hour passage which covers between eighty and one hundred miles. Two days at sea for a crew of three experienced hands is no hardship in good weather and such a passage would take them most of the way down-Channel. For the small cruiser it would be rare to have it easy for much longer than that, and the long passage cannot be reckoned on—one can only take the chance if it arises.

In a fortnight an experienced crew might cruise from, say, the Solent to Cherbourg, down to St Malo, back to Weymouth, and thence to the Solent again. A total distance of about 250 miles but including two

Channel crossings and perhaps three or four nights at sea in light weather. A total sailing time of between a possible 70, or in light weather a probable 115, sailing hours which divided up means something like an average of 8–9 hours a day for a fortnight. The essential thing about this type of cruise is to have time in hand in case you are delayed by the weather.

Plans must be made on the chart if estimates are to be realistic. It is safer to call fourteen days nine actual sailing days to allow for delay, poor weather, and so on, and of the nine, perhaps only four will be real distance-coverers.

Prevailing wind is important. A one-way cruise from Falmouth to the Solent would be far more likely to come off than the same distance from east to west. For the same reason, a cross-Channel passage to, say, Le Havre from the Solent is more likely to go according to plan than one from Chichester to Alderney—the first is a reach and the second a close fetch in prevailing westerlies. The return passage must be remembered, of course, and time kept in hand once more.

It is unwise to arrange a cruise to coincide with top Spring tides especially in such areas as the Brittany coast or Bristol Channel where heights rise to 30 or 40 feet (Bay of Mont St Michel). Seas are rougher, many shallow-water anchorages dry out, anchor scope is much greater and it will often be impossible to make headway against foul tidal streams. Important also to note times of ebbs to avoid when entering rivers.

The matter of the weather is anybody's gamble, but it is possible to gamble a little upon the likelihood of certain months of the summer being better than others. According to records taken over the years May is likely to start with a cold spell and end with hot sun and thundery tendencies. June is famed for cold nights, sunny days and frequent rain. Thunderstorms in July, hot and dull days alternating, ending up with a questionable few weeks when gales so often cause havoc among yachts. The first weeks of August tend to be stormy too. Mid-July and mid-August would seem to be hot spell periods frequently.

Late August and early September are likely to give troubled weather—hot days sandwiched between rough patches. A settled spell often arrives after the first few days of September and may last until the middle or last week of the month. This is the time for small craft to be content to stay around home waters as the equinox arrives with a tendency to bad gales. If a late autumn cruise is planned, early October is often safer if the bad weather has passed by.

Trailer cruising is becoming ever more popular. Using the boat as a caravan, there are big advantages in trailing to some ideal cruising area, or for that matter trailing on the Continent. The A.A. and R.A.C. can give advice upon cost of shipment and so forth.

## Foreign Waters

The to-ing and fro-ing of small yachts between Great Britain and the Continental ports has become such a large-scale movement nowadays that any tendencies to restrict them by imposing undue rules and regulations have long since been ironed out. The requirements are few, but some of them, Customs formalities for instance, are not to be dodged.

Although one *may* enter foreign waters without notifying our own Custom and Excise people in advance, clearance outwards should be obtained when the yacht is leaving a British port specifically to go abroad. She can, of course, seek shelter in any port, whether originally intended or not. If, on the other hand, the crew includes an alien, outward clearance from a British port is required by law. Good cameras and binoculars or any article bought abroad on a previous visit should be cleared outwards for the sake of the receipt as re-entry may pose a problem later. The matter of bonded stores hardly applies to the very small yacht cruising in Home Waters unless she returns from abroad with foreign bond, as will be mentioned later.

Whenever possible, entry of a foreign country must be made at a port large enough to issue the necessary clearance and levy the usual dues. A British yacht, for instance, cannot make straight for some tiny fishing hamlet without first clearing inwards at some recognised port of entry. Once officially 'in' she may then proceed. (A Certificat d'Identité is needed for France, obtainable from R.Y.A., Victoria Way, Woking, Surrey.) Although it is necessary by international law to fly the yellow 'Q' flag requesting clearance, some French ports have a sort of unwritten law that you don't do so. Certainly they raise no objections if a crew make port and go shopping instead of sitting in purdah aboard their yachts until the Customs officer pays his visit, but until the drill at any particular port is known it is better to play it by the book.

In addition to the 'Q' flag, the cruiser must fly her own Red Ensign (NOT a Union Jack), and it is normal courtesy to fly at the crosstree a small national flag of the country visited.

Dues payable will be small, a matter of a few pence as a rule. Foreign officials are not much interested in ship's stores, but immigration authorities may be more searching. This is very much the case in Jersey, which has a very rigorous immigration department, no doubt due to its position as an easy hop for the ungodly.

Although every British yacht should be registered as a merchant ship if she is to claim the protection of her flag against seizure, very few of the very small craft are registered. (To appear in Lloyd's Yacht Register does not constitute official registry.) Some form of document which proves ownership of the vessel should be aboard in case of any complications, even if it is only a bill of sale or the insurance policy.

Personal documentation in the form of a passport and visas, if necessary, must be carried, although the latter are not needed for entry into France, Belgium, Holland, Ireland, etc. The matter of finance alters constantly, but any bank will supply up-to-date information. The Traveller's Cheque is the best way to carry currency, but it is very inconvenient to arrive foreign without even a small amount of cash in hand to pay for a meal ashore, as banks may be closed and not all hotels will be able to cash a cheque.

Many foreign ports will permit small yachts to take on bonded liquor and cigarettes at spectacularly low prices, providing the stuff is escorted to the ship by a policeman. In Cherbourg, for instance, there is such a weekend rush to do this that many regular British customers actually mail their order in advance of arrival. This is all quite legal, but the rub is that no matter how much hooch at duty free prices is taken aboard, only a limited amount can be brought back into this country by concession.

## Re-entry of a British Port

It is a requirement of the law that re-entry is made at a standard port where there is a customs Water Guard which can give clearance. In the event of bad weather, naturally, a vessel is entitled to seek any shelter she may but—and this is the crux of the matter—no member of the crew must leave the yacht and no person from the shore must board her until she has been officially cleared. Of course the case of a yacht in distress takes priority at the time.

Once within territorial waters, the yacht must fly the 'Q' flag where it can be seen and keep it flying until given permission to take it down. At night she must, if requiring clearance there and then, show a red light above a white one (not more than six feet apart).

The owner and master is responsible for his crew on the count of smuggling. The Water Guard are very kind to yachtsmen, but they will stand no nonsense. They also have a very sharp nose for smuggling, and it is extremely hard to put one over on them. More important than the risks of seizure perhaps, which is in any case a personal matter, is that the fair name of yachting is at stake. Hence, a smuggling offence may mean expulsion from your yacht club. Declare everything bought abroad and all is well. Owners who carry their pets to sea should remember that risk of rabies makes it a grave offence to re-enter U.K. waters after visiting foreign ports without notifying Customs that there are animals aboard.

What must be remembered, as a final thought on the subject, is that the Customs concession *is* a concession and not a 'right'. In short, the Water Guard can reward shirtiness by taking away all concessions and black-listing the yacht.

# Chapter Ten

# Night Sailing

THERE is nothing particularly alarming about sailing at night. Whether by accident or design every cruising yachtsman finds himself at sea in the dark sooner or later. As long as he is prepared for it, a night passage lengthens cruising scope and broadens his experience.

The main differences between day and night sailing boil down to a few important details. The danger from big ships increases but landfalls are usually easier by reason of coastal lights. Judgement of speed, wind strength and sea conditions is harder, the man overboard risk becomes more serious, chart-reading and coastal comparison, although easier on the score of identifying buoys, become harder in reckoning distances. And the weather can change without anyone noticing. To all this must be added the sense of emergency which most first-timers are apt to feel; and the important point that man is not a nocturnal animal and has to readjust his habits and instincts.

It is very unwise to attempt a night passage until basic chart-reading is not only mastered, but has become a habit. The need to have a 'feeling of position' on the chart is more necessary than ever, since there is no recognisable feature of land to cling to, and all the navigator has by way of substitute is a panorama of lights, some moving, some flashing and others fixed. By day, one can look at the coastline some eight miles away and be in no doubts of a safe offing. By night a powerful lighthouse to the inexperienced eye looms uncomfortably close, and in no time at all one hears breakers where none exist—which is the first step to hollow-eyed despair and fun all round.

## The First Night Passage

If possible the first night sail should begin in daylight, allowing the darkness to come upon the yacht when she is already nicely under way, her course tracked on the chart, the buoys of any channels already noted, and so on. This also offers a chance to watch the lights of large shipping and get some idea of distance by relative height and width between lights. The crew will have settled down and the ship will be in good order with everything in readiness for darkness.

Leaving the moorings in darkness means wholesale confusion and much coming and going with torches, looking for gear, groping about in lockers for almanacs and so on. The outcome of it all is that by the time the yacht is well under way and there is time to think about the little matter of navigation, she will be in the thick of that panorama of lights and the navigator will be hard pushed to sort himself out.

If, for no better reason than that man is not a nocturnal animal, night sailing demands an even greater degree of care, but just at the time when this care is really needed, yachtsmen are most likely to be sunk in cold and sleepy apathy caring little how they steer and less how they navigate. More offshore races are lost by night than by day. The crew which may be on the ball all day may subside into lethargy soon after dark so that by dawn better crewed yachts are lost in the distance ahead.

Brilliant moonlit nights are a joy at any time, but unfortunately they are the exception rather than the rule. Dark nights play havoc with sense of proportion and the yacht seems to be tearing along in a rising wind and sea when she is probably sailing well in moderate conditions. It is easy to doubt one's common sense. Lights will be seen where none could be and even the compass may be suspected. There is only one answer to this state of affairs, heave-to and think it out.

Most nights at sea can be divided into three phases. The early part of the night when tiredness is yet to come and when people are alert and warm and sailing the yacht, next the state of intolerable sleepiness when it is almost impossible to keep the eyes open, and thirdly the early hours before dawn when apathy sets in. One becomes cold and a prey to sea-sickness, and the reluctance to move an inch from the cockpit results in many a yacht drifting under double-reefed main in a falling breeze or conversely being dangerously over-driven. It is only by understanding the likelihood of these conditions that a skipper can stay in proper control.

## Watch-keeping

Sleep on a night passage is only vital if there is any likelihood of having to remain at sea for an indefinite time. This is mild heresy, of course, for the reason that one never can tell how long a passage may last, but there are plenty of times when with settled weather and shelter in easy reach along the line a fair guess can be made. The point of the argument is that it is a silly habit to let sleep for sleep's sake rule the ship. The man who lies in his bunk gloomily ticking off the hours of sleep which *he* has missed (the others have always had more) becomes so obsessed with the thought that nothing else can possibly matter. One night at sea without more than a nap or two is no hardship. As long as a man can lie down and rest for his spell below there is no need for panic. The fact that he can't get to sleep simply means that he's in no desperate need of it. By the next day he will be able to sleep, and if a second night should follow, he will have only to close his eyes and that will be that. On a single night-passage it is far more important to change watches often, every hour even, and keep the ship sailing than it is for the two- or three-man crew to be determined to get their sleep during their watch below, and to hell with what's happening up top.

Watches are essential of course. A man must *know* that he is free to have a rest. The all-night marathons with everyone hanging around in the cockpit feeling that it is in some way 'not quite cricket' to go below are bad seamanship and lead to ill-feeling. Systems vary, a three-man crew of experienced people may choose to work a two-hour trick, which means a clear four hours of rest for each. No beginner should be left entirely alone on watch though. With only one experienced hand (the skipper we trust), it may be better to let the other two share a watch until midnight with the skipper on instant call, after which he can take the 'graveyard' watch until dawn when he calls the other two again.

The essential about this second arrangement is that 'instant call'. It must be absolutely understood that the skipper is to be called for anything which is in the least sense unusual, change of wind force or direction, appearance of lights or any steamer seen close enough to distinguish her side-lights. In thickish weather of course the skipper will have an all-night session. No skipper has the right to resent being awakened on a false alarm, because it is only the knowledge that he can be sure of being given a shake which allows the system to work. For a three-man crew a stand-by system works well if all the crew are of fairly equal experience. One man stays on watch for three (or four) hours, according to the expected duration of the passage. He then comes off watch, or off the tiller at least, and stands by while the next man does his trick. He then goes off and goes below for three or four hours while the third man comes on watch and the second man does stand-by duty. The system means that each man is on watch for a spell, available for a spell, and definitely off for a spell. During his stand-by, he can doze, cook or relieve the helmsman so that he can feed. The plan also ensures that nobody comes on watch half-asleep to take charge of the ship unprepared.

## Preparation for a Night Passage

It is bad policy for a skipper to decide on a night run purely on the spur of the moment. Ordinary people who spend a third of their lives in bed lack the adaptability of the professional seagoer. After a day of energetic swimming or dashing about ashore, it is poor preparation to spring a night passage on them just as they are getting ready to turn in. This sort of thing may, or may not, be tolerable for the larger crew of an offshore racer but certainly is not good policy for a three-man boat. Since the decision to go or stay usually rests upon the B.B.C. weather forecast at two minutes to six, there is plenty of time to warn the rest of the crew in the afternoon giving them a chance to rest up in advance. Once the decision is made, either way, there should be no vacillation. The 'shall we, shan't we' skipper is a pest.

A really good, though not outsize, supper is important. A celebratory rich meal with drinks is a bad foundation for night passage, such a meal will only cause sleepiness and probably sea-sickness. Take the opportunity to fill thermos flasks or to mix the ingredients for cocoa so that successive brew-ups only need hot water adding. Sort out oilskins and spare warm clothing and stow them where they can be found without disturbing the resting watch. Sort out the charts in the order they may be needed and mark in courses and distances for easy reference, page-mark the Pilot Book after carefully reading any appropriate bits. You will need to read it all again, but later, when the mind is fogged by sleepiness, it will help to be reading what is already familiar. Note any prominent light buoy characteristics on a separate scrap of paper or pad and keep it in a pocket. Knowing which light sequences to look for without repeated scrambles to and from the chart makes it easier to watch for them as they come up.

The tidal stream situation will be checked in the ordinary way, but notes on when it changes, etc., save wearisome checking by artificial light. See that torches, flares, spare bulbs and batteries can all be found easily. Check over the gear on deck and see that reefing pennants are rove off. Not having to search for a single thing is the mark of a well-run ship no matter how small.

Night sailing is often cold and wet. Even if there is no rain, it is surprising how wet one can get from dew-fall. The only true protection from cold is plenty of proper feeding beforehand. Multiple layers of clothing on the upper part of the body are not really satisfactory. Clothing should keep the wind out and the body-heat in, therefore loose wool under oilskins is warmer than tight clothing. Looseness is the real secret. Plenty to do and plenty to chew is a sound rule for a night watch. Regular log entries and shortish watches, plenty of nuts, raisins, boiled sweets, glucose and so on. Incidentally glucose is no more energy-giving than sugar but it is less thirst-promoting and is digested more quickly. Let the change of watch brew-up be a routine as long as weather permits. In quiet weather the ritual of putting on the kettle helps to make the last of the watch go quickly and a hot drink for both oncomers and offgoers is good sense.

## Steering

Steering by night is the true test of sailing instinct. The man who is a slave to the burgee is at an immediate disadvantage. The sails are only a pale blur, there is very little help to be had from the eyes, and one sails by the feel of wind on cheek or neck and by the sensed speed, tiller pressure and angle of heel. The rattle of a luff or leech brings hearing into a new importance, perhaps, but keeping a good windward course is much more a matter of feeling.

Most small compasses rely on luminous marks for their lighting. The snag about this that the brightness wears off in time, and whereas the card may be easy to read on a very dark night, it will be too faint to see in semi-darkness or bright moonlight. This is not quite the serious drawback that it may seem. Compass staring is a habit to shun. All that is really necessary is to glance at the card occasionally—it should be easy to read naturally, but with practice one can manage fairly well by having a small torch with a red bulb (so not to spoil night vision) and keep it in one hand the whole time.

'A star to steer her by' is very practical poetry. It is rare that the sky is completely overcast at night and any star which is at a convenient height to line up with some part of the rigging will serve as a steering-mark. The procedure is to glance at the compass to check course and then look for a star, say between cap shrouds and mast. The movement of the yacht will cause it to arc wildly back and forth, but the mean of the swing can be judged and the course steered by it.

One must remember that most stars are moving across the sky, and it is bad to steer for too long without checking the course. From time to time it may be necessary to pick out another star. If the course is a windward one, and making ground is therefore the only important thing, it is far better to forget the compass completely save for noting the average course made for the navigator's benefit. This will mean that every little lift of wind will be used instead of ploughing along like a shopper with a basket on wheels, indifferent to anything but direction.

## Night Vision

Night vision must be protected at all costs, and if by any remote chance the compass has an electrically-illuminated binnacle, it should be fitted with a rheostat to control the degree of light. A glaringly bright compass ruins night vision and also hypnotises the helmsman. In fact it can put a tired man to sleep.

It may take five or ten minutes to accustom the eyes to darkness after scrambling into oilskins by the light of a torch on the cabin sole. The old watch should never hand over and bolt below to the blankets without hanging on for a while until his relief has got used to the darkness. It should also be the practice to point out the sights and advise him of any peculiarities of the wind. The sort of thing might go as follows: 'I half-imagined a loom from Berry Head over there and that's Torquay reflecting from that cloud (the town lights). There's a steamer crossing safe ahead but I've been watching one astern for some time.' The briefing can be more detailed but some sort of 'picture' is essential to the man who has just come blinking sleepily into the cockpit.

One sometimes marvels at the difference between the night vision of an old hand and an inexperienced yachtsman. The difference is not in better eyesight but in knowing what to *expect* to see. If a particular light is expected and overdue one can begin to see lights everywhere. Looking for lights should never be a matter of straining to see. The best way is to let the eyes wander almost lazily backwards and forwards across the horizon. The light is more likely to be spotted through the corner of the eye than by direct sight. This is because the most sensitive part of the retina of the eye is not exactly at the centre.

On a small yacht cruising at sea—and let's stress the word cruising—the helmsman is the best look-out. His gaze is ceaselessly roving from ship to horizon, back and forth. He is alert and in control, he has the best opportunity to gauge his speed against that of other shipping and he has sense of direction to help in spotting lights. Incidentally, if a landfall light is expected, it is wise to look now and then in the 'impossible' direction—odd things happen.

## Coastal Lights

Many years ago I received two sharp and never-forgotten lessons about coastal lights. The first taught me to discriminate and the second taught me scrupulous care. On that first occasion I had the watch while sailing along the West Brittany coast. Suddenly it seemed that

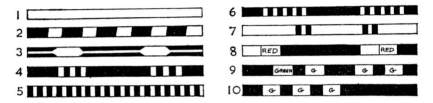

FIG. 55. White indicates period of light, black period of eclipse. (1) Fixed. (2) Flashing. (3) Fixed and flashing. (4) Group flashing. (5) Quick flashing. (6) Group interrupted quick flash. (7) Occulting. (8) Alternating. (9) Wreck buoy, leave to port. (10) Wreck buoy, leave to starboard. Note also new sequences in the IALA system.

the coast became alive with lights—flashing, occulting, fixed and moving. I panicked. Inside five minutes I had taken ten different bearings and couldn't plot one of them. I called the skipper. He looked, grinned, identified three lights, took their bearings, plotted them and then went back to bed. The lesson learned was that faced with a mass of lights one need only pick out those which assist. The rest, unless they lie athwart the course, can be left alone.

The second lesson I gave myself. We expected to pick up a distant lighthouse at a certain time. Dead on time the helmsman called out that he could see it. I asked for a bearing, plotted it, altered course and patted myself on the back. Within half an hour we were squared away and sailing hard with the engine running flat out trying to get clear of a sluicing tide and a reef—my distant lighthouse had turned out to be an unexpected buoy near at hand. We had been off course on landfall, and I had neglected to check and time the light. Moral, never 'guess' the identity of a light without checking it.

Lights of buoys, lightships and lighthouses, shore beacons and harbour lights are all identifiable by their colour, character, timing and range. The chart informs and the almanac lists them. On the face of it there should be no difficulty. The loom (glow from below the horizon)

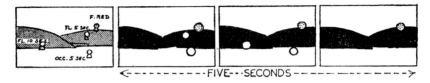

FIG. 56. Although four lights are visible ashore, each has a different characteristic and it is extremely unlikely to see all 'on' at the same moment. In five seconds the pattern might alter as shown and the eye must try to retain a picture of how they lie in position to each other so that comparison with the chart is possible.

of a distant lighthouse or lightship gives long warning of its identity. Next comes the river mouth or harbour entrance with a sequence of lit buoys or beacons. Then there are leading lights which may need to be kept in line (transit) during the approach, or perhaps taking the form of a sector light which shows a safe white, with red and sometimes green sectors on either side. There are quick flashing, group flashing, fixed or occulting lights. Individually they are simple to understand, collectively they are liable to be as perplexing as twenty masters to one dog.

Viewing the coast by night and looking at the chart of that area brings out one major difference. The lights marked on the chart can all be seen at once, but in actual fact they can only be seen in irregular groups just as they happen to flash at that particular moment and second by second the picture alters (Fig. 56). Add to this the altering angles caused by the moving ship, the loss from view of some lights as they are obscured by an island or headland and the emergence of new lights as the coast opens up, and the confusion becomes easy to appreciate.

The surest proof of the good navigator, compared to the beginner, is his chart after a completed passage. The one will show only a track-line ticked here and there by a neat three-point fix, the other will be smothered in little wigwams—indication of a constant taking and plotting of bearings which continues from dusk till dawn. By knowing where you are at the start and 'feeling' your position relative to the chart, it is usually possible to con the ship by eye alone, working from a previously noted list of buoy timings and watching them as they appear and disappear along the coast.

A stop-watch is not essential to night sailing but, as I have mentioned before, for the beginner it is a great help. Looking at the sweep hand of a watch means taking one's eyes off the buoy and it is easier if there are two on deck, so that the mate can keep his eye on the flash and call out 'now'. Lights are timed from the first flash of one group to the first flash of the next, whether occulting (light on all the time and going out at fixed intervals, flashes of darkness in fact) or group flashing. With practice the timing can be done by judgement alone. Some people count seconds by saying 'One thousand two thousand three thousand' and so on, note the absence of punctuation. Others favour 'I-reckon-that's-one-I-reckon-that's-two,' etc. Try out both methods against a stop-watch. The tendency is to count too fast.

One of the disadvantages of navigating a very small yacht is the low eye-level. Buoy lights which are seen steadily flashing from a higher platform are often seen intermittently as yacht and buoy rise and fall among the seas (Fig. 58). This doesn't stop you from seeing the light,

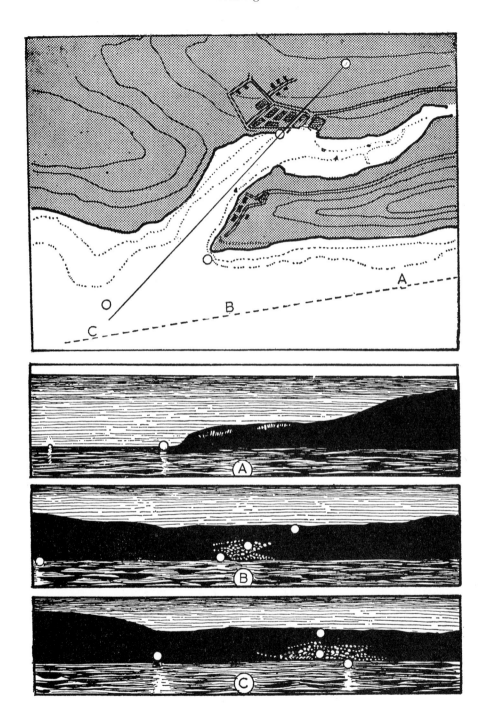

Fig. 58.

but it does play hell with the light sequence. For instance a buoy may be expected to flash four times every fifteen seconds. One count may show two flashes, another gives four and a third three. Sooner or later the whole sequence is seen, but the temptation is to guess. Sometimes ships' lights (such as fishing vessels off the French coast) can be confused with navigational lights, when they dip regularly in the swell or the troughs of seas.

The height of the eye above sea-level is a good thing to know since the 'Table of Lights Seen and Just Dipping' can be used to estimate distance away. A shortened table is given at the end of the chapter and the use is self-explanatory. Knowing height of eye and height of light from the chart or Almanac Lights' List, the appropriate cross-reference provides distance away. This naturally means the actual light and not the loom, which varies in range according to the weather. Sometimes it is possible to see both St Catherine's Lighthouse on the Isle of Wight and the Barfleur light on the French coast when in mid-Channel, although naturally this can't be relied upon.

The 'Lights Seen Dipping Table' comes into its own on a cross-Channel passage. Once the loom of the light is seen it is only a matter of standing and waiting for the first blink of the light at sea-level as it climbs the curvature of the horizon. While on the subject of dipping lights, a warning. Fixed shore lights, nothing to do with navigation, sometimes give a convincing impersonation of flashing lights when seen from low down. Car headlights on a busy road, sweeping around a bend do much the same thing, and to the beginner it all adds to the confusion.

Fig. 57. As the yacht sails past the coast not only do the lights alter second by second, but they change bearing as well. The chart shows four lights in the region of the small port, two of them, shown by the solid line, are leading lights one at shore level and the back light higher up the hill. The dotted line is the course line. At position 'A' the loom of the town lights are seen above the shoulder of the hill and the two buoys off the river mouth, one faint and the other close to. At 'B' the leading lights are seen above the lower point, but as yet wide open. At 'C' the leaders are 'on' and the yacht can turn on course to enter.

FIG. 59. The light is still dipped from watchers on deck but at varying heights above deck on a big ship it could be seen as the ship draws nearer. On small yachts convenient height of eye might be 5 foot and 10 foot for the purpose of calculating distance off by the Lights Seen Dipping tables.

A navigator must not forget to take the power of lights into account. He expects to find the buoy which appears in a prominent position on the chart more easily than the rest. It may be of minor importance or there may be others nearer to his position at the time. What he sees is a line of lights some faint and others bright; the one he wants may be insignificant. After looking the chart over the temptation is to pick out the buoys as you expect to come to them and ignore anything five miles beyond. This doesn't always work out. As long as you can identify enough lights to fix your position and keep an eye on your track nothing else matters much. Tick off the lights as you pass them, and pass them on the proper side unless they are merely marking a big-ship channel.

## Approach

Landfall and arrival in darkness are usually easier—for identification of the coast at least. In practice, many people feel far happier to be bowling inshore in daylight, searching for their marks along a hazy and anonymous coastline than they do at night when the way in may be unmistakable. By daylight they can see how far away they are, but night gives a feeling of sailing straight ashore, when, as like as not, the yacht is still five miles off. Dawn is the best time for an approach, because it means that you have come inshore on the lights and have the strengthening daylight to help you to navigate the narrows.

Coming to anchor in the dark is another big test of judgement. Shore lights dazzle, and the reflections across the intervening water destroy all idea of distance. A common error is to over-estimate distance. Don't just tear into a river or harbour and unload with a splash, nose around a bit and get well clear of the channel.

Anchored among local yachts, which are probably on their own moorings, there is rarely need to hang up a riding-light, but no cruising yacht can afford to be without one aboard. The chances are that the time will come when the only vacant berth for anchoring is on the fringe of the yacht anchorage and bordering the navigable channel. A riding-light may make the difference between safe sleep and a bad crack from a returning fishing-boat. Oil-lamps are messy but quite reliable. The hurricane lamp from the local ironmonger is definitely not proof against a fresh breeze, let alone a hurricane, and a proper yacht riding-light is the only safe type. An electric light run off a 6-volt bell battery is effective, but the fittings must be watertight, and a stock of spare batteries carried, as they soon run down. A simple make-shift is to lead the wire flex from the battery below deck up to the bulb and holder which are contained in a pill bottle with the neck corked. Better is proper engine-charged lighting and a wandering lead to the light.

## Safety at Night

Although the alarms of navigation and weather are more pressing on the imagination, by far the greatest dangers at sea are from being run down by a big ship or the risk of going overboard. There is only one safe rule for navigating steamer lanes by night or in thick weather in a small boat and that is to *assume your own yacht to be invisible.* The value of the radar reflector is discussed in another part of this book, but suffice to say now that no yacht should go to sea without one—having said that, the rule of invisibility should still be acted upon since the radar reflector is *not* a guarantee of safety.

The rule that 'power gives way to sail' was made in the days of the big commercial sailing ships which handled slowly and couldn't hope to manoeuvre clear of a power ship. Today, there are such matters as Traffic Separation Zones and local dock and harbour board regulations to consider, which frequently give full rights of way to large commercial ships.

Most yacht's sidelights may not be visible for more than a mile. (One cheap plastic combination light powered by torch battery was visible at fifty yards on a rainy night.) The big ship steaming at twelve or fifteen knots or possibly much more has only a matter of a couple of minutes or less in which to do something after a light is sighted. Suppose then that the look-out sees 'something' ahead. He phones the bridge and the officer of the watch takes his night glasses and walks to the wing of the bridge. He has to decide what it is and *which way* it is travelling, then he has to give an order to the quartermaster on the wheel. A very young officer may hesitate for a minute—big ships are not to be swung off course at a whim, especially if there are other big ships ahead. The

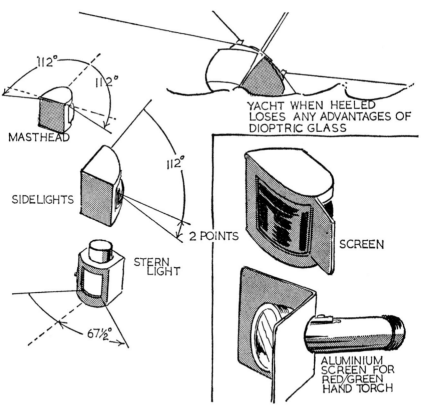

Fig. 60. Dioptric glass directs the light beam and on a heeling yacht it will mean that the leeward light shines into the water. Although the small cruiser is unlikely to be fitted with separate lights, the arcs of visibility are laid down according to international ruling for any form of lighting and the use of a torch with coloured screens must be governed by this.

small yacht may have been holding course and speed in accordance with the rules, relying on the Law instead of interpreting it with common sense. Alternatively, to play safe the skipper of the yacht may begin flashing a torch and this, from a steamer's bridge, may completely destroy all idea of which way the yacht is moving or indeed that it is a sailing craft in the first place.

Small sidelights on a heeling yacht are pointing at sea and sky respectively. They are also gyrating wildly and half the time invisible by reason of lost direction. Pulpit lights of combination pattern rarely have a satisfactory dividing screen with the result that, seen from nearly ahead, they show alternating red, green, red, green. This confusion completely destroys any notion of direction. Tri-colour masthead lights, now accepted under International ruling, are the best answer.

The safe rule is to decide very early whether the two vessels are on a collision course and, very early, shape to pass astern. This need only mean altering course until the bow is aimed at the big ship's stern and following her round.

The rule for recognising a collision course is quite simple. A bearing taken on the other ship will read the same when taken some minutes later if they are converging. If the bearing has increased or decreased you will be passing clear ahead or astern. A simple rule-of-thumb method which can be used to save routing out the bearing compass (the steering compass isn't always suitable), is to settle the yacht on as straight a course as possible and sit quite rigid. Let any part of the yacht's deck or rigging fall in line with the distant ship and then, remaining motionless, watch carefully to see if the lights of the big ship draw ahead or fall astern (Fig. 62). Naturally if there is much sea movement this 'bearing' will be no more than an average line-up, but the odds are that any doubts will be resolved one way or the other.

It is misleading to waver and haver at such time. Assuming that you have been seen (for once) you should think carefully, alter course if

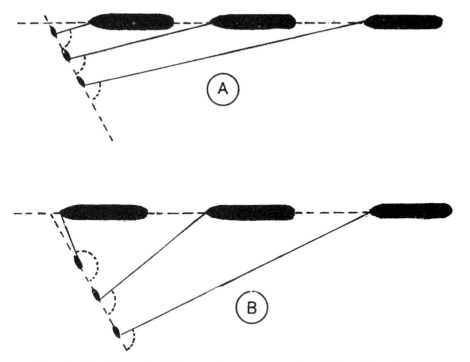

Fig. 61. Bearings taken 'A' remain constant and a collision is imminent. Bearings taken 'B' vary rapidly and the big ship will pass ahead.

necessary and then sail straight. The sight of pin-point lights changing colour and angle back and forth is dangerous. As mentioned earlier, flashing of torches is harmful too. Shine a torch steadily at the ship and, when she is closer, pan it slowly on to the sails and then slowly back to the ship. Even this hallowed routine is of questionable value. The only sure and safe course when in actual danger of being run down is to light a white flare. These flares can be bought from any good yacht chandler for a small sum and a stock of half a dozen (you may need several in a real emergency) is as fine an insurance as all the navigation lights on sale. Big ships recognise the meaning of a white flare as a warning of presence and they won't attempt a forceable rescue. A Very pistol is firm favourite with a lot of people and as a distress signal it may be fine, but any sort of sky-rocket is bound to invite investigation. I have even heard people who advocated firing at a steamer's bridge if they came too close, but then how daft can people get?

Becalmed and helpless a sailing vessel has to do *something* and the white flare is the answer. Do remember, though, that it must be shown in good time, giving the big ship a chance to alter course. Once the

Fig. 62.

flare is finished, keep a torch alight and have a second flare ready in case she doesn't seem to be altering.

Judging the distance of a big ship at night is very difficult for the inexperienced man. At a distance of about $2\frac{1}{4}$ sea miles, an ordinary larger freighter crossing ahead looks very large, but also remote. With the little finger at arm's length both her masthead lights can be covered. It is this appearance of remoteness which is most misleading. Take the case of an express train seen approaching from the distance and head-on. For a long while it is visible as a black vertical rectangle which simply grows gradually larger. It is only in te last quarter of a mile that it suddenly seams to accelerate, and then it does so breathtakingly.

The big ship at sea is much the same to watch. First the remote pin-points of light at the mastheads, next the red and green sidelights and then a long spell during which they steadily grow wider apart and higher. Quite suddenly the lights develop haloes, light spills from portholes, deck lights are seen and the black bulk of the superstructure. In an instant it has become a vast, reeling, shimmering mass of movement, her engines are heard and the intervening water is lit by her reflection. If she is head-on it will be too late to bother about flares, only your cool action at the helm can avert the danger. On a rainy night the blurred lights are even harder to judge.

Ships at sea by night show direction firstly by the position of the two masthead lights, the lower of the two being forward and thus giving the clue to her direction of travel and secondly by the sidelights. It takes quite some while before a beginner can glance at a cluster of lights and say at once, 'Passing safe astern port side to.' Distance away is less easy, since one has no idea of the size of a ship beyond the number of lighted ports and her speed relative to her apparent size.

Whatever you decide to do about avoiding her or revealing your own presence, do be sure to glance in the opposite direction as well. The whereabouts of any other big ships, though no concern to you, may dictate how the steamer is to be turned. Other more distant ships may not know why your steamer is suddenly bearing to port, but they will probably have to alter course as well, and you are in the middle.

For much the same reason never be too sure that a big ship has seen you just because she may have 'seemed' to alter course. She may be altering to clear another big ship miles away and there is no guarantee that she won't suddenly swing back if the distant ship has behaved unexpectedly. Having seen yourself clear, keep an eye on the ship until you are quite safe.

Not all lights are easy to identify. Fishing-boats are one of the inshore hazards for the coasting yacht and here there is no question of forcing a right of way, sail versus power. You are expected to know (or at least do some lightning thumb-work in a book and find out) the significance of any unusual arrangement of lights, and the trawler with her gear down or the drifter lying to her nets must be given a wide berth. Not only are they not under proper command since they can't manoeuvre, but their gear extends beyond them and often at surface level. The arrangement of their lights makes this quite plain. The cluster lights which illuminate the decks for working are the first clue to the fisherman, unless on passage, of course. Even under way and not fishing the lights may be in use for clearing the catch and they may be so bright that the navigation lights are quite hard to distinguish. The biggest illusion is in thinking a small fishing-boat to be a big ship far away and then suddenly see her roll and pitch dead ahead and close to. The inshore fishermen are wonderful friends to yachtsmen, but woe betide the man who transgresses the fisherman's rights at sea.

Tugs towing at sea, naval craft on manoeuvres, behaving in a very odd manner and, of course, fellow yachtsmen, all add their quota to the endless puzzles of lights in combination. Yachts meeting yachts can be the biggest headache of all sometimes. Many people sail without any lights at all, reasoning that as they can't be seen by steamers, what the hell? Others have a nasty habit of switching on a masthead or spreader light for identification. Both are risky habits, and the latter is illegal. Sailing yachts are required to carry only sidelights and a sternlight. In yachts under 12 metres they may be combined in a single lantern at the masthead. The sidelights must be visible from 1 mile and the sternlight 2 miles. Sailing vessels over 12 metres must carry the same sidelights and sternlight as a power driven vessel of their size.

A yacht under power becomes a power-driven vessel. If she is also carrying sail and *behaving* as a sailing vessel under the Rules and an accident occurs she may be liable; if she behaves as a powered vessel

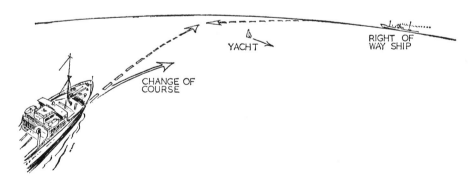

FIG. 63.

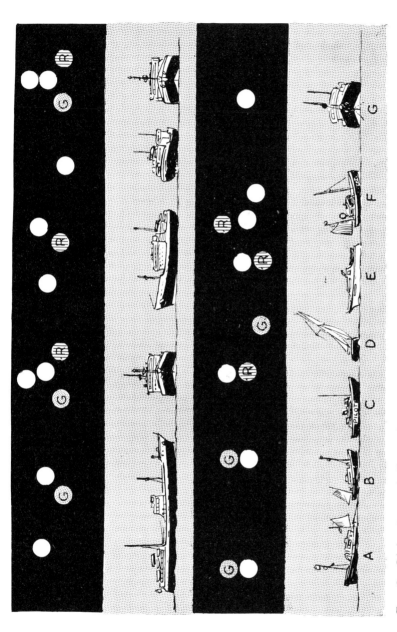

FIG. 64. Light clusters indicate the course and type of vessel. Vessels approaching bow to bow will pass safely if sidelights show green to green or red to red. Bottom strip shows 'A' and 'B' trawlers with their gear down, 'C' Pilot boat on station, 'D' sailing yacht, 'E' small power vessel, 'F' drifter with her nets extending not more than 150 m. Above 150 m a lower white light indicating the direction of the gear. 'G' vessel at anchor (black ball by daylight).

she must make the fact plain, if necessary lowering sails. At night she must show a white light on the mast with a forward arc of 225 degrees and at least 3 foot above her sidelights.

Crossing a busy estuary channel at night is about the nastiest part of navigating in the dark. Big ships are, by reason of narrow fairways, restricted to straight courses and in certain port areas, such as Southampton Water, they have absolute right of way. The small yacht

FIG. 65. Lights in a busy channel can be confusing. Each group must be assessed carefully so that the direction of movement is understood. Often it is the apparently inconspicuous cluster which suddenly becomes the threat.

must wait her chance to cross much as a pedestrian waits at a busy crossing. A good plan is to make for one of the channel buoys and stay close to it (don't sail round and round it) until there is a chance to cross the deep-water channel. Once in the middle it may even be necessary to alter course up or down stream so that a big ship can go by. Whatever happens don't begin zig-zagging around. Try not to tack across a channel at such a time, take it full-and-by and get across fast and then work up the opposite shore in shallow water and safety.

### Additional Notes

*Lights just seen or dipping:* Find a position where the eye is either five or ten feet above sea level, look up the lighthouse or lightship in the Lights List (*Reed's Nautical Almanac*) and find the height of the light.

The heights of lights are given as height above *high* water. Thus any discrepancy in range or distance off due to applying the table at a time other than high water will have the effect of putting the navigator 'nearer' than he actually is—a safety factor.

In the event of the light being relatively low in height while the range of tide is unusually great, the range of tide (if at a time other than H.W.) should be *added* to the height of the light if greater accuracy is needed.

| Height of Light in Feet | Height of Eye | |
|---|---|---|
| | 5 feet | 10 feet |
| | *Distance off in miles* | |
| 40 | $9\frac{3}{4}$ | 11 |
| 50 | $10\frac{3}{4}$ | $11\frac{3}{4}$ |
| 60 | $11\frac{1}{2}$ | $12\frac{1}{2}$ |
| 70 | $12\frac{1}{4}$ | $13\frac{1}{4}$ |
| 80 | 13 | 14 |
| 90 | $13\frac{1}{2}$ | $14\frac{1}{2}$ |
| 100 | 14 | 15 |
| 110 | $14\frac{1}{2}$ | $15\frac{3}{4}$ |
| 120 | $15\frac{1}{4}$ | $16\frac{1}{4}$ |
| 130 | $15\frac{3}{4}$ | $16\frac{3}{4}$ |
| 140 | $16\frac{1}{4}$ | $17\frac{1}{4}$ |
| 150 | $16\frac{3}{4}$ | $17\frac{3}{4}$ |
| 160 | 17 | $18\frac{1}{4}$ |
| 170 | $17\frac{1}{2}$ | $18\frac{1}{2}$ |
| 180 | 18 | 19 |
| 190 | $18\frac{1}{2}$ | $19\frac{1}{2}$ |
| 200 | $18\frac{3}{4}$ | 20 |
| 210 | $19\frac{1}{4}$ | $20\frac{1}{4}$ |
| 220 | $19\frac{1}{2}$ | $20\frac{3}{4}$ |
| 230 | 20 | 21 |
| 240 | $20\frac{1}{2}$ | $21\frac{1}{2}$ |
| 250 | $20\frac{3}{4}$ | $21\frac{3}{4}$ |
| 260 | 21 | $22\frac{1}{4}$ |
| 270 | $21\frac{1}{2}$ | $22\frac{1}{2}$ |
| 280 | $21\frac{3}{4}$ | 23 |
| 290 | 22 | $23\frac{1}{4}$ |
| 300 | $22\frac{1}{2}$ | $23\frac{1}{2}$ |
| 310 | $22\frac{3}{4}$ | 24 |
| 320 | 23 | $24\frac{1}{4}$ |
| 330 | $23\frac{1}{2}$ | $24\frac{1}{2}$ |
| 340 | $23\frac{3}{4}$ | $24\frac{3}{4}$ |
| 350 | 24 | 25 |
| 400 | $25\frac{1}{2}$ | $26\frac{1}{2}$ |
| 450 | 27 | 28 |

*Light abbreviations—and observations on types*

Fixed (F) Steady light, white or coloured, also used in pairs one above and behind the other as leading lights. Seen on harbour entrances (small harbours). Easy to confuse with ordinary shore lights.

Fl. (flashing) White or coloured. Regular flash with the interval of darkness being just a shade longer than the duration of the flash.

F. Fl. (Fixed and flashing) A light which shines steadily and periodically increases in brilliance, sometimes with a brief interval of darkness.

Gp. Fl. (Group Flashing) A number of flashes repeated at a set interval timed from the start of one group to the start of the next. In British channels, port and starboard hand buoys (IALA system) carry red and green lights respectively, any rhythm. Those not yet converted from the Lateral system are even numbers of flashes white or 1, 2, 3 or 4 red (port) and odd flashes white (starboard).

F. and Gp. Fl. (Fixed and Group Flash) The light is steady and increases brilliance in group flashes.

V. Qk. Fl. or VQ (Very Quick Flashing) Constant flashing of 120 or 100 a minute.

Qk. Fl. or Q (Quick Flashing) Constant flashing of more than 60 in the minute.

Gp. Int. Qk. Fl. (Group Interrupted Quick Flash) Bursts of quick flashing with longer periods of darkness in between.

Occ. (Occulting) A fixed light which goes out at regular intervals giving an equal or shorter spell of darkness between light.

Gp. Occ. (Group Occulting) A steady light with 'flashes' of darkness. Timed from the beginning of one eclipse to the beginning of the following group. The group occulting light is an easier mark for taking bearings as it remains in view most of the time, whereas the flashing light, especially if it has a long period, is easy to lose in the compass sights. Seen from a small boat though, rise and fall in a seaway can create false eclipses.

Gp. Occ. (2) W.R. 10 secs. showing white and red in different sectors.

Alt. (Alternating) Changing from white to red (or green) at regular intervals. Failure to note this characteristic on the chart can lead to confusion.

Other common abbreviations likely to be found on the chart are as follows:

Obscd. (Obscured) Some lights are not visible from certain directions. The arc of visibility is marked around lighthouses and a vessel crossing from a dark area can get a rough position line as the light opens up. This is not to be relied upon without a bearing as well.

(U) (Unwatched) Not to be relied on too much as the light is not under constant inspection to see that it is working.

Ldg. (Leading Lights), Occasl. (Occasional) A light which is exhibited by arrangement, perhaps for incoming shipping.

Lt. (Light), Bn. (Beacon), Lt. V. (Light Vessel), Lt. Ho. (Lighthouse).

L. Fl. (Long Flash) A light appearance of not less than 2 seconds duration. *IALA.* Now being introduced to supersede both the Uniform Lateral and the Cardinal systems, this system uses red buoys to port in a channel and green to starboard, with matching lights of any rhythm. A particular hazard may be marked by cardinal type black and yellow buoys with white V. Qk. Fl. or Qk. Fl. lights of the following rhythms: north continuous; east V. Qk. Fl. (3) 5s or Qk. Fl. (3) 10s; south V. Qk. Fl. (6) +L. Fl. 10s or Qk. Fl. (6) +L. Fl. 15s; west V. Qk. Fl. (9) 10s or Qk. Fl. (9) 15s (remember the clock face for 3, 6 or 9 flashes). Wreck buoys are discontinued and are marked by IALA cardinal buoys, or by isolated danger buoys having Gp. Fl. (2) W characteristics.

*Lights:* In vessels of less than 12 metres length, sidelights must have a minimum range of 1 mile, masthead lights and stern lights 2 miles. Vessels of less than 12 metres may carry a combined masthead light. Oil-lamps with proper cone glasses may meet the above requirements although the dioptric lens usually accompanying them concentrates the light beam along a horizontal band which, when heeled, may be shining into the water on one side and upwards on the other. The biggest problem is to know whether your lights have been seen; very often they have not. The safest assumption is that they have not been seen and it is wise to behave as if this were so. Yacht batteries are another problem. Few yachts cruise with their batteries better than in a state of half-charge and by the early hours of the morning they are frequently so weak as to be useless.

*Flares:* White and green hand held pyrotechnics are used to draw attention to position and presence. Blue flares for summoning a pilot. Red flares, distress. White flares can be ordered from any chandler. A fire-arm certificate is needed for a Very light pistol.

*Lifebuoy Lights:* Usually operate by capsizing into float position, thus tripping switch to dry battery. Bright flash. Should be tested regularly.

*Lifebuoys:* Onazote type preferable to kapok-filled. Horseshoe shape is usually kapok-filled and must be kept dry or at least not left permanently on deck. Buoys which are extra light in weight should have some sort of small sea anchor or drag to prevent the buoy blowing away across the water.

*Rule of the Road:* Vessels meeting head on. When red and green you see ahead, steer to starboard, show your red.

Converging: Green to green or red to red, perfect safety go ahead. (*Note:* maintain a close watch for any change of course.) White lights are four times brighter than red and five times brighter than green. All lights on the chart are white unless otherwise stated. Range of lightship rarely more than 11 miles. Compass lighting: Do not use a single wire and an earthed bulb, run the wires in a pair close together or the compass magnet will be deviated.

*Avoiding collision:* Read and understand the International Regulations for Preventing Collision at Sea. The rule dealing with two sailing vessels meeting, has been altered of recent years and beginners under instruction by experienced but out of touch old-timers may be wrongly informed. The present rule is that the vessel with the *wind on her starboard side*, whether running or beating, has right of way. If both vessels each have the wind on the same side (whether both on the port side or both on the starboard side), the vessel which is to *leeward* has right of way. Thus a vessel beating on port tack gives way to one running with the wind on her starboard (her boom to port) and a boat beating on, say, starboard tack has right of way over one running on starboard. *Note:* under the *old rule* a closehauled vessel had rights over a running vessel in all cases.

*Traffic Separation Lanes:* In areas of concentrated shipping, 'lanes' have been established which (should) channel heavy shipping along eastbound or westbound (north or southbound) lanes thus minimising the risk of head-on collisions. Strict rules forbid transverse crossing and where this is unavoidable craft must cross as nearly at right angles to the traffic stream as possible and at the best speed. Small yachts shall NOT impede big ships in such waters.

Having regard to the difficulties of slow moving small craft in strong tides, the problem may exist at times in which a course to cross at say, 45 degrees, is faster than one at 90 degrees. The yachtsman must do his best to hasten his crossing time, using his engine to this end but, as stated at the end of the next chapter, heading up too much to allow for tide may confuse approaching shipping as to the real course.

# Chapter Eleven

# Fog

ALTHOUGH anyone with a choice in the matter and some previous experience of being at sea in a small boat in fog would settle for staying at anchor when the visibility begins to drop, fog is such a stealthy danger that one is often at sea when it begins to roll. The typical sea fog accompanied by faint airs and perhaps the swell which is the aftermath of an earlier blow is the most damnable of all conditions. Avoid it at all costs, but if it can't be avoided, concentrate if possible on piloting the boat out of the way of the big ships and let passage-making take second place.

If the approach of fog is stealthy at least the conditions giving rise to fog can often be noted, and an eye kept lifted for the disappearance of the horizon or the long flat-topped bank so often mistakenly put down to 'steamer smoke' until the true extent of it is realised.

A fog bank is really a cloud. Warm air holds moisture but as it cools—perhaps by coming into contact with the cooler air rising from the sea—the moisture has to be deposited and the cloud rains. If the cloud is already at sea-level the droplets have insufficient distance to fall to gain size and become raindrops and so they remain as drifting vapour. A fine 'mizzle' often accompanies fog.

Warm wind blowing over cool water, sea haze, the sun a yellow ball or a warm, soggy-feeling wind, all are fog signs—signs that the warm air has almost reached 'dew point' when the moisture will begin to be squeezed out. The night-time cooling of the earth can give rise to fog conditions. A slowly moving cold front coupled with night cooling is also a cause, although the arrival of a warm front is more usual. It is possible, especially along the western Brittany coasts, to come up with thick fog driving in on a gale-force wind, quite terrible conditions.

There is often a fog tendency during settled weather, and if weather forecasts repeatedly give fog warnings in certain areas they can be anticipated in other areas if the conditions seems to be spreading. The warm steady wind, warmer than the water, and the sudden muzzy appearance of lights at night, are signs that the navigator should take a set of bearings while there is still time.

The constant checking of position is the wise navigator's only

19. Visibility less than one mile. Those conditions by night are often much more treacherous than real fog since the yachtsman may not be aware of the decreasing visibility and steamer lights suddenly appear before he has time to gauge their speed, angle and distance. Morning haze or an approaching rain belt produce conditions of this type, both are more common than real fog.

20. A moderately large sea in the open Channel following a gale. The white water has subsided and the sea is no longer dangerous. In fast tidal waters, shallows or overfalls it would be dangerous however. Note the lifeline rigged for the occasion.

armament against the fog. He knows that he can be lost in a bank while the rest of the coast is still clear, or the reverse can be true. It is the true test of accurate dead reckoning, since the only visual assistance is the compass, the chart, the water, log and lead.

Hearing in fog becomes the most important of the senses while being the one most subject to trickery. The yachtsman must be able to hear. If he is unlucky enough to be out among big ships he must hear and hope to be heard.

The decision which so often has to be made is whether to drift under sail at a couple of knots or less, straining to hear every siren, thump of engines, ringing of bells, and so on, thus having some idea of the nearness of other ships (if not their direction) or whether to use power and motor as fast as possible out of the danger area while being deafened to all save the clatter of an outboard. There can be no single answer. The owner should bear in mind two things. Whether it be sail or power he *must* have smart steerage way on his craft at all times if he is caught in dense shipping, for it will be *his* action which will avert trouble in an emergency. The second point to remember is that hearing a very distant siren is no assurance that the ship can be dismissed as unimportant. Many big passenger ships today actually minimise the use of siren in the interests of passenger comfort. Relying on radar, they move through the fog quickly and silently. The yachtsman has only his ears and his eyes.

## Radar

The old radar bogey is slowly but surely taking a proper significance in the minds of seagoing yachtsmen. For some years we thought we were safely visible on the radar screen of every ship in the locality. We were visible in just the same way that a particular pebble is visible in a photograph of a section of beach—it can be seen if you look for it.

Wave crests give a yacht-like echo—a confused and indistinct signal which takes second place in importance to the big echo of another vessel of similar size. The advice of one Trinity House Pilot was that, in fog, the radar screen should take a secondary place and more reliance should be put upon seamanship and sound signals. In fact, there are cases of ships moving through thick fog at 18 knots. Collisions between the giants are becoming more and more frequent and the reason is usually one of speed and the difficulty of deciding whether the signal on the screen is moving to port or to starboard. The clever development of 'True Motion' radar shows the picture as though the observer were at the base instead of in the centre of the screen and gives each echo a little tail which suggests direction of travel. It has provided new standards of safety among the big ships, but for the small ship the situation remains a matter of luck.

Wood is a bad reflector, even waves are probably better. Beams are absorbed instead of being thrown back and even when a yacht is visible to the naked eye, and in quiet conditions at that, the radar picture may be too indistinct for positive action to be taken by a steamer's bridge. Metallic paint is no good as a reflector since the overlapping flakes of alloy which comprise the paint simply absorb instead of reflect. An aluminium mast, caught when it is vertical, provides a good reflector, but as soon as it heels, the reflective properties become poor.

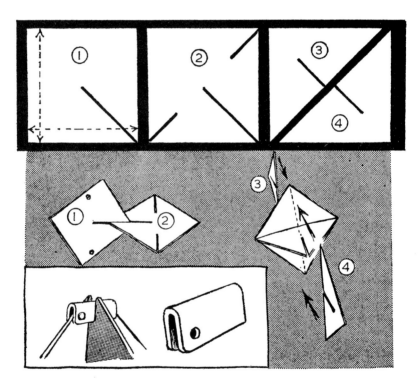

FIG. 66. Making a corner reflector. Zinc, galvanised sheet or aluminium may be used, the thickness depending upon the material, but tending to be heavy as a safeguard against loss of shape. Ten-gauge aluminium is about right, but by folding the edges, lighter gauges may be used in other materials. The corner catches must be a tight fit and may be assembled with two bolts per corner instead of one if the reflector is not to be dismantled. Holes are provided for hoisting shackles. 12 in. × 12 in. sides are a suitable size.

If the scanner is (let's say) tuned to picking up targets at close range such as channel buoys or fishing vessels then the small yacht can expect to be seen, but a big ship at sea is like a car on a motorway—the drivers are looking far ahead. Again, clutter control can be used to isolate important signals from the mess of wave signals and the weak reflection of canvas and wood is lost along with the wave clutter. As wind and sea increase, radar range decreases. From being able (when desired) to pick out a rowing boat three miles away, the radar loses the echo of an eight-ton yacht completely in as little as a Force 4 breeze—or in the sea which goes with it at least. In a gale, quite large coasters can be missed.

Nevertheless, the radar reflector offers such amazing improvement in the chance of being picked up by a big ship scanner that there cannot be any choice in the matter of whether it is worthwhile carrying one. Any yacht even remotely liable to fall foul of the steamer lines in fog or thick weather should have one. The eighteen-inch corner reflector set in the rigging can give a reflection equivalent to a two-hundred-ton ship even in a Force 4 or 5 wind and sea.

One might argue that at that rate why not be content to look like a fifty-ton ship with a four-and-a-half inch reflector? It just doesn't work that way. The smallest size practicable might be one foot in breadth but, when one considers that the echo is then similar to that of a sixty-foot hull while a *two*-foot reflector gives an echo similar to that of a one-thousand-ton ship, the disparity in size becomes trifling and a thing to be gladly borne.

The principle of the reflector is that of a prism. It offers a series of right-angle corners wherein the radar signal is caught and bounced back, and it follows that the angles must be exact right-angles if it is to work. For this reason home-made reflectors, and they are simple to make, must be accurately cut and put together and protected from damage when aloft.

The biggest problem on the small yacht is where to hang the reflector. If it is hoisted on a signal halliard the motion of the yacht causes it to snatch and jerk so badly that it is destined to come crashing down within the hour and it may easily damage somebody below. Perhaps lashing to the standing backstays (if fitted) is a safer alternative. It is of great importance to hoist the octahedral corner reflector in the right aspect. If such a reflector is simply placed down on deck or table, it automatically assumes its correct aspect. Hoisting 'point-up' is absolutely wrong and reduces efficiency—so also does inaccuracy of the angles and 3 degrees out of true in any corner reduces effectiveness by up to 50 per cent. Height above sea-level should be at least 15 feet and the higher the better. Remember too that a wet sail will screen a reflector completely.

## Sound and Sight in Fog

The effect of fog upon sound is to distort it. Sound may be loud one moment and soft the next. The 'lanes of silence' where a complete loss of sound is possible may block off an approaching siren only to allow it momentary startling volume. Direction is even less certain. Some attempt to narrow down the sound by listening through the wrong end of a voice trumpet or rolled-up newspaper is worth trying, and it should be remembered that to blow a foghorn from behind a sail or in only one direction is limiting its effectiveness.

Sound is often heard more clearly from above the deck or up the mast—a little impractical on the small cruiser. It is also possible to hear bell-buoys or submarine fog signals by pressing an ear to the hull below water level, but only the very roughest idea of direction is possible.

A small boat is a surprisingly noisy place when serious listening is needed. The movement of sails and water, rattle of gear, clunk of rudder, and so on, make it very hard to concentrate. The momentary lulls in the noise make it even worse. Listen in each direction, cupping the ears and shutting the eyes—not a pretty sight perhaps but a great aid to concentration. Better is to have two people listening, both to say aloud 'There' if the sought-for siren is heard. The 'snap' effect then disallows prompted imagination.

Look aloft often in fog. If the blue sky can be seen the bank is obviously a shallow one—it may be very little higher than your mast, which means that big ships can possibly see each other if not you. Seek constantly to judge the range of visibility. With nothing but fog and water around this is very hard to do. An empty box fifty yards away looks for an awful moment like some huge, square tanker looming up.

FIG. 67.

Drop overboard a rolled up paper ball or a bean tin and watch it to see how soon it vanishes. If the visibility is, say, two hundred yards you can reckon that sighting another vessel is going to leave no time for second thoughts, ten or fifteen seconds at best.

The first glimpse of a large vessel in fog is like a sudden densening of the fog. In a flash there are gleams of white from paint and bow-wave. In that moment you will have to form an impression of her heading and decide what to do. The position of the bow-wave may be the real clue, central below the denser mass of fog if the ship is head on, to one side or the other (Fig. 67) if she is shaping to pass ahead or astern or to port or starboard of you.

Careful adherence to the Separation Zones is mandatory but it is also plain good sense and all yachtsmen should know where these rules apply.

Land seen through fog can develop just as rapidly. A first glimpse might be a row of semi-detached villas apparently built among the clouds and a depressing foretaste of the Life to Come. I have sailed slap into a tiny bay when attempting to round a headland, and seen sheep high overhead and seagulls standing on rocks just yards away.

Fog can also affect the true contour of the land by enveloping the

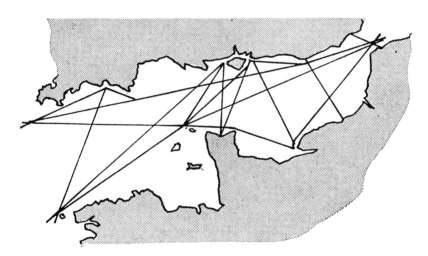

Fig. 68. This plan gives some idea of the main shipping routes in the English Channel. Note the comparative emptiness of all bays and the tendency for ships to converge upon important headlands and ports. While the routes between ports often depend upon the Ship Master's decision in the circumstances, the bulk of the traffic will follow pretty set lines. In addition to these routes there are, of course, the coasting craft which may follow much the same courses as the small yacht in fog.

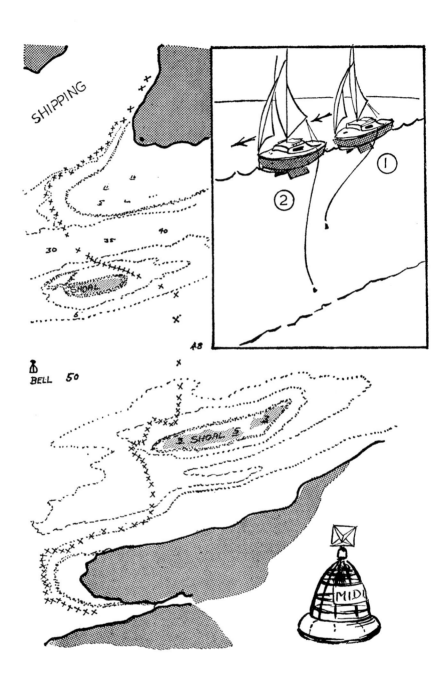

SHIPPING

30  35  40

SHOAL

A8

BELL  50

SHOAL S

MID

background cliffs and leaving the low sand-hills standing importantly and deceptively high.

In the main then the first concern is to get clear of steamship routes. Far offshore this means having some notion of where they lie, but with the slow-moving cruiser it may take many hours to sail into one of the few relatively quiet areas and a pretty accurate D.R. plot to ensure that you are in one. For the coasting cruiser the aim is to get into shallow water and stay there, to avoid headlands where shipping tends to converge, and to be on the look-out for inshore fishing craft and coasters.

It is obviously not always practicable to steam straight inshore and into a mass of rocks and reefs, especially where strong tides are running, but it is also unlikely that any big ship will venture even remotely near such a coastline. If it is possible to lie to a kedge on a long—very long—light nylon line so much the better. In conditions of calm this sort of kedging is common ocean-racing practice and, at all events, it is safe if not particularly comfortable in a swell. There is the added advantage that once the anchor has taken hold, the rate and direction of tidal stream becomes known which is very important to navigation in fog.

## Echo-sounder in Fog

Contour navigation is particularly valuable in thick weather. Basically it consists of a steady series of soundings taken while studying the chart depths in the area where the yacht is considered to be. She may be approaching the coast along a course which should take her into a bay, but due to the usual regrettable little inaccuracies in the pilot's ancient art her approach may be along one of several possible lines. She may be heading for the point or she may be missing the bay altogether. A study of the chart shows how the sea-bed rises towards the land in each area. Along the D.R. plot it may rise from twenty fathoms to five fathoms in the space of five miles, but to east and west it may rise abruptly within

FIG. 69. Use of the echo-sounder in fog. Sailing on a dead-reckoning course the yacht feels her way over and around the patches. If the rate of tide is not known it may be worth anchoring on a kedge so that it can be estimated. Note that arrival at the shore (*bottom of sketch*) sees the yacht working along a contour line until she finds the river mouth. (*Inset*): If hand sounding, swing well ahead of the yacht. If she is moving fast it may be necessary to slow her by luffing while the cast is made. Note whether any channel buoys are equipped with radar reflectors and if so either stay in the shallow water or proceed with extreme caution.

the distance of a mile and a half. By sounding until bottom at the twenty-fathom line is found, noting the log-reading and time, and then continuing to take soundings at say quarter-mile intervals, a picture of the sea-bed is built up. This can be plotted with an even greater degree of accuracy along an uneven sea-bed which, plotted down on tracing paper to chart scale, can be juggled around on the chart until trace fits chart. The soundings must be reduced to datum figures by adjusting them for height of tide in each case, of course. The echo-sounder offers enormous advantages. The navigator can literally watch the rise and fall of the sea-bed and thus there is no chance of a sudden and tell-tale change of depth being missed. Most cruisers of 20–25 feet l.o.a. are fitted with them nowadays as an essential.

It can also be used to even greater effect if the cruiser is faced with having to cross the mouth of an estuary in thick fog. It should be pointed out yet again though that if this involves crossing a busy steamer route it is best left untried. If the channel buoys are fitted with radar reflectors then it is a fair bet that some small coaster at least will be buoy-hopping to catch his tide to the docks.

If the crossing is to be attempted, a careful study of the course in advance will show what is to be expected if the yacht can be kept to her course. She may cross shallows for two miles, hit a deep patch for half a mile, cross a bank and another deep, then the main channel and so on. Making due allowance for cross currents to stay on this track, the possibilities *of not* staying on it must also be allowed for, and the course laid down-tide of any dangers such as wrecks or drying banks. It will be very hard to have faith in the tidal allowance which may appear necessary since nothing will be seen but the seemingly motionless water around the cruiser. If it is possible to lay the course to include channel buoys so much the better, but faith in a carefully plotted course is preferable to time wasted searching for buoys which may be only a hundred yards away yet invisible.

## Signals

By International Law a sailing vessel in restricted visibility is required to sound a whistle (or foghorn) at not more than two-minute intervals, giving one prolonged blast (4–6 seconds) and two short blasts (1 second each) regardless of which tack she is on.

Horns sold for yachts tend to be toy-like and very directional. There are compressed-air or gas horns which last a whole season on one container and are of very high volume, and, of course, the usual collection of bugles and honkers of one sort or another. The note best suited to carrying through fog cannot be fixed upon. Sometimes with a two-note fog signal one or the other, but not both notes may be heard. At anchor yachts over 12 metres in length must sound a whistle, while those under this length must make 'an efficient sound signal' (winch handle banged on a metal mast or even coins rattled in a cooking pot) for 5 seconds at intervals of no more than one minute. Remember that two small vessels navigating in silence are in as much danger from each other as two large ones.

The sound signals of the big ship manoeuvring should also be understood. One to starboard, two to port, three for 'engines going astern' are the basic signals when in sight. A ship under way but stopped in fog may sound two blasts roughly two seconds apart, repeating the signal at roughly two-minute intervals or thereabouts. When two vessels are in sight and one is unsure of the other's actions, five short blasts are given; vessels which can't manoeuvre properly including fishermen, and tows give one long and two short blasts every two minutes. A vessel of under 12 metres length is exempt from the above but if she wants to join in she should sound off an 'efficient' sound at not less than two-minute intervals. For we small craft with small foghorns perhaps the important thing to remember is that it may not be heard.

At anchor the use of a bell is further supplemented by a gong of a different note which is situated at the stern of any vessel exceeding 100 metres.

Sound signals of lightships, lighthouses and buoys vary a great deal in type and value. It is worth remembering the effect of wind force and direction. A fog signal heard from leeward in a moderate breeze may have double the range of the same signal heard from up wind of it. On the other hand the expected signal may not even be operating. The lighthouse, perhaps, is in clear visibility while your vessel is in thick fog. Again, such is the deceptiveness of sound in fog, that a signal which has been clearly heard for some miles, may grow gradually fainter as it is approached.

Many foghorns are directional, particularly those facing seawards from a river mouth. It is quite possible to be tacking to and fro across the signal, losing it and hearing it grow in volume each time the bearing is crossed. When this effect is consistent it is safe to 'home' on it.

In general each type of signal has its characteristic, as well as an identifying interval. The diaphone with its final grunt, the thin note of the compressed-air siren, and the high note of the reed. Electric foghorns, powerful and medium in tone, may in fact have several sound frequencies. Some lighthouses use the fog-gun which is an acetylene affair giving a brilliant flash at the same time. Others fire explosive signals in mid-air.

Submarine signals which give a high note are not of great importance to yachtsmen, but the inshore bell-buoys or whistle-buoys should be noted on the chart even though both are dependent upon the motion of the sea for their effectiveness. The whistle, incidentally, is usually more in the nature of a 'moan'.

## *Additional Notes*

*Foghorns:* Clarion compressed-gas type gives 100-decibel volume (300 two-second blasts per container). Hand-operated or mouth-horns at lesser volume. Compressed gas horns may 'freeze' at the reed in dense fog and in doing so become almost useless.

*Visibility:* Mist and fog are low cloud, haze is formed by solid particles suspended in moisture. Range is as follows. Thick fog visibility limited to 1 cable (200 yards). Fog, limited to 2 cables. Moderate fog, less than $\frac{1}{2}$ mile. Poor visibility, under 2 miles. Moderate visibility under 5 miles. Good visibility, under 10 miles. Very good visibility, under 30 miles. Excellent visibility, over 30 miles.

Check the range of visibility in thick fog by dropping a crumpled newspaper overboard and timing its disappearance against the speed of the yacht. At night a ball of paper soaked in paraffin and set alight can be timed.

*Traffic Separation Schemes:* The amount of big ship movement in Separation Scheme traffic lanes is nowadays such that it is highly dangerous for a yacht to attempt a crossing. She is unlikely to be seen either by lookout or by radar. When visibility is good enough to permit crossing, a yacht should cross at her best speed, under power and as nearly at *right angles* to the advancing traffic as can be managed. Heading up to allow for tide is risky, as approaching shipping may become confused as to her real course. A yacht has NO right of way and yachtsmen have been fined for Separation Scheme traffic lane contraventions.

# Chapter Twelve

# Choosing Your Weather

IF there is any one subject which merits extra study by the small-boat man it is meteorology. Unfortunately single-observer met. study can present only a very limited view of the whole weather jigsaw. Nevertheless what is happening there and then in one small part of a large-scale weather pattern and what is likely to happen within the next hour or so are important for the lone observant yachtsman to know.

The broader picture of the weather situation is provided by the shipping forecasts, but important though these may be, they are several hours old by the time they are broadcast, and in rapidly developing weather systems several hours can mean the difference between deciding to make a passage and staying in shelter.

For the very small boat, bad weather is not restricted to gales. A Force 5 breeze, under certain conditions of sea, is gale enough for a family cruiser. It is the ability to glance at the sky and the barometer and make a shrewd guess at what is likely to happen within the next few hours that really matters.

No small boat should be put to sea in the face of a truly bad forecast. The trough mentioned on the shipping forecast may mean no more than cloud and a shift of wind. On the other hand it can develop quickly, the bottom can drop out of it, and it may give rise to six hours or so of truly nasty weather. The observer at sea notes what the professionals tell him and takes over from there to draw his own conclusions in his own particular bit of ocean.

To watch the weather one must watch it all the time. To perk up and become a weekend weather-prophet while ignoring the shift and change of weather during the rest of the week is only playing with it. The man who owns three barometers, one on board his boat, one at home and one in the office, may seem to be making rather a meal of things, but his weather-picture is a non-stop one. He notes the weather map in his daily paper, glances at the sky whenever he happens to think of it and maybe hears the shipping forecast before he sets out for his office. By the weekend he can go aboard his boat aware of the present trends. The fine Friday, curse of the week-ender, is a fair example of this. With a chain of small lows chasing in all the week, a sudden calm and sunny day on Friday is often an ominous sign—a ridge perhaps, heaped up before yet another depression. The observer who has been watching cynically all the week may choose to ring up his local airport Met. office if the official forecast sounds cagey. At all events he is on his toes.

It is always depressing to embark upon a study of met., learning the typical formations of 'fronts' and trying to identify ideal cloud shapes from the pictures. Our weather is such a mess that such identification is usually about as difficult as trying to distinguish a Dutchman from a Frenchman by racial characteristics. Now and then comes the perfect example, but most of the time it is the general character of the sky which is our guide. Anyone can forecast a thunderstorm. Sky, atmosphere and general feeling cannot be mistaken. To the old-time fisherman almost any weather change was as obvious. Now and then he was absolutely wrong—wrong to the extent of heavy loss of life, but then he had no shipping forecast to fill in the background story. We have that one great advantage, but we cannot afford to stop thinking for ourselves as well.

## The Sky

As a sure indication of weather-to-come the sky is very unreliable, more often than not a collection of odds and ends of cloud, left-overs from weather patterns which have passed by. Each alteration of temperature and humidity brings forth a fresh crop of clouds of one sort or another. Some, but only some of them, are significant to the layman. On the whole, it is held that soft and cushiony looking clouds are associated with or precede fine weather and moderate winds, while those which have hard, jagged edges, or appear to be greasy are forerunners of wind and rain. Clouds taken as confirmation therefore have value. A forecast of coming bad weather, due to arrive maybe some time the following day, might be viewed with more urgency for the present if the sky took on that distinctive lowering of the cloud base. On the other hand, of course, it might just be a trough running in advance of the true bad weather and due to be followed by a narrow belt of finer weather before the real low comes in. From this it can be seen that to assume the bad stuff to have come and gone might lead to a risky decision to go to sea and hence the importance of close link between forecast and observation.

The ragged clouds which look like torn paper and which the East Coast fishermen used to call 'bawlies' are a good indication of wind to come, not necessarily gale force but the stiff breeze of high summer.

Flying across an otherwise still sky first thing in the morning, bawlies are rarely wrong. They are in fact just what they look to be—tattered scraps of cloud blown off the top of some slow moving bank and fore-runners of a general fill-in of the wind in that area.

The much quoted rhyme about 'Mackerel skies and mares' tails making great ships carry low sails' is a true enough warning of an approaching depression. The ice cirrus cloud of a high altitude wind is the jet stream whipping off the top of an advancing storm front, but it isn't always so easy to be sure of defining the signs correctly. Some people prefer to describe this type of sky as being 'scratched by a hen'. It is a piece of the jigsaw which may fit the general picture.

Sky colour is perhaps of more use than cloud type. The 'red at night' which is held to be the sailor's delight must not be truly red, though, and, in fact, livid sky colours at any time are something to be wary of. A pink or rosy sunset may be good, a bold yellow one bad. Pale yellow tinged with green is a sign of rain. In the latitudes of the British Isles a deep, hard blue sky is a sign of wind too. Pale blue on the other hand is a fine weather sky. Grey, early morning skies are usually a sign of a settled day to come, but the low bank on the horizon, held to be sure sign of fine weather, is a bit uncertain, at best it is a negative sign. If the morning cloud-bank is high, though, high wind may well follow.

The thundercloud bears careful watching. If it is high and the top is rounded it is a potential squall-maker. The warm lower air rises, becomes unstable at high altitudes and plunges down to spread out across the water in all directions. A black cloud isn't necessarily a sign of a squall, although one must keep an eye on the water beneath it for signs of wind. The familiar anvil-shaped thundercloud is usually a safer proposition than the high one, since it is a thundercloud which has started to disintegrate.

The all-too familiar solid mass of low cloud associated with nothing in particular and thoroughly gloomy in appearance which covers the skies for so many days in one of our average summers is usually a sign of stable air if nothing else. Stratified cloud is usually a sign of stable air conditions—not that there is much to be said for the alto-stratus which flies in advance of bad weather. The big, beautifully sculptured cumuloform clouds often mean unstable air liable to result in squalls as warm lower air rises and then returns in a down-blast. If the upper cloud is moving in a contrary direction to the lower cloud these squalls may give rise to sudden wind shifts, but when both layers are moving in the same direction the squalls, though constant in direction, are likely to be harder. The hazy sky is a sign of air stability and the hard, clear horizon a sign of instability.

The circle round the moon is a pretty reliable warning of dirty weather. Here, warm air forced up by an advancing front has formed a steadily thickening layer of high cloud, which gradually gets lower as the front moves in. This accounts for the rider that the bigger the halo the sooner the blow. If this advance cloud is low enough and dense enough to give rain it is a sign that the low is to be of some importance and hence another old couplet, 'Rain before wind, sheets and halliards mind.' Again—'When stars hide soon rain will betide'—is a somewhat vague way of saying the same thing. All in all, it is a reminder to watch the night sky as well as the day sky.

# Chapter Thirteen

# Wind and the Barometer

SHORT of cribbing from half a dozen serious works on the science of meteorology, and trying to write a seventh and less valuable book on the subject, the most that can be done in a single chapter is to skim over the basic principles.

By 'weather' the yachtsman is really speaking about wind, and wind is the mass movement of air. It moves from high to low pressure areas like water running down a mountainside and the steeper the slope the stronger the current. The face of the earth is covered by warm and cold belts according to the location from equator to poles and like oil and water these warm air and cold air regions are reluctant to mix. Instead of graduated slopes of pressure from poles to equator, the two warring bands of temperature meet and swirl, causing bulges in the frontiers. Up goes warm air above the cold, forming a low pressure area and the air begins to whirlpool.

Due to the rotation of the earth it circulates in an anti-clockwise direction in the northern hemisphere. The cold air sweeps around forcing the warm air to rise above it (the 'front'). Ahead of the shovel-like cold air goes the warm mass in a wedge, leading the bulge and giving a 'warm front'. Sooner or later the cold air overtakes the warm front and shoves it up above sea or ground level. The depression is then said to be 'occluded' and is beginning to spend itself.

The whole system is on the move. It moves along rather like a spinning top. The hurricane, which is a depression on a grand scale, follows a fairly well defined route—but by no means so clearly defined that it can be dodged with certainty. The depressions which affect the British Isles come whirling down from the North Atlantic. They are mapped and reported as they pass over weather ships and observer stations, and usually pass to the north of these islands. The average rate of travel seems to be around 25 m.p.h. with the winds blowing slightly inwards towards the vortex rather like water going down a plug, and in just the same way the speed of the wind gets higher and higher as it nears the centre.

This whirlpooling is the reason why the yachtsman in his boat may experience in the second part of a gale a possible wind shift from south-east to south-west followed by another shift into the west and a final petering out of the blow from a nor'westerly direction. The centre of the depression would be to the north of him in this case. Should he be right in the line of travel, however, he might experience a vicious southerly which falls to an odd calm before coming in from a northerly direction, or, if he's to the north of the centre, which is the exception in these waters, the wind shift may be from south-east to north-east and finally blowing itself out from north or north-west.

It is plain to see why knowing where the centre lies is very important to any yachtsman faced with staying away from what may turn out to be a lee shore. Lacking a shipping forecast or a positive idea of which way the depression is heading, the rule for locating the centre is to face the wind, when the centre will be on your right hand. Naturally it is important to know that the wind you are experiencing is actually a part of the depression.

All this time the barometer has been reacting to the pressure gradient. It may fall steadily and rise steadily as the depression wheels past leaving the yacht in its fringe; on the other hand it may fall slowly at first and then pitch. It may then rise sharply as the centre passes over and with the rise a sudden, savage blow from the northward which soon falls lighter. 'Sharp rise after low soon foretells a harder blow' runs the old jingle, and how right it is!

The approach of the warm front with its drizzle, the gradual backing of the wind (backing means changing direction anti-clockwise, e.g. west to south) and the increase in velocity with that murky yet strangely translucent greyness all around typify the path of the depression. This is the time to watch the barometer closely. The steady decline over a period of perhaps a day or so will have suggested a large low-pressure system ('long foretold long last, short notice soon past'). The sudden sharp drop, though it may only be a small one, is just as important to the small-boat man, for it hints at a small, though very active, depression moving in quickly—the type of small low which so often slips by the forecasters as an inconspicuous trough and later suddenly deepens.

The occluded front with its unstable warm air shoved skywards over the wedge of cold air can produce a squally type of weather which, while lacking the greater threat of a very active and deepening low, can stand close watching. So too can the sudden shift of wind which follows the passage of a front when a sharply defined 'low' is followed by a steep ridge of high pressure—sudden torrential rain and vicious squalls which may end rapidly and leave a clearing sky and a steady breeze from a totally different quarter.

The appearance of the sky after a low has passed is often quite distinctively 'nor'westerly'. Colours seem to be brighter, the sea shows deep, dark blue wind ruffles, the sky is deep blue and dotted with the tattered white clouds which have replaced the low altitude stratus.

Since most depressions pass to the north of the British Isles with their familiar sequence of the passing fronts, should they pass south of us the weather pattern may be puzzling. There are no such fronts to be experienced, just the wind shifts and change of barometric pressure. They are none the less dangerous for that.

High pressure systems, ridges and anticyclones as opposed to troughs and cyclonic systems, are generally looked upon as the good fairies of the weather world, but the rule that any steep slope means fast running 'rivers' of water or air must not be overlooked. A very steep 'high' can produce strong winds around the outer edges. In a depression the winds blow round the centre and slightly inwards in an anti-clockwise direction. This is the exact opposite in the case of the anticyclone.

Anticyclones *usually* mean gentle breezes with the whole system moving along slowly, sometimes remaining stationary for days at a time and gradually declining. Settled, hot weather in summer or perhaps hazy, overcast but warm weather. In the early part of the year and in the springtime, an anticyclone can mean bitterly cold winds and grey murk, particularly if settled to the north and bringing down Arctic air as it circulates.

The small, steep high, the 'dog-day' which so often appears between lows, the 'weather-breeder' as the old-timers call it, is often the only chance a yachtsman may have of making his quick passage home before the next low hits him. He must not be fooled by it. It may last twenty-four hours, but it may be less. This is the time to watch the weather and not over-strain his luck. The low which follows one of these smiling days is often a big one.

It often happens that the sailing area is between two systems, say a high to the south and a low to the north. One might be forgiven for assuming that being halfway between them, moderate weather would be the result. But very often a 'gear-wheeling' effect occurs. Clock-wise winds to the south and anti-clockwise winds to the north produce a strong westerly wind between them.

This is a very bare summary of the way the weather works. For the most part it consists of a variety of half-day heat-waves, pocket gales, rain, cloud, shifting winds and a barometer which twitters uncertainly up and down. The troughs, cols, wedges, ridges and so on which drift and swirl around us night and day are impossible to isolate, for the layman at least. The broad understanding of it all is the only thing possible. Just as a seaman can distinguish the tide-rip from the regular movement of wind-driven water or the ripple over a bank from the ripple of a light breeze, so he must be able to recognise trouble in the air when he sees it.

## The Barometer

One barometer without any other information can only tell you about half the picture. But it cannot be dispensed with. The ideal form of instrument is the barograph, since the wanderings of the needle are traced upon a dated and time-recorded chart. At a glance we can see how the barometric pressure is behaving. As it is the steepness of a system which causes the winds to be strong, and as an observer is constantly on the watch for a sharp fall or rise, it becomes a matter of luck whether his haphazard tapping of an ordinary glass is rewarded with such a dramatic piece of weather evidence.

Here a point about tappers: strictly speaking one should never tap a barometer, but should set the dummy recording hand at fixed and frequent intervals during the day (and the night!) and graph the rate and extent of movement between times. In practice, the majority of yacht barometers are inexpensive instruments which are by no means as delicate as they might be and can stand a *gentle* tap. A sudden jerk upwards or downwards just *may* be caused by a sticky movement suddenly freed. This is particularly likely when one goes aboard after a week of absence and non-tapping.

Continuity in fair weather and foul is important. One man only should re-set the hand of the barometer. If everybody is fiddling with it (unless there is a written log of its movements), it will be impossible to know what is going on. Morning, mid-day and evening settings are the minimum but on passage the barometric pressure can be logged each watch—this is quite as important on a small craft as on a large one, and moreover it is something for the watch-keepers to do.

In Home Waters the average sea-level pressure is around thirty inches, which means pretty settled weather on the whole. A slight fall is by no means a sign of doom. The glass may fall for the collapse of a small ridge or the arrival of a shallow trough, which in itself may mean no more than a cloudy day. Warm air or moist air (even in the absence of a definite warm front) cause a slight fall and cold, dry air brings a rise. Diurnal rise and fall, a normal daily occurrence of no other significance than the passage of night and day, should be ignored.

The famous generalisation laid down by Admiral Fitzroy is well worth repeating. Barometers rise for northerly winds including winds from north-west through north to north-east. They rise for dry or drier weather, for less wind or for several of these changes. The exception is when strong winds bring rain or snow from the north.

Barometers fall for south winds (south-east through south to west), for wet or strengthening winds or for several of these reasons, save when moderate winds with rain or snow come from the north.

Direction, wind force and humidity affect the barometer, and the greatest falls come when all act together, reading lowest when wind and rain come together with southerly winds and reading highest in cold, dry northerlies.

From this it can be seen that with the barometer should go the thermometer if readings are to be interpreted with any precision. To go further, a hygrometer to record humidity should come into it. Obviously, an owner will need to be making a hobby of the study to go to these lengths. That it is worthwhile goes without saying, but a small yacht makes such demands upon her crew that detailed met. study becomes impractical on a three-man boat.

## The Forecasts

To listen to an area shipping forecast and disregard all areas except the one in which you happen to be sailing is no way to get the best information from the weather picture as a whole. The experienced man can be seen listening to a forecast with both hands—literally so. The general situation may show that there is a low to the west of him and turning north while deepening. He at once begins trying to visualise the overall effect this will have on his own area, how the wind will behave as it passes and changes direction—hence the hands. He uses them as an aid to imagination.

Ashore, the synoptic charts printed in simplified form in some of the more earnest dailies are a splendid follow-up to the shipping forecasts. Better, from the point of view of study, than the television weather maps for they can be saved day by day and watched as the low pressure and high pressure systems advance and retire, grow and diminish.

There is a similarity between a weather map and an ordinary land map which gives contour lines, since the purpose of the contours is to trace the height of the land in one instance and the height of the barometric pressure in the other. On the weather map these lines are called isobars and the general effect is to create an impression of hills and valleys. The closer they are together the steeper the slope and the stronger the wind. But the wind flows roughly along rather than directly across them. A watch on the Atlantic weather maps reproduced in the newspapers gives a general guide to what may be developing. Sometimes a line of lows can be seen coming in one after the other. Not all may affect the British Isles, since they may be diverted further north, but it does seem that once a run of depressions begins there will

Fig. 70. The shipping forecast areas. (Crown Copyright. Reproduced here by kind permission of the Controller of H.M. Stationery Office.)

be a period of one day fine two days of foul weather with the wind shifting constantly between south and west. 'When the wind backs against the sun trust it not for back 'twill run.'

At sea, and denied both television and a morning paper, the alternative is to jot down the area forecasts on a blank chart (tear-off pads are on sale at most big yacht chandlers). The circulatory flow of wind and the strength in each area can be noted and the degree of visibility, temperature and so on fill in the details of the picture. Thus a yachtsman in area Wight may hear of a low approaching from the Atlantic. He may be in some doubt whether to make a short hop to the next port. His barometer is falling slightly, the forecast for Plymouth–Biscay is bad but *his* weather is still fine. Should the Coastal Stations' report give drizzle and low visibility at Start Point he can be fairly sure that

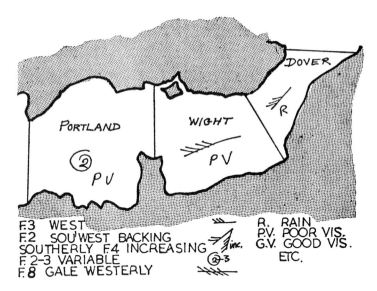

F.3    WEST
F.2    SOU'WEST  BACKING
SOUTHERLY  F4  INCREASING
F.2-3  VARIABLE
F.8   GALE  WESTERLY

R.    RAIN
P.V.  POOR VIS.
G.V.  GOOD VIS.
ETC.

FIG. 71. A simple form of notation which can be taken down at normal reading speed. A comprehensive picture of the whole forecasting area is built up giving a better understanding of the general situation.

he is in for the treatment—this is when he begins to look closely at the sky—sunrise, sunset, height of cloud, hardness of horizon and so on. He will expect the wind to back towards the south and freshen a little, he may even note a long ground swell moving in over an otherwise smooth sea, forerunner of the disturbance. Incidentally, ground swell is not a certain sign of bad weather because the depression causing it may alter course. It can also be caused by moderate winds close at hand rather than a more distant storm, but it is one more shred of evidence.

If he is wise he will either stay where he is in his little cruiser or make the passage a short one. It is a decision which may take a very great deal of courage to make, if the sun is still shining.

### Additional Notes
*Clouds as warning of advancing depression.*
CIRRUS, high, delicate-looking tufted or feathery white cloud spreading in from the west to become Cirro-stratus or a thin veil which haloes the sun or moon, and later forming lower alto-stratus which is grey and fibrous-looking. When the sky is covered to seven-eighths bad weather is imminent. In general the steady descent of the cloud base is a sign of bad weather. Haloes can occur with fine settled summer weather, but a check of the general situation is wise. Isolated patches of blue sky in a clouded bad weather sky are a sign of improvement. Damp winds may often be observed by feeling the ropes and

sails as a guide. These tend to swell and feel clammy. This may be a sign of an advancing front.

*Barometer* (generalisations only):

Rapid rise: unsettled weather.

Gradual rise: settled weather.

Rise with dry air and becoming colder (summer) wind from north. After rain an improvement.

Rise with moist air and cold: wind and rain from north.

Rise with southerly wind: fine weather.

Steady glass with normal temperature for the season and dry air: good weather continuing.

Rapid fall: stormy weather.

Rapid fall, wind westerly: stormy weather from the north.

Fall with northerly wind: storm with rain or hail, snow in winter.

Fall with increasing dampness in the air and humidity: southerly wind and rain.

Fall with dry air: becoming colder (snow in winter).

Fall after settled warm weather: rainy squalls.

*Storm Warning:* A black cone (a few also show three lights in a triangle at night) hoisted on a signal mast gives warning of a local gale. Point up: Gale from northern half of the compass. Point down: Gale from the southern half of the compass. If the gale is expected to change from one direction to the other the cone is reversed. The cone may also be hoisted for strong winds. Choose an anchorage bearing in mind that southerly blows are liable to fly into the west or north of west. Less likely for northerly gale to veer south of east (clockwise). Easterly gales tend to fly into the north.

*BBC Radio Met. information:*

Shipping Forecasts Radio 2 (1500 metres), Mon–Sat at 0033, 0633, 1355 and 1755. Sundays at 0033, 1155 and 1755.

Forecast for inland waters at close-down of Radio 4 around 1245 (Scotland 2335).

BBC Radio 3 (464 metres) Mon–Fri at 0655 and Sat–Sun at 0755, gives detailed synopsis and local area forecast.

GPO local dialling listed under 'weather' also gives useful local area forecasts.

Local information also available from the following:

| | | Tel: |
|---|---|---|
| NE Scotland | Kirkwall Airport, Orkney | Kirkwall 2421 |
| | Aberdeen Airport | Dyce 2334 |
| | Kinloss, Morayshire | Forres 2161 |
| E Scotland | Pitrevie, Nr Dunfermline | Inverkeithing 2566 |
| NE England | Newcastle Weather Centre | Newcastle upon Tyne 26453 |
| E England | Manby, Lincs | Louth 2145 |
| SE England | London Weather Centre | 01–836 4311 |
| S England | Southampton Weather Centre | Southampton 28844 |
| SW England | Plymouth | Plymouth 42534 |

| | | Tel: |
|---|---|---|
| Jersey | The Senior Met Officer—Jersey Airport | Jersey Central (0534) 23660 |
| W England | Gloucester | Gloucester 23122 |
| S Wales | As above | As above |
| N Wales | Valley, Anglesey | Holyhead 2288 |
| NW England | Liverpool Airport | 051–427–4666 |
| | Manchester Weather Centre | 061–832–6701 |
| | Preston, Lancs | Preston 52628 |
| W Scotland | Glasgow Weather Centre | 041–248–3451 |
| N Ireland | Belfast—Aldergrove Airport | Crumlin 339 |

*Local Forecasts:* Most regional radio stations around the coast offer good local forecasts and the value of these and the local forecasts obtainable by dialling a GPO number should not be underestimated. The shipping forecast areas cover great tracts of sea and while a forecast may be very accurate over the major part of the area, local coastal regions within it may be experiencing very different conditions.

*Tape Recordings:* The speed at which shipping forecasts are read is often too fast for the untrained yachtsman to write or record on a Met chart. The use of a battery powered tape recorder is recommended. Thus the listener can note down as much as he is able and then play back at his own speed later on.

# Chapter Fourteen

# The Effect of the Land on Wind

COASTWISE sailing puts a yacht within the influence of the land which affects the course of the general wind direction. Far out at sea a true and steady wind may be blowing, but inshore, direction, strength and general character may be quite changed.

The obvious cases are the land and sea breezes of hot weather. Most people know that as the land masses warm up more quickly than the sea, hot air rises from the coast, flows seaward at a higher altitude, cools and is drawn inshore again in a circular movement—the result is a sea-breeze. It may not begin to make itself felt until the day is well advanced. It may not materialise at all and it is rarely felt more than ten miles offshore even in the Mediterranean. The land breeze of late evening is a reversal of the same system, land cooling rapidly, sea temperature cooling slowly and air flowing offshore at sea level and back inshore at a higher altitude. Just now and then the yachtsman meets this lovely offshore breeze, and the fast night passage over calm water and in a warm, fragrant wind is something to rave about. Long before the night is half over he may be left becalmed, of course. It needs to have been a very hot day for the land breeze to be felt in force. In both cases the nature of the land affects the wind behaviour. Fields and built-up areas heat up more rapidly than densely wooded land.

More often than not the true sea or land breeze caused by land-heating becomes diverted by the influence of the existing weather systems. An offshore breeze due to some passing high or low can result in a flat calm as soon as the hot air circulation begins, the onshore breeze which *should* be blowing being stalemated by the opposing force. By the same token, the light *onshore* breeze of early morning which develops into one of those boisterous half-gales that lash the coastline in hot and brilliant sunshine can be no more than the sea-breeze aiding and abetting it. The old cry 'They only forecast Force three' is usually inspired by something of this kind. By early evening the wind has steadied down and by dusk, when the offshore wind begins, it meets that same little onshore breeze and a night of flat calm follows. The man who can recognise this sort of weather for what it is and plan accordingly can go to sea and enjoy some spirited sailing.

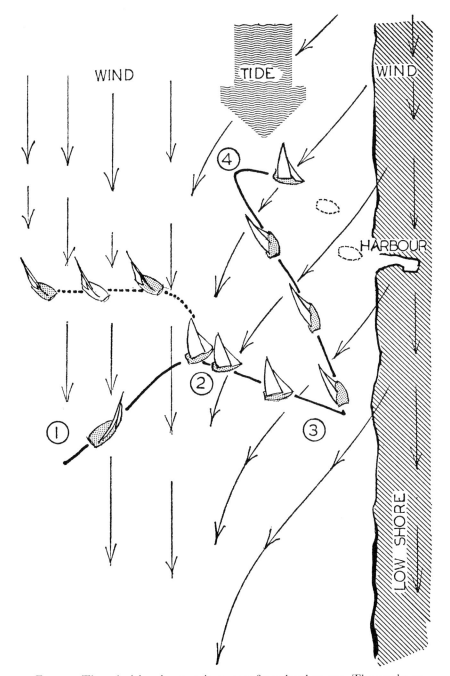

Fig. 72. The wind has bent as it crosses from land to sea. The yacht at
(1) has tacked inshore and been headed. (2) She has gambled on finding
a steady, freer wind on the next tack and she goes about at (3) to work
up the coast over the tide. She sails well above her harbour (4) before
going about. If, on the other hand, she had followed the dotted track she
would have made little ground as the tide strengthened.

On the whole, winds are more stable at night. A cold layer forms and permits upper winds in warmer air to slide over the cold base. It is when these conditions are reversed, cold over hot, that unstable conditions develop and the down-blasts of cold air cause squally weather. It is even said that cold air is 'heavier' of impact upon a sail and that waves become steeper in unstable conditions.

Land 'bends' the wind, as anyone who has raced a dinghy will know. If a wind is blowing down the coast and parallel to it, we are likely to find that close inshore it is blowing diagonally *across* the shoreline (Fig. 72) from land to sea. In a river this may be the other way round and at each shore the wind will bend and blow diagonally across it towards the land. If, at the same time, the onshore breeze conditions are in force this bend may be much more acute. The wind may be almost dead onshore along the coast and further out it may be blowing practically at right angles and dead down the coast. It often pays to explore a little. Though knowledge of met. may be too light to predict with certainty that such is the case, a long leg inshore may prove that it is so. Many people, tacking up the coast, stand inshore, and when they begin to meet a heading wind and lose ground, they promptly go about. It may happen that by standing in still further they may be able to carry the next tack right along the shore.

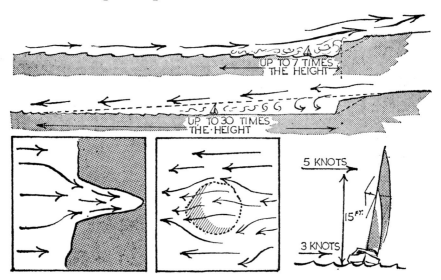

FIG. 73. The effect of onshore and offshore breezes over a cliff. The wind tends to accelerate as it funnels and it bends to flow round and over an island. Surface friction has a slowing effect on wind speed and even the small cruiser is subject to considerably increased speed at the upper part of her rig.

When the wind is blowing from land to sea or sea to land, it almost invariably bends as it crosses. It also divides to blow around each side of a headland or island (Fig. 73). High cliffs cause the wind-flow to lift from sea to land, leaving a dead area immediately offshore. An offshore breeze crossing cliffs also leaves a dead area to leeward, which may extend to as much as thirty times the height of the cliff, but in each case a sloping cliff of less than 45 degrees will have little effect on the wind. A cove or river mouth can produce an accelerated force of wind particularly if it is funnelling down from hills. The yacht which is *just* able to cope with the wind force offshore might well have another roll pulled down if she is to be tacked into such a river mouth.

## Wind Force

Although this is a particularly gloomy chapter, well studded with dire head-shakings, and perhaps too preoccupied with what one shouldn't do rather than with what one should, the short answer to bad weather in such small boats is that there is only one really relevant 'should': to stay in shelter until the sea smiles again. After all, we go afloat for pleasure. We can take a reasonable amount of teeth-gritting, but saturation point is in every sense soon reached in a small cruiser.

The Beaufort Scale is a constant delight to yachtsmen. We hear of a fourteen-foot cruising dinghy being hove to in a Force-8 Channel gale while her crew shelter happily 'below'. We hear of threshing into a Force-6 breeze and scudding before Force-9 squalls. It is all good fun. Fortunately these tales are almost invariably just wild exaggeration. Small cruisers *have* come through gales safely, but more often than not the wind forces which blow around the club bar are in reality well down the Beaufort Scale. The fact that gale force winds may be forecast is no proof that the actual wind when it comes attains that velocity.

In the open sea or in wide estuaries where tidal streams run strongly a full Force 5 is all the small boat can handle with any degree of comfort—and very uncomfortable it is! Force 5—the 'fresh breeze' blowing at 17–21 knots may raise a possible six-foot wave in open water—smaller and steeper inshore, showing many crests and some blown spume. A weather-going tide may produce a bigger and toppling form of sea. Add a low, ominous sky and some rain, and it is easy enough to imagine that the wind is much stronger.

Forecasts giving a possible Force 5–6 but with nothing worse in store may be perfectly safe on a passage off the wind, providing the waters are free of ugly tide-rips and easy to navigate, but a beat to windward in these conditions is likely to be so gruelling that only the shortest of port-to-port passages in sheltered waters should be tackled. Force 4 is the favourite and even this will give 'a lively passage to windward in open waters, while Force 3 with a fair tide carrying a beating yacht to windward is a nice working breeze for a little boat.

By all means let the small-boat man look upon Force 5 as a gale. By proportion *it is* a gale, but he must get a proper perspective about the true gales of the forecasts and leave them to bigger boats.

*Additional Notes*

*The Beaufort Scale*

(0) Below 1 knot. Calm. Sea mirror-like.

(1) Up to 3. Light air ripples like dimples. Steerageway.

(2) 4 to 6. Light Breeze. Wavelets but no crests. Good handling breeze, gives maybe 3 knots.

(3) 7 to 10. Gentle Breeze. Large wavelets and small crests, waves 2 ft high. Cruisers heel and sail well 4 knots.

(4) 11 to 16. Moderate Breeze. Small waves getting longer with white crests up to $3\frac{1}{2}$ ft. May need one reef at sea, excellent sailing.

(5) 17 to 21. Fresh Breeze. Moderate waves, white horses and some spray. Two or three reefs and smaller jib. Heavy going to windward at sea.

(6) 22 to 27. Strong Breeze. Large waves forming and white horses everywhere with spray. Fully reefed and storm jib. Bad conditions in a fast weather-going tide.

(7) 28 to 33. Near Gale. Heaped sea with foam in streaks. Small cruisers should be in shelter or making for shelter with care if running. Main down to 5 ft or stowed. Storm jib.

(8) 34 to 40. Gale. Moderately high waves, spindrift and foam blowing down-wind in long banners. Small cruisers may have hove-to or scudded with fenders, coils of rope, etc., towed astern long before this but in the open sea they must now do so if the sea is big.

Above Force 8 the scale continues Strong gale, Storm, Violent storm and Hurricane (9, 10, 11 and 12). In the open sea, Force 8 can raise an 18-ft sea, but if there is land to windward it will be far less. Height of sea increases rapidly as fetch or distance offshore increases. Tide and nature of sea-bed also affect the size and type of sea. In any wind force above 3 to 4 the small cruiser must stay well clear of tidal rips and overfalls.

# Chapter Fifteen

# Rough Water

WAVES, with a few exceptions, are wind-driven water. The further they are able to travel without meeting land the higher they become. The depth of the sea and the effect of tidal currents impose restrictions on the wave form which alter its character.

A swell being either the subsiding wave pattern after a blow or the movement of water in advance of wind is of no inconvenience to a yacht at sea, but close inshore in shoal water it tends to shorten and steepen until it plunges and breaks across a bar or shallow patch.

Increasing from catspaws to ripples, then wavelets of glassy appearance followed by larger wavelets of maybe two feet in height with a tendency to break (Forces, 1, 2 and 3), the waves begin to be built up by the increasing wind in a regular pattern. Through Force 4 they become longer, and white horses begin to move among the smaller waves, increasing in number and length through Force 5, with spray blowing and larger foam-capped seas appearing at Force 6. Thereafter the character changes rapidly. A heaping sea with foam blowing to leeward from breaking crests, and later the true blown spindrift whipping in banners from crests and long, orderly streaks of foam patterning the longer backs of the seas—this is the Force 7–8 gale. Above this it is all beyond the scope of the small cruiser; it is all bad and to be out in it will be to lose all academic interest in the exact force of the wind at the time.

## Shoal-water Waves

Quite apart from the big seas raised by high wind, the question of shallow-water seas must be remembered. In a fresh breeze, or even a moderate breeze if it has shortly been preceded by much wind, shallow water in the entrance to a river in the form of a bar often produces conditions dangerous to small craft.

There is no question of advising how to set about surf-riding in over a shallow bar; you just don't attempt it without the knowledge and the right sort of craft. There are the borderline instances though, the occasions when, having gone in so far, it is no longer possible to turn back.

From inshore, where the height of the seas can be properly judged, a breaking bar always looks worse than it does from seaward, and hence to the small-boat man happily standing in for the river without a care in the world. At a certain point the yacht will suddenly seem to drop bodily into a big trough, then astern of her comes a huge comber, advancing like an express train. It will lift her, and she will begin tobogganing down the forward face of it, bows deeply immersed, stern in the foaming crest. She will either broach to and be overturned, or she can allow it to pass ahead of her without trouble. Alternatively it may fill the cockpit and the following sea will catch her out of control.

The only action to take is to *keep going*. Never, at such a late stage, attempt to turn and make offshore again in panic. Keep absolutely straight, keep the fore-and-aft trim a little by the stern and crew weight low and most of all keep the speed down. Drop the mainsail in a heap and let the jib carry her in if there is time to prepare. There will be a distinct line of breaking, fast-moving crests, and then there will follow an area of white water where the seas have expended their force and it will be over. Better that it should never have begun, perhaps.

Approach all bars with foreknowledge gained from the Pilot Book. Take stock of the forces of the wind and the recent weather history. Note the presence or otherwise of a distinct swell, check the tide height and state of tide because a fast ebb against an onshore wind is to be avoided. Remember that most bars, most of the time, are passable, otherwise the place would be completely shunned by yachtsmen. Don't be spooked by a white crest or two but sail up and down and examine the situation if there is any cause for doubt.

The small shoal-draft yacht is less likely to hit the bar than a deep-keeled vessel, but the risk may be there and must be considered as it would certainly be the finish of her. The simplest way of checking in advance that a bar carries enough water for safe crossing is to take a there-and-then sounding at some fixed position just offshore, such as a cross-bearing taken when the ship is centred on leading marks or close to some beacon or buoy. If the chart shows a least depth at that known point of say two fathoms and the lead reading gives three and a half, then obviously there is one and a half fathoms to be added to the soundings shown on the bar. Further, it is safer to deduct half the estimated height of the seas (in fact, it is less than half) from the expected figure to allow for sinking in the troughs but naturally such fine limits are to be avoided as you must have a margin of safety. Such calculations should be in the nature of reassurance.

The effect of wind upon a fast tidal current has been mentioned time and again in this book, and it cannot be over-stressed that tide races, rips and overfalls are best avoided (and usually very easy to avoid). The seas in such places rise in sharp pyramids and fall flat on their faces only to jump up again a few yards away. Big sleek swirling 'smooths' appear which spin a boat around in defiance of her rudder and troughs seem deeper than usual. There is rarely much need to bother about these horrors in gentle weather. In fact it is educational to shoot a race providing there is enough wind to give normal control, but in anything above Force 4 the small cruiser does well to stay clear.

## The Pocket Gale

Although it may seem that the only safe behaviour is to be like the candlestick fisherman who stayed ashore because there was too much wind if the flame blew out and stayed ashore becalmed if it didn't, the frame of mind which finds alarm in every puff of wind is something to be avoided like the plague. Worry is tiring and it is contagious.

Inevitably the small cruiser will hit patches of rough going which may not have been foreseen. They last a few hours, or just as long as it takes to round a headland, but they can be worrying to the inexperienced. Faith in the cruiser, and trust in good gear are the essentials for peace of mind. Worry about either takes all the fun out of yachting. The weaknesses may be inadequate staying, or neglected wires, poorly fastened fairleads, worn sheets and old sails. To be watching and fussing over such things for fear they may fail is to be ill-fitted to cope with any outside troubles.

Any normal boat will tell you when she is being pressed too hard. She should have enough sail to go to windward easily without smashing and flinging her bows around, staggering and lurching. A long beat should only be undertaken if the crew is strong enough to do justice to the boat and, for most people who are unused to being offshore, this may mean that by the time each of a three-man crew has done a two-hour trick one at least will have had enough of it. The owner who takes account of this will budget for an outside eight hours of rough going and lay plans to have shelter under his lee at the end of it. In all probability the wind will ease or shift by then, and he can take a second look at his crew before tackling a longer leg.

A few bigger yachts can carry full working sail in Force 5–6, but not many. A modern ocean racer may work to windward in Force 7–8 and may not need to be hove-to until the wind reaches 40 knots, and it is an odd fact that in an offshore race small yachts often keep going to windward longer than large ones. However, this cannot be carried down the scale to the small cruiser. A fully reefed 18 footer is well pressed in a Force 5 wind at sea, but given sail reduction to 'storm' proportions she can keep going in stronger conditions.

It seems to be very seldom that one can take a fair tide on a beat to windward without having to roll down a couple of reefs and the stronger the tide the more necessary this becomes. The reason is quite simply that a 12-knot breeze becomes a 20-knot breeze when you have a 4-knot tide under you sailing to windward (Fig. 74)—a simple fact which accounts for many a 'yachtsman's gale'. More important, though, is that under such conditions (and remember that the breeze is really only a moderate one) the sea will have become broken with white horses possibly four or five feet high and the going will be extremely uncomfortable. With such a tide to help it is sensible to shorten sail right down to a snug rig.

It must again be stressed that it is wrong to sit out in any small cruiser. Beyond sitting to windward in the cockpit it is a sure sign of being over-pressed if she seems to need still more weight uphill. Sailing too fast in hard weather tends to make some of these craft bury their bows badly and this in itself is but one step from losing control in a seaway.

The slower you sail the more comfortable it tends to be, and the longer the passage, of course. One must strike a medium. Short water-line hulls lacking overhang do not benefit by being threshed along on one ear like a Six-Metre. In a tumble of waves and a moderate to fresh breeze, it is far better to slip easily past the seas rather than try to smash through them. A good full-and-by course (no matter how much higher

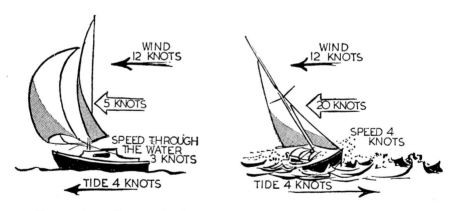

FIG. 74. According to whether the tide is carrying the yacht to windward or to leeward the wind force experienced will be increased or decreased. A fast weather-going tide is responsible for many a 'yachtsman's gale'.

she may *seem* to point) is the fastest in the end. To stick a small cruiser tight to the wind, and expect her to generate power enough to bulldoze her way through, is to induce that tiresome hobby-horse motion which gets you nowhere. One sees people with an outboard motor wowing away on the stern, head to wind and making no way, but it is poor seamanship except as a last hope of rounding a spit in a foul-turning tide. If there is plenty of wind and the boat won't go it is unlikely that she will do any better under auxiliary power. The engine and sail combination is acceptable in the tubby 20–25 footer, but only to help her through a short head sea—sail is her main power.

## Bad Weather and the Crew

Noise and movement are the enemies of endurance. A three-man crew leaves no reserve for lame ducks. Should two men fall low the safety of the cruiser is undermined, since there is a limit to the time that one man can keep going without rest and food.

The food question in heavy weather is critical. Food is warmth and energy, optimism and level-headedness. Without it a man begins to fail. The belief that food must be cooked is open to doubt. There is really no reason to suppose that hot cooked food is more nutritious than raw or cold. The struggle to cook on a very small boat often results in making the cook seasick quite unnecessarily and, while the moral value of a hot meal counts for a lot, it is far more important for all hands to stay well and take nourishment in some other form. In fact, it may not do any harm to go for twenty-four hours without eating—water they must have, but shore living will have left them well nourished. The danger lies in reaching that point when appetite no longer functions as a warning to re-fuel.

A diet of brown bread, raisins, cheese and so on is of far more value than the usual tinned lash-up stew, and water is far less likely to induce seasickness than tea or patent coffee.

Small meals (not snacks) are easier to digest and easier to organise. They also give the queasy a fighting chance to stoke up during his occasional periods of well-being.

It is a sound plan to have a heavy-weather ration kept aboard in one particular place, never to be touched at other times, but ready in the emergency. Self-heating soup is expensive, but one tin can restore the morale of a weak crew. Horlicks produce a variety of scientifically prepared food concentrates specially for hardship conditions such as mountaineering, lifeboat survival and extended trekking. These heat- and energy-producing foods are high in carbohydrate and fat, and low in protein. Curry and meat in brick form for heating with water, stew bars, concentrated oatcake and special non-thirstmaking fudge typify the sort of foods available from them.

Alcohol is a useful food used with discretion. It is an immediate energy and heat producer, but the letdown afterwards is fast. It should be saved for the man who is going off watch when a quick slug of Scotch will help him to make the most of his one- or two-hour stand-easy. Nuts are another quick energy producer, chocolate, of course, and plenty of raisins. Sugar in any form, and fruit if you've got it. Plenty to drink is important. Five hours without liquid, and a man is already beginning to experience the first symptoms of dehydration. The often-heard cry 'I'm dying for a cup of tea' has an element of truth.

Seasickness is the arch-enemy, though, and allied to noise and movement, cold and hunger. All too often a man will go sick simply because he is hungry and morbidly mistakes the hollowness of hunger for *mal-de-mer*. Eat and keep eating as long as you can, night or day.

There is still no cure for seasickness. Marketed drugs help some people more than others, but there is no guaranteed cure. Most of them induce intense drowsiness, which, while being fine for anyone who can die happily in a deck-chair on a steamer, is poor compensation to the man who must struggle to stay awake at the tiller. It is no use being unsympathetic with the sufferers—they are usually beyond shame, any-how. Now and then a person may be quite seriously ill after constant retching, and it is unwise to treat all horizontal shipmates as malin-gerers. By the same token many a crew has been bullied back to work and incidentally back to health by a skipper who can discriminate.

Warmth and fresh air, the familiar horizontal position and food if it can be taken are the only things which seem to matter. Too much liquid can cause sickness, and tea seems to be particularly bad. Sitting down below instead of lying down can bring it on, or, for that matter, any smell, taste or sight of food at a critical moment.

Keeping warm and dry is a never-ending bother. Loose woollen clothing, long woollen pants and vest, long-tailed shirts and in general all the most unlovely garments you can think of seem to be the best. Certainly it is useless to expect to stay warm with six sweaters on top and a thin, damp pair of jeans on the lower half. Wool socks and loose boots—even half-filled—seem warmer than wet canvas shoes, and a pair of wet-suit gloves kept somewhere on board will one day become valu-able.

Oilskin suits should always be bought big. Try the smock on over a sports-coat and imagine trying to struggle it on over wet wool. Trousers should come high but never the elastic-waisted things which leave a bare section of back exposed when you bend. The one-piece boilersuittype oilskin suits are best of all, perhaps, as they are easy and quick to get on and off—an important matter in conditions which make dressing-up a performance likely to take as much as fifteen minutes each time.

The wet oilskin worn below-decks is an amazing water-carrier. Dry accommodation becomes saturated in a very short while, but to stipulate that the watch below should strip off on deck is a little harsh when conditions are bad and there is very little room to do it anywhere else. An old towel to rub off the worst of it before diving below to strip off properly saves quite a lot of drips.

## Bad Weather

In a suitable type of craft, well equipped and with the right type of crew we don't *fear* bad weather in summertime, but unless we are racing we avoid it, because it is hard on our sails and gear and because it is highly unpleasant.

Unfortunately, the preliminary to bad weather is often a four- or five-hour spell of magnificent sailing. With shelter ahead this may be splendid, but on a passage outwards it is a bait to lure the yacht further and further from shelter. The question of seeking shelter is one of the oldest of all seafaring problems. The land is a deadly enemy unless the vessel is under full command and able to be beaten offshore again if anchoring is not a safe policy.

Very few yachts are powerful enough for their crews to beat off a lee shore in an onshore gale once they are close in and among confused water. A crack ocean racer could do it, perhaps, but a tiny cruiser might not.

In theory any lee shore which has a convenient river mouth leading to shelter ceases to be a danger to the yacht scudding in with a gale astern. The problem is to be sure of finding it. Such a hell-for-leather race for shelter might begin in clear visibility, but there is no assurance that driving murk will not close it to a few hundred yards long before she gets close—and if she misses she is in bad trouble.

The bigger seagoing yacht offers a choice. She can stay out, well offshore, in reasonable safety (save for the risk from steamers), or if she is turned down-wind on a run for shelter. The better facilities for navigating and the fact that she is better able to beat back out of trouble give her a good margin of safety.

It follows then that any run for safety must have an easily attained goal, a wide estuary with deep water, a bay or a headland. In the English Channel, for instance, there is a natural abundance of shelter from westerly weather all along the English coast mainly in the form of headlands, but the easterly blow is a different matter, and so is a southerly. This type of open-sided shelter, however, is not particularly safe for very small craft if there is a chance of the wind backing and cornering her, blocking her escape.

If she is going to run for a difficult mouth it should be long before the bad weather is on her. Remember that a 'low' will be moving at about 25 knots, the yacht may make six or seven. If she has forty miles to go and the weather is already thickening she just won't make it.

This doesn't preclude her owner from having a shot at it if the shelter he is making for can be reached obliquely—if it is not a dead lee shore, in fact, or if the wind is not likely to back southerly and make it into a lee shore by the time he gets there. He can run for it while running is safe under normal sailing conditions, scud under a small jib or bare mast for a little longer than that, perhaps, but once the seas begin to break and wave-planing begins it is time to take stock. If shelter is still beyond reach, the temptation to keep running wildly, to hang on and hope has to be put well aside. Lack of bad-weather experience is a great nuisance here. It may be possible to run safely for several more hours, but one dollop of water in the cockpit and the frightened owner thinks he has been pooped. Knowing no better he very wisely rounds up.

Such a run, with wind and tide under her, perhaps, very often leaves an owner unprepared for the real weight of wind when he does at last think of rounding up. Very few small cruisers are ever reefed down to the tiny scrap of sail which is all they may carry in even a moderate gale—some will be unable to carry any sail whatsoever. Running under four or five rolls plus working jib may seem exhilarating, but on the wind in a real blow she may take no more than six feet of main plus a jib no larger than a shirt. Not one small cruiser in fifty carries real hardweather sails in her lockers, and certainly no proper sheets and fairleads for them.

Heaving to in a gale means lying often almost beam-on under a tiny scrap of sail or no sail at all and letting the ship lurch away to leeward as she will. She may well have to be handled the whole time since lashing the helm of such lightweight craft liable to be spun and chucked in all directions is hardly as practicable as it is in a displacement hull. Under a storm trysail, it should be possible to keep a small cruiser more or less heading the seas with one bow and sailing slowly. The aim is to see that she takes them under her shoulder, climbs and rolls down the other side. In no circumstances should a helmsman luff full into a sudden big breaking sea for fear of the cruiser being stood on her tail and pitchpoled backwards.

Lacking a storm jib, a good terylene mainsail rolled right down, or provided with a deep enough reef, will certainly keep her head up, and by adjusting the tiller and lashing it she may lie to under it, but the sail must not be allowed to flog. The deafening crackle of a flogging sail in a gale rarely continues for long without loss of the sail.

If such small boats are to come safely through a bad gale at sea without the proper sails they must be allowed to exploit the buoyancy which is their redeeming feature. To drive them is impossible, to maintain them at an angle to the seas which allows them to ride up and over means keeping headway on them by carrying sail, and to run means that their empty-paper-bag characteristic must be offset by towing some bulky object astern on a long line. The sea-anchor is practically impossible to rig from scratch in a very small boat handled by inexperienced yachtsmen, and in any case it is no guaranteed solution. Built-in buoyancy to make the yacht unsinkable is a last extreme comfort, but a bulkhead sealing off the cabin from the cockpit, and cockpit drains, all tend to make her a fairly safe floating object, providing that she is not burdened by too much sail or subjected to solid water falling upon her lightly constructed decks with force. Keep the water out and the crew in are probably the only aims in a last extreme of weather.

An along-shore gale, although seemingly safer than the deadly onshore gale by far, may still mean that a small cruiser sailing under bare pole or a scrap of mainsail and using her engine may find it impossible to turn at right angles to the wind for the purpose of entering a narrow harbour entrance or sheltering river. As soon as she brings the wind on her beam she is laid flat and she cannot be headed up for the entrance.

Scudding downwind parallel to the land it may not occur to anybody that the shelter now in sight may prove to be the real danger. It is wise to try turning the boat across and half into wind well before reaching the entrance just to see how she behaves. In any event, it will probably be necessary to turn in well before the entrance has opened up. It is also vital to note whether the ebb is running out of the haven, because the cross sea created may be dangerous to a small craft. It is considerations such as these that mark the wise and careful seaman.

Heaving to under bare mast with helm lashed a-lee or scudding under a bare mast while towing a mattress bundled up on the end of a warp (warps alone are too light) are both possibilities which must be proved. The important aim is to do anything to keep the boat sailing slowly, to let the sea overtake her or pass harmlessly under her. At such times the passage is of secondary importance. Shelter may be no more than a few miles distant but the ship must be handled as though it were a hundred miles away.

## *Additional Notes*

BREAKERS may begin in 2 fathoms with an onshore wind and ebb tide. Wave height is reckoned as two per cent of the square of the wind velocity in knots; thus a 10-knot breeze gives a 2-foot wave. Estimate by sighting as the crests come into line with the yacht in the trough. Calculate eye-level above water line.

Open sea waves average 50:1 length:height. When shoaling water equals half the wave length in depth the waves begin to alter form. By the time the depth is ten per cent the wave breaks. Breakers can be reckoned to form in water which is as deep as the wave is high.

A yacht running before a sea must be overtaken. If she tends to dwell on the crests she is in danger of being broached.

*Heavy Weather Sailing* by K. Adlard Coles (published by Adlard Coles Ltd) is a classic work on yachts in bad weather. It relates mostly to slightly larger craft and it is quite frightening in parts. For the conscientious owner of a small boat it is essential reading though.

*Motor Sailing:* It is not always advantageous to use the engine and sails together in order to punch to windward in a blow. Unless the propeller is deeply immersed in solid water and relatively slow turning, large and of coarse pitch, the heeling and pitching of the yacht combine to keep the propeller racing in light water near the surface. Better to motor dead to windward albeit very slowly. Motor sailing, with a minimum of sail tightly sheeted may however be more comfortable. The use of the engine with sails to help the yacht to point up and make ground in short, steep seas is another matter. In this case the engine is run at half revs (or less) and it serves merely to help her carry her momentum.

# Chapter Sixteen

# Distress

I T seems a little unfair to follow up so dismal a chapter with an even more depressing subject, but while the reader is in sober mood the matter of dealing with real trouble may be received with deeper attention.

Of all the yachts which fly distress-signals it is some comfort to know that only a small proportion of them are in genuine trouble, beyond their own ability to cope. Moreover, the reasons for their predicament are in most cases due to carelessness rather than the dangerous nature of the sport. Figures of lifeboat rescues are a bit frightening until the assistance rendered to rowing dinghies, Lilos and motor boats out of petrol are deducted. The instances of yachts in dire distress due to extremes of weather are rare. More often than not it is a case of frightened, cold and seasick people who have run out of seamanship and enthusiasm. In the light of this, maybe it can be seen why this book nags so much about combining seaworthiness of boat with sea-fitness of crew, and staying within the limits of skills and endurance whenever there is a choice.

Troubles seldom come singly. A block jams, the cruiser luffs, hits a buoy, holes her bow, etc., etc. Usually some quite small failure can bring about a state of disorder, and this leads to faulty decision and poor handling. Good gear, forethought and a clear appreciation of how serious or otherwise the situation may be will avoid at least fifty per cent of trouble. Good sails of all things are trouble savers, a blown-out mainsail means a down-wind course and heaven only knows where that may end.

Ultimately, practically all trouble at sea dates from a wrong decision somewhere back along the line (and this excludes the decision to buy a boat). Somewhere there was a choice of doing one thing or the other. There is only one way in which an owner can shuffle his ideas into correct focus at the time of making that decision. It is to range his facts in order of importance rather as though he was sitting in judgement upon his own actions. Whether to gamble on a tricky river entrance or sail twenty wet and weary miles further on, whether to go to sea in face of a bad forecast to be back in time for work on Monday. A weighing up of consequences and penalties leaves no doubt of the wise choice.

There is one great fallacy of the coasting yachtsman that needs knocking on the head right away. It is that no matter how hard it may be blowing, a coasting passage, down wind with plenty of rolls in the mainsail, is safe enough so long as you can 'nip in' to shelter if it gets too bad. Under a bare mast or scrap of jib the small cruiser may be able to scud safely enough for hours on end providing the following sea is not breaking dangerously, *but* should the crew try to put her on a reach in order to fetch into a river-mouth, she will need some mainsail and, scrap though it may be, it may put her down flat on her ear, so flat that she cannot stagger the short distance into shelter. This has happened over and over again, not always disastrously, perhaps, but usually it has been a lucky lull which has brought the boat through it. With a following tide sweeping along the shore it may be even more difficult to claw inshore.

Another risky delusion is that you can always run her ashore in the event of bad weather. In a fresh breeze and on a suitable sheltered shore this may be so, but it takes a very experienced man to decide when and where. Obviously, a rocky or cliff-bound shore is a suicidal place to beach a boat in onshore weather. The 'soft' shoreline can be equally dangerous. A beach which is steep-to will be fringed by plunging surf which will dump the boat, draw her back, dump her again and so on. It is often quite impossible for a man to haul himself out of the water due to the under-tow of receding surf even though the distance may be a matter of yards, unless of course there is a shore-party of rescuers waiting who know their stuff backwards.

A beach of normal slope may mean the boat striking or being overwhelmed at some distance from the shore. She may broach to in the surf well before she has reached easy swimming or wading distance. Perhaps the safest way to get ashore would be to let go the anchor and hope that she drags it steadily into the shallows, this way she should stay bow-on to the advancing breakers and move very slowly astern, which is almost the proper manner of tackling surf in an unsuitable craft.

The long, shallow shoreline offers the only reasonable chance of beaching in safety, but it is a gamble unless the shore is known. As the boat comes into shallow water—and it may take her a mile or more—the seas grow correspondingly smaller and less dangerous until she finally grounds in little more than wavelets. The crux of the matter lies in the state of tide and whether there are any offlying banks. At high water, the long, shallow shore may be fringed by a steep seawall or groins which could be highly dangerous to hit. The offlying bank may result in a smashed hull. The intervening stretch of deeper water remains to be crossed somehow—this, incidentally, is where the boat with built-in buoyancy offers a reserve of safety.

Beaching is something to be undertaken only as a very last resort. That it must be considered is only part of the business of being a seaman, but it should only be considered judiciously.

In the final outcome, the decision to fly distress-signals must be made boldly. Either the owner considers his ship in danger or he isn't sure, just worried. He must make a definite signal while there is a chance of being seen and while there is time for rescue forces to get into action. He may lose his mainsail with shoal water to leeward. He can motor while petrol lasts and just hope to claw off, but if failure to do so may mean stranding with darkness ahead and danger of breaking up it is foolish to gamble on a small anchor holding him off. It may take some hours for a rescuer to reach him, so the decision to signal is plain. On the other hand, with a tide about to turn and carry him clear it is a fair gamble to take.

At least six red distress-flares and at least one daylight smoke-canister should be carried by any small yacht going offshore, preferably many more including a hand-held starshell pyrotechnic, or so. It may take many fireworks to attract attention and several more to guide rescuers to the spot at night. A really powerful torch should also be at hand.

Once a flare is sent up, the yacht is at once acknowledged to be considered by her owner as in distress and in need of assistance—a point to be remembered before pooping off for any superficial reason. This brings up the question of salvage, which is discussed later on in the chapter. By daylight the hoisting of clothing in the rigging or the flying of the ensign upside down are both hailed as signals of distress, and anything in the nature of frantic waving with both arms by one or more people amounts to the same thing. Lacking proper flares, yachtsmen have often attempted to summon assistance by setting light to a drop of petrol in a can and in a large number of cases they have managed to set fire to the ship as well. If the need is so pressing that this risk seems worthwhile, the 'cresset' should consist of rags bound round a boat-hook, the whole thing can be held aloft and dunked over the side if necessary.

Perhaps one of the sanest plans for the small-boat man is to keep a friend ashore notified of his movements when long passages are involved—it must be a sailing friend, though, who understands the chances of delay and can hunch when delay seems ominous. Coastguards and R.Y.A. urge that all small craft should have the name of the yacht painted in large letters somewhere on the hull or coachroof so that in the event of an alarm, wild goose chases can be eliminated and time saved. At all events, any small craft which is unduly delayed at sea should be reported to the local harbour office on arrival just in case a search has been called. The number of yachtsmen who go in ignorance of their supposed loss seems to increase by the year. What they may little realise is that a small craft on a coastal passage in tricky weather is often reported from one watch house to the next all around the coast, a service which all too often is rewarded by a 'mind your own business' attitude.

The organisation behind sea rescue services is a tight one. A yacht in distress off the coast may be reported by coastguard, police, other shipping unable to get close or the holidaymaker on the beach. The message is passed on to the controllers who decide whether rescue by helicopter is possible. In winds exceeding 45 knots, during darkness or fog or at a distance of more than sixty miles air rescue is not practicable. Likewise if the assistance of a lifeboat is needed to tow a vessel clear of danger towards which she may be drifting, either it or both services may be brought to bear.

There is a great deal which the yachtsman can do to help above and beyond waving his trousers about and setting off rockets. In daylight, a smoke-signal either of the Wessex type or some improvised cresset can be made ready for when the helicopter is sighted. If the yacht is in the sort of trouble which is not likely to be obvious from the air, such as leaking fast beyond the ability of her crew to cope, any deliberate disorder of gear on deck—lowering the mast, streaming sails over the side and so on will help. If other yachts are anywhere in the same area, although perhaps not visible from the water, this is more than ever important.

For the actual rescue, if the yacht can be kept head to wind so much the better. Helicopter crews have one great fear—that the lifting wire they lower may get tangled in the rigging of the yacht or, for that matter, be made fast there by the yachtsmen in their ignorance. Such a thing could easily wreck the aircraft. To this end, any backstays, topping lifts and so forth should be cleared away to leave the after part of the yacht bare of snags. If sails are still set these must be lowered because the slipstream could capsize a small yacht. In some cases the aircraft may even lower a rubber dinghy or a member of the crew, but if the yachtsmen can stream astern in their own dinghy—if it is of a suitable type—the lift may be made easier without extra trouble. Lifting gear consists of a belt which loops under the armpits with a toggle to slide down to the chest, but a pick-up net may be used in the case of children or people incapable of helping themselves. The readiness of helicopter crews to go out on a rescue operation is something to be thankful for—they may even welcome the chance of getting some live practice, but this in no way detracts from the gratitude we owe them.

If helicopters are concerned with saving our necks for us, the lifeboat service is concerned with saving both our necks and our boats, and on this matter the yachtsman does well to know his facts. To the R.N.L.I. life comes first. No risk is too great for the volunteer crews to tackle. Their record of lives saved is around 80,000 in the course of the service's history. What is not so generally known is that the crews are allowed to launch the lifeboat for purposes of salvage—an arrangement which is completely separate from the R.N.L.I. They pay for any damage to the boat and pay their own court charges, but if there is salvage to be made then make it they will.

Against this ominous ring is the fact that the owner of a very small boat is unlikely to be socked hard by these men. But they are working men, who can use money, and they are entitled to make a few pounds where they can. The small boat towed to safety by the lifeboat may be a fair salvage claim, which may or may not be pressed by the salvors. It is up to the owner to see that he acts fairly and behaves sensibly.

Insurance companies seem to be unanimous in saying that the Royal Navy is sharper off the mark on matters of salvage than the lifeboatmen and both, oddly enough, are sharper than the fishermen (who are more likely to do you down for a pint of shrimps and rescue you for your gratitude and a five pound note).

## Salvage

The essential matter is that salvors must be able to show that without their efforts the vessel would stand to be a total loss. The firing of rockets is proof that the owner is worried, but he can still bargain for 'assistance' rather than admit complete loss of control. One must use sense over this. A truculent attitude in a tight spot is not the right line at all. If he is in serious trouble let him leave the job of rescue in more experienced hands and not impede the rescuers, but by the same token he must be ready for the unscrupulous who paint a lurid picture of fictional perils when all that is required is a simple tow from A to B.

Whenever possible a price for assistance rendered should be agreed on the spot, and the owner should keep dark about whether or not he is insured—witnesses should be present at any such deals. The owner must remain in command of the whole works too, so that the tow-boat becomes no more than a form of power. He should pass his own tow rope and remain at his own tiller.

A salvage award will depend upon a Court's decision, and this will be based upon the dangers and difficulties of the job, risks involved, and time and trouble expended. If the owner is able to arrange a private sum instead of allowing the salvage claim to materialise he should pay up on the spot and be content. Nevertheless, the salvage award, which may amount to half the value of the yacht, is still a cheaper way out for the insurance company than footing the bill for complete replacement.

A sense of proportion is needed throughout. An owner should recognise genuine kindness with gratitude and reward it with a proportionate sum.

The danger lies in innocently accepting assistance without arrangement. Even the loan of a big anchor can become salvage if the case can be proved. Keep the insurance company informed, for their interests and the owner's are closely linked. But at all costs don't jeopardise the safety of your crew in an attempt to be smart.

A great deal more damage may often be done to a boat in the course of an ill-planned rescue than she may suffer as a result of the emergency. Tow-lines made fast to forestays or shrouds, the arrival alongside of a rough fishing-boat hull, towing at high speed and berthing afterwards in some commercial dock, all can result in damage to topsides and deck or even holing of the hull and loss of mast. The same holds true for the rescued crew. Attempts to leap for safety should be strictly avoided. Danger from the screw of the rescuer to yachtsmen unwise enough to attempt to swim for it and even superficial injuries following an unnecessary scramble are usually avoidable if all keep their heads.

The old truth that yachtsmen should never, never attempt to swim for the shore can bear repetition. For as long as the yacht remains afloat—and this may be indefinitely—the safest place is aboard her, whatever else may be going on. There will obviously be the exceptions, but the rule is the thing to remember. That lifejackets should be aboard for each man of the crew is basic common sense.

## Fire

There was an instance of a yachtsman who filled a kettle with petrol in the dark and burnt out the yacht—he was lucky to get away with a whole skin. The fault lay in using identically shaped jerry-cans for water and fuel. There are innumerable cases of explosions and fires great and small, but not one single case which was unavoidable.

Gas-bottles, as everybody knows, can be allowed to leak, and the leakage being heavier than air trickles down into the bilge. Paraffin stoves can be allowed to flare up, methylated spirits can be spilled and cause a blaze, and so on, *ad infinitum*. Wooden boats have been potential bonfires for hundreds of years, and only care can prevent trouble. In fact, very few yachts are ever totally destroyed, but many are badly damaged by fire. Prompt action by the crew can minimise the damage.

Half a cup of neat petrol in the bilge can blow a boat apart, the vapour can lie undetected for days. Fill cans and tanks over the side, and keep empty cans stoppered if they are stowed in lockers. Mop up even the smallest spillage; and, should any petrol go below, pump out the bilge at once and open up the cabin sole, lockers and hatches to ventilate the bilges. Even a tank which is filled carefully without drips is dangerous if the breather pipe is *inside* the cockpit, as the filling process drives out vapour which immediately goes below. Don't fill the outboard in the cockpit or even on the stern in a light following breeze and certainly douse all naked lights.

Bottled-gas stoves are quite safe as long as they are efficiently used. Trust your nose and suspect everybody else of carelessness. Make 'turning off at the bottle' an instinctive reaction, and don't regulate the burner heat by turning the flame low or it will blow out.

If there is paraffin, petrol and water aboard, see that each liquid has a distinctive and differently shaped container and label each one.

Fire extinguishers are usually far too small in capacity. Nowadays conscience is placated by installing just one small aerosol extinguisher on the bulkhead. This is fine if there are three or four more in a handy locker. Most yacht dealers supply approved types of extinguisher, but some are to be avoided whatever their efficiency, since they produce dangerous fumes. $CO_2$ extinguishers are safe and effective, but methyl bromide and chloro-bromomethane extinguishers are bad, while water, though adequate for simple fires, should never be used on fuel blazes.

In the event of a fire at sea, draught must be kept down to the minimum, and usually this will mean putting the yacht on a run at once and closing the forehatch once everybody is abaft the fire and out of the cabin. If the fire is right aft, naturally this will not be practicable as the flames will be blown forward and spread.

## Serious Leaking

No bilge-pump which cannot be worked constantly without undue fatigue should be installed. A big pump in a small boat may look disproportionate, but it is an important extravagance. On the modern glued ply hull, moulded ply hull or glass-fibre boat there is very little chance of serious leakage unless it results from a collision or stranding on a rock or underwater wreckage. The only possible action to take is to rip out the interior carpentry until the damage can be reached and the hole or crack stuffed with a towel. This is less easy than it sounds unless something in the nature of a crow-bar is kept aboard—rather an unwelcome item on a small cruiser.

The splintered area should be pushed back into shape where possible and to do this may mean shoring it from inside in some way. To this end a hammer and a handful of assorted nails are worth carrying in the bosun's bag. An adjustable strut can be made by lapping two lengths of wood (bunk sides perhaps), joining the lap at one end with a single large nail and by using the 'hinge', insert the strut with a dog-leg in it and straighten it to exert the pressure. A lashing then holds the parts together. Soap is a good filler for cracks or builder's Sylglas tape. A cushion or pillow makes a good leak stopper.

## Insurance

It is an extravagance to sail without insurance cover. Not *your* actions may cause damage but those of some unknown person.

The company takes the condition of your boat on trust, quoting after assessing your case, taking experience, age of boat and engine, etc., into consideration. Cover applies to a specified cruising area and some companies are reluctant to cover the small cruiser for offshore passages, a fact to be ascertained at the beginning. Loss or damage by fire or accident—collision, wreck, heavy weather, etc.—also theft, are covered; but masts and sails when racing or sails when set are not usually covered, and neither is damage to an engine unless part of a larger claim. If sails are damaged while stowed, or damaged as a result of a collision we'll say, compensation is usually given. Risk of loss overboard of an outboard may have to be covered by a separate arrangement.

It is possible to cover for total loss only, but this is a doubtful saving, especially as damage may entail virtually rebuilding the whole cruiser. Some people undertake to stand the first ten pounds of any claim as a means of getting a lower premium, but in a bad season, or for a beginner, this may add up to more money in the end than the loss of a no-claims bonus.

Marine insurance companies are very fair and very human. They hate to be served a fast deal and react as one might expect. They like notification of any shift of boat while laid up at the lower laying-up rates, and the yard that slaps in a big bill for 'handling' a yacht during a blow should be referred to the company at once. Never leave a stranded boat to her fate simply because she is insured, the underwriters just may not wear this one. They will be very sympathetic, on the other hand, to an owner who does all he can to save his boat even if she ends as a write-off. In any fracas with another yacht—just as in motor insurance—an owner should find out the other company involved.

Third party insurance is vitally important. An adequate cover makes only a slight increase in the premium, but the number of cases which have recently arisen, and which involve owners in huge sums of compensation for injury, make third party cover an urgent necessity.

# Chapter Seventeen

# Singlehanded Sailing

THERE is a temptation to think of the singlehander as being a person of great stoicism crossing oceans, alone for weeks at a time and given to other eccentricities. In truth, a person is singlehanding every time he or she lets go of the tiller and allows the boat to sail herself for a moment or two while another job is attended to.

Having the helm under your hand is a delight most of the time—one of the reasons for sailing at all is that controlling a sailing boat is a satisfying thing to do. There are times though when it becomes not merely tedious but exhausting and there are other times when being *unable* to let go of the tiller means the neglect or the skimping of something more vital too, perhaps safety. A typical example might be the husband who badly needs five minutes in which to study his chart very carefully; he cannot do so because there is nobody he dares to trust (perhaps on a dead run) or because his relief crew companion is seasick or perhaps urgently involved with young children. If he could become a singlehander in the full sense of the word he could save himself a worry and perhaps avert worse trouble.

## How Does She Behave?

Before any considerations of wind vane or other automatic steering gear comes the basic consideration of boat behaviour. What will she do at any particular moment if you simply let go of the tiller and stand aside? Cruisers vary a lot. Some will proceed, slowly changing course as they luff up into the wind. If closehauled some will continue to steer as good a course (or better) than when under the helmsman's hand. Yet other cruisers will swerve violently into the wind within seconds of the helm being released and either lie head-to-wind a'shake or fling themselves round on to the other tack and lie hove-to. Still others may carry lee helm in lighter winds and they will bear right away until they gybe themselves all-standing. Under engine yet other characteristics emerge. A big propeller and its paddlewheel effect will drive some craft round in a steady curve, others, and many modern boats, will curve off slowly at first and then fling themselves into a full helm attitude, turning so rapidly that a man can be flung overboard by it. In every weight of wind the characteristics will change.

Not only is it very interesting to know the characteristics of your own boat and fun to find out, but it is essential to know before we can begin to singlehand. For instance; a cruiser may be sailing along on a broad reach in a steady Force 3-4 breeze and the helmsman wishes to make a quick trip forward to check the anchor lashings. If he doesn't know his ship he will lash the tiller amidships and then dash at great speed up the deck and back again hoping to get back to his helm before she does ... what? To begin with one should *never* make quick dashes along small and lively decks, it is far too risky. Next, how much does it really matter if she does stray off course a bit?

Lashing a tiller to hold an exact course is only practicable in a cruiser of such steady directional character that she barely needs it lashed. Usually, one spends minutes deciding on the exact angle at which it should be held and then by shifting one's weight from aft to forward, the trim is sufficiently upset to alter her sailing balance and the carefully selected helm position becomes useless. In the case mentioned, slacking off the mainsheet *and* the headsail sheet together and allowing the boat to slow right down, sails shaking and lying beam to wind would be more sensible. It is no great effort to sheet in again and the helmsman would have time to *walk* and time to carry out a proper inspection forward.

Practically all yachts will lie beam-on if they are (1) Slowed down by freeing the sails before letting go of the helm and (2) If the helm is held a little to leeward; we are talking now of a tiller of course. In my own boat I have two lengths of rubber cord, one from each side of the cockpit and each has an eye seized in the end to slip over the tiller. We might call these helm a'lee holders our first piece of singlehanding equipment.

## Ordinary Singlehanding Equipment

Ordinary, because it is simple every-day stuff modifying existing ship's equipment. Whether the purpose is to facilitate singlehanding or not, anything that makes the working of the ship easier, simpler, has a place aboard a family cruiser. There may be plenty of willing hands to handle the sails and gear in fine weather but all too often and like it or not, the skipper, like the Mate of the Nancy Brig (remember Bab's Ballards?) may be cabin boy, navigator, cook and foredeck hand rolled into one when the seas begin to roll.

Working from bow to stern the singlehander's additions may be as follows: A stopper such as a split cotton reel seized around the forestay to prevent the lower jib hank from jamming on the splice of the forestay (if spliced); a length of rubber cord seized at its middle to the foot of a pulpit stanchion, which has an eye in one end and a toggle in the other. This provides a rapid lashing for a sail which is lowered in haste. The singlehander can lower, lash and be at the main halliard inside seconds. Failure to lash the headsail means that it will blow half-way up its stay again, fill and handicap the manoeuvre. The halliards too have their bitter ends secured to the deck so that they don't escape and there are toggle lines to hold the coiled rope safely. Hitching over the top of a cleat is fine but sooner or later off comes a coil.

If the headsail sheets tend to snarl up on a mast winch now and then something must be done because there may be nobody to send forward to free them while tacking up a crowded anchorage. Another (thick) rubber cord rigged when under way, running from mast down to foredeck cleat will act as a deflector. If rope is used it also makes a good handhold. The singlehander will have pockets for winch and reefing handles and a place for a knife with spike or a shackler right at the foot of the mast. The loss or the lack of any of these may mean precious time lost on a trip aft.

Nowadays, 'slab reefing' is finding much favour over roller reefing especially for singlehanding. I can haul down a deep reef in 60 seconds quite unaided and I can recommend it (see end of chapter notes). With reefing comes the allied task of stowing the mainsail. When singlehanding this is a job which takes precious seconds at a time when time is pressing. The ship may be shaking sail off preparatory to a mooring pick-up or she may be bringing up at anchor; either way there is much to attend to and all that is needed is a quick stow good enough to hold the sail down and tidy up loose and trouble-fraught bits of line. Canvas sail tyers are as quick as the man who uses them but if used, they, or a couple anyway, should always be hitched to the cabin top grab rail at sea, using a slip hitch. Better in some ways is to run parallel lengths of rubber cord along and below the boom, if the sail is to be slab reefed, each seized to the other at 2 foot intervals with a plastic hook strung on one side in each section. To use this method one simply grabs the cord from each side, up over boom and sail and engages the hook.

The mainsail luff has slides. A luff groove attachment to a mast means that the whole sail spills out of the track at every lowering, blowing everywhere and prohibiting a quick re-hoist should it be needed. A luff fitting sail can be converted by fitting toggles and any sail maker will do the job.

On the coachroof top a small car-type compass can be mounted instantly when required; this obviates the need for the proper compass on short coastal passages and gives a rough heading. Much of a single-hander's navigation is by eye and he glances from chart to land constantly, gauging angles and offings as he goes. The car compass aids his visualisation although it is *not* trusted for important bearings.

The cockpit has a couple of open pockets fixed to the forward bulkhead for the purpose of stowing safely any small object that might be in his hand at a moment when something urgent needs doing—a gin glass in particular. There may be some quick method of closing the open companion against a sudden shower, such as a canvas flap on Velcro fasteners and there will be a good deal of non-slip material laid on locker lids, side decks and steps—as elsewhere on deck, because falling, let alone falling overboard, is a grave risk for anybody who is quite alone.

In addition to the rubber cord helm a'lee lashings there is the tiller lashing. This can be rubber cord or terylene line, either way it spans the cockpit, it is instantly detachable and the tiller is engaged and held by means of a jam cleat or a complete turn of the cord around the tiller. The aim is that it should be possible to ease the tiller fractionally one way or the other until the exact position is found which holds the ship on course—with the proviso mentioned earlier that a shift of weight can play hell with the setting.

The boathook lies along the deck held by instant release rubber cord lashings, fenders, a warp, a heaving line and a collection of useful short ends of rope live in one place in one locker, instantly available.

The above is the basis of it and it varies from boat to boat. There is nothing specialist about it; many hundreds of ordinarily crewed cruisers carry it or something like it. The individual boat and the ingenuity of her owner dictate what you'll find but the aim is always the same—save seconds.

## Stop the Boat

We have reviewed one method of stopping her—by freeing sheets on a reach. One can achieve the same by backing the headsail and slightly freeing the main, with helm lashed a'lee, or by lowering the headsail and freeing the main or indeed by lowering the main or perhaps *half* lowering to destroy its shape and drive. In all these cases we are left with a ship which is still under control by sail, which is not the case if we simply drop the sails completely. This should be the aim, and whether the engine is reliable or not, we should never 'switch off' one source of power and control before effectively switching on another.

Knowing the behaviour of a boat under bare pole is important though. One can be moored or anchored in wind-against-tide conditions and know that anchor can be raised or mooring let go, usually with perfect safety under bare mast alone (she pays her bows off down wind with enough steerage to be held against or steered across the current) or again, failure of the engine while motoring with sails stowed can lead to a critical situation if you don't know what the boat is likely to do. Almost always, she will turn her stern into the wind and drift half-beam-on down wind and slightly ahead—*almost* always. This is something to find out about because it may make all the difference between knowing that the ship can be controlled for long enough to investigate the cause of engine stoppage or knowing that you have no control and a limited time to do *something*.

It is a mark of the good singlehander that he does know what his boat is liable to do and, to the second, just how long he has to do this or that job before the helm needs his attention. Stopping a boat is an everyday requirement for the coastal singlehander. Where another skipper may sail flat out into an unknown river, steering with his backside while trying to digest pilot book and chart and to con his way past unfamiliar marks and buoys, the singlehander will round up, lie to and sort himself out before proceeding. Not bad procedure for anybody.

There is nothing antisocial about singlehanding, indeed most of the ocean crossing breed are very extrovert people who love a party; they have an aptitude for self-sufficiency and loneliness, although it may bother them at times, it is just a price they pay for their complete and utter independence. Their *self* dependence is something else. They cannot talk over a problem and if they come and go at their own whims, the mental and moral exercise of having to keep their own council is something which makes for a better and indeed more considerate skipper in a crewed boat. The family cruising yachtsman or woman who sails alone occasionally knows how to give a reasonable order to others, neither does he issue a stream of them, some countermanding others. He also learns to plan a few steps ahead in every move he makes.

## Forward Planning in Singlehanding

A good case in point would be the laying alongside of a cruiser by a singlehanded yachtsman as compared to the same operation performed by a somewhat tardily crewed family boat. In the former case the lone crew must lay out the fenders and warps, have ready a heaving line and boathook, perhaps clear away his anchor ready to drop if his engine is at all temperamental and, for the same reason, see that his sails are ready for hoisting and held by a couple of tyers with slip knots. The latter outfit make for the berth with, perhaps, fenders out and trailing and a bunch of people obscuring the view by standing on the foredeck. The heaving line will be got out hurriedly and not re-coiled ready to throw, warps will be in a similar state, there will be much shouting of orders and should the engine stop the circus will be coming to town.

Exaggerated a bit perhaps but it happens. The moral is readiness and the singlehander *has* to be ready. At other times he applies the same forward thinking. He pagemarks his almanac and pilot book, rings round inconspicuous dangers on the chart, fills the kettle whenever a spare moment arises, stacks his sails in the best order for use and sees that they will come out of their (correct) bags tack first. He takes his meals when he can be sure of enjoying them in peace, he leaves his oilskins in easy reach, thinks out alternative options for making for shelter, lays out his sleeping bag ready for use, hauls up anchor chain and restows it prior to reaching the anchorage (to ensure that it will run freely) and he may even inflate his dinghy and ready a kedge and warp if entering a shoal river on a falling tide. It adds up to old fashioned seamanship. He *has* to do these things to stay out of trouble and it becomes second nature to think ahead. The ordinary family man can only benefit by singlehanding for a couple of days now and again.

## Vane and Automatic Steering

Many cruisers can be left to sail themselves closehauled but virtually none will do so on a reach or a run without special arrangements or equipment. There is a simple arrangement of lines and cords (Figure 75) which utilises a spare headsail and which will suit many but not all craft, otherwise a self-steering gear of some type is needed.

In broad terms there are three main types. There is the automatic helmsman which is based upon a special compass which, once set to the course required, signals an off-course port or starboard and cuts in an electric motor to apply rudder as required. There is adjustment for the width of the on course band and provision to overcome the tendency to 'hunt'. Such auto helmsmen are designed to limit the motor use and so conserve electrical power but naturally the cutting in and out of an electric motor is the guts of the operation and it will be more or less according to whether the yacht is lying to an easily held course in a smooth sea or a wild, yawing course in a tumble of following waves. The other two types are both wind vane arrangements.

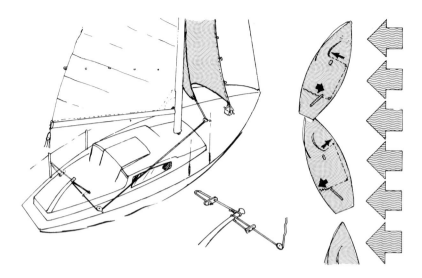

Fig. 75. A spare jib rigged as shown will allow most boats to self-steer on most courses, other than when the wind is well abaft the beam. Rubber shock cord is rigged on the tiller to port (in this case) and adjusted to suit the conditions.

The more basic is the vane which is mounted on an horizontal axis and which is set up edge-to-wind. Any deviation from course causes the vane to present one of its surfaces to the wind and in so doing flop over under the wind pressure. A system of lines conveys the wind power to the tiller, which is moved accordingly and the necessary amount of rudder is applied. The essential weakness of this type lies in the fact that while a strong wind provides plenty of power, a light wind offers very little power. This might seem to be acceptable on the assumption that the wilder the weather the harder the work and the more power needed but it is *apparent* wind that we are concerned with. A boat making five knots to windward against a 20-knot wind could be expected to produce an apparent wind of around 25 knots and the same boat, running before the same wind at 5 knots would experience a *15-knot* wind. It often happens that a sailing cruiser may need to be steered down wind in a tumble of a following sea and in a relatively light following breeze; the horizontal axis type of vane then lacks the power to cope with the amount of rudder work required.

The third main type of gear is the wind/water powered mechanism. A wind vane again senses any deviation from course and moves as it is deflected but this time instead of being linked directly to the tiller it is linked to a blade or 'paddle' which is hinged in such a way that it projects downwards into the water at the stern of the boat. As the boat sails, this paddle trails edge-on to the wake but if the vane is deflected by a deviation from course, it *twists* the paddle which instantly swings out sideways under the pressure of water against its inclined surface. The power generated thus is substantial and a clever linkage transmits it to the helm. Even a slight deflection of the vane in a light breeze therefore is enough to twist the paddle and release its powerful action. There are a great number of vane steering gears all related in some form to these basic ideas. They vary from 'sticks-and-string' arrangements to very sophisticated pieces of engineering.

Yet another variety combines both the automatic helmsman with its electrics with the wind vane. In this case the vane is tiny, no bigger than the palm of a man's hand and its deflection sets in motion an electric motor which operates a push-pull arm linked to the tiller. At least one such (Autohelm Plus) also combines a compass unit, thus giving a choice of compass or vane control at the flick of a switch and a quick resetting of the control column. A big advantage here is that the boat which may have made a passage under vane, getting the best out of a closehauled course perhaps, can, upon entering the river, be switched to compass for a course dead down the middle. Vane steering, in the tricky puffs and slants of a river wind, would send the boat swerving all over the river obedient to the shifting wind direction. Current consumption is no greater than that of, say, a navigation light and for singlehanded coasting, creek crawling and ordinary passage making this type of gear has about everything. There remains the sole snag that, *should* it go wrong, there isn't much that one can do about it whereas the 'Meccano' construction of the pure vane leaves the handy man some scope for improvisation.

No gear is instantly useable. It has to be fitted, adjusted and understood. One man may curse the same equipment that another man lauds. Properly adjusted a vane steering gear will steer a far better course to windward than a human helmsman because it is more sparing with the helm movements. Such gears are really tiller *holders*; the boat shifts off course, the device finds a new position in which to *hold* the tiller and when found it doesn't move again until a new hold is needed; the human tends to move the tiller constantly.

Self-steering gear set up to maintain a course which may last for days on end is one thing but gear which is used off and on during the busy hours of a short coastal passage, among traffic, around obstructions and in and out of rivers is very different in application. If it takes ten minutes to set up for a long haul it doesn't matter; if it can't be set up within seconds for the short term stuff it is more nuisance than help. This ease of use is something to examine in the light of the sort of sailing envisaged and something to be taken into consideration when buying.

Self-steering gear of any kind or design shares one great weakness; *it can't see where it is going*. There is also an uncanny tendency for such gear to single out the one other boat, the solitary buoy, beacon or rock in sight and make straight for it. I have watched my own gear at work and marvelled at this particular aptitude.

## A Singlehanded Coastal Passage

We'll assume that the owner of a 30-foot auxiliary cruiser is about to make a short passage between rivers. He makes his assessment of wind, tide and weather in the ordinary way and bends on an appropriate headsail. He may, if the wind promises to freshen, bend on a smaller headsail *below* the first, hanking it to the stay by leaving off the bottom sail hank of the sail in use and lashing it in a tight, neat bundle clear of the deck along the pulpit. To change sails he will merely have to (*a*) lower, (*b*) transfer halliard, tack and sheets, (*c*) unhank the first sail and (*d*) hoist.

He will have looked up his tides to see how they affect his passage, made notes of rise and fall times at the place she is making for and pre-read pilot book instructions; he will read them again as he makes the approach but, having read them earlier, they will be familiar and more easily digested. If the passage is to be a busy one or a rough one he will have prepared a few sandwiches, filled his kettle, put a teabag in a mug and other such domestic jobs. His oilskins will be laid out on a bunk and everything below will be stowed as if for gale conditions.

Under way, he heads down river. If he has one, he may cut in his self-steering gear on the straight reaches but more likely it is that he will enjoy sailing his boat; later when he gets busy and a bit tired is the time when he will look to it for help. Under self-steering gear there is a big temptation to wander around catching up with small maintenance jobs—none too wise in a river crowded with moorings. To this end it is an advantage to have a forward facing port light so that when below he can take an occasional peep forward without having to keep popping up on deck.

At sea, course laid, he sets up his self-steering and relaxes. It is now that he can take time and care in his coastal pilotage, wander around looking at the set of his sails and generally relax himself, but he will still be keenly aware of the real danger of self-steering gear, namely the risk of falling overboard and being left astern as the ship sails on placidly. He may or may not wear safety harness the whole time. There is much argument about this. My own theory is that one should wear it always at night and in roughish conditions and at other times according to circumstances. With self-steering there is time to move slowly and carefully. One cultivates (or should) an instinctive catch-and-grab mode of walking the deck; one hand never lets go before the next clamps on—even at the mooring. To work, there is always an arm around a stay, a spine wedged for balance, a knee locked against a mast—or one sits down, instinctively. An almost bigger risk than falling overboard is in falling back into the cockpit, down the main hatch or against some sharp projection with an ensuing injury that for a singlehander can be a grave danger.

As he approaches the destination he decides whether he is going to make for the marina or dock or whether to anchor. He may be able to make a decision but if he can't, he prepares for both. He hauls out warps and fenders, recoils and lays handy in the locker. He hauls out a few fathoms of anchor cable and runs it back into the locker, ensuring that when needed it will come out in a clean run. He may stow his anchor at the stemhead. He may also give his engine a short run to warm it up (if it responds to that sort of treatment) and he has a last good look at the chart—henceforth he will be having to take hasty glances at it.

His approach to the chosen anchorage is typical. He may well decide to find his spot under engine. He positions his boat in that part of the fairway that gives him the greatest available time for sail handling and slows her right down on a reach, lets fly sheets completely and lashes the helm a'lee. If he had been beating up the fairway this manoeuvre would have been started well over to one side of the channel or on the windward side if one favoured more than the other. He can now lower and stow headsail and mainsail, securing both with temporary, easily slipped lashings. He makes ready all for letting go anchor and puts the engine, which was at tickover, into ahead.

He may circle the chosen anchorage several times, sizing up swinging scope and distances, depths and the consequences of future wind shifts once anchored. This circling is well worth while because the aspect alters constantly as seen from different angles and the singlehander above all doesn't want to make extra (3 a.m.) work for himself.

Such is the typical singlehanded coastal passage. It *should* be little different to any crewed passage—except that it may well be a great deal more seamanlike.

# Chapter Eighteen

# How to Test-sail a Small Cruiser

MOST yachting magazines carry test reports on new cruisers but these seldom amount to more than a mildly effusive description of the boat and her performance. The best of them make a genuine attempt to describe what the writer experienced at that particular time. To test a boat thoroughly it would be necessary to sail her in fair weather and foul, smooth water and rough, to live in her and to spend nights at sea in her; no magazine can afford to do this. Don't therefore accept wild generalisations by magazine writers. Take the information they have to offer and suspend judgement.

An owner-to-be will have narrowed his search to two or three boats if he is buying new and perhaps to only one if on the secondhand market since he is dependent upon what is available at the time. Almost all builders offer test-sail facilities—or should, but a trial sail in a second-hand boat is not always possible as the transaction may be taking place during the winter and the buyer must rely upon information about the class of boat, obtained maybe from owners' associations or by writing to an owner listed in Lloyd's Yacht Register and asking for an off the cuff opinion.

Since he has narrowed his search the buyer in the market for a new boat goes for his test sail already slightly biased in favour of the boat; he *wants* to be able to like her. Probably his wife will be with him and she may take to or against the accommodation layout—again affecting his final summing up. He should have weighed up the all-in cost of the boat by the time essentials and extras have been added to basic cost and he should be solely concerned with the handling performance.

He must be fair to the boat and to the salesman. If she is a true *pocket* cruiser of less than 20 foot overall length, he should resist the temptation to take a crowd of friends with him because his party plus salesman, and maybe one other, will overload the little craft and distort her true qualities. For this reason it is as well to ask in advance whether he will be having to share a sail trial with another buyer.

The salesman may be an employee or he may be the actual builder—he may be a yard boatman. The extent of the trial sail is a bit affected by this. A builder or designer will have no objection to a very thorough trial, but there may be a shade of resistance from the boat-man, who wants to get home by knock-off time. The weather must be considered and the restrictions imposed by having to catch tides and so on. On the other hand the prospective buyer is perhaps about to lay out a great deal of money. There are nuisances who go around taking sailing demonstrations and who have no real intention of buying—the

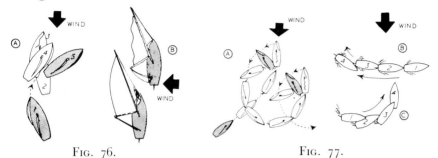

FIG. 76.                                         FIG. 77.

FIG. 76. When a sail test takes place in a river where manoeuvring space is limited some indication of handling aptitude can be gained by tacking her very slowly. In light airs this will be apparent anyway, but in a smarter breeze ('A') she can be pinched to slow her and then brought slowly head-to-wind and tacked. If she gets out of control it will then be instructive to note how easy or difficult it is to get her sailing again. Choose a spot clear of moorings or dangers and warn the salesman what you intend to do.

At 'B' she has the main well off (bottom) and the jib down. Many handy craft will continue to sail themselves quietly on a reach with the helm unattended and not even lashed. The upper sketch shows her sailing unattended with jib eased and main let right off while being reefed. While some cruisers are too delicately balanced to do this, it is a bonus to the singlehanded owner or to the man who does most of the work while his wife is watching over small children.

FIG. 77. At 'A' the cruiser under test has gone about leaving her jib aback. With the helm still held hard over she pays off and bears away until she gybes. The helm is still hard over so that she comes up into the wind and tacks again (jib has not been altered at all), continuing to gybe and tack more or less indefinitely. This test of manoeuvrability will be more effective in a moderate breeze and while it is no proof of a good or a bad boat it gives the helmsman a 'feel' of the boat early in the test.

At 'B' a cruiser is being handled under power. Put her across the wind and let her lose way completely. Go hard astern and note how her stern kicks—probably to port with a right-handed propeller—try steering her *straight* astern. At 'C' she is making a tight turn from stopped by heading up into the wind. Many craft refuse to bring their heads up for quite a long time. Note the turning circle with helm hard down and engine at $\frac{3}{4}$ throttle, then try her the other way round.

builder or his man will have suffered them in the past. The aim is to be considerate regarding the length of the sail, but adamant about the things to be done during it.

If time permits or maybe between making or taking in sail, try her under jib alone and main alone. In light airs she may not handle very well, particularly if she is a twin-keeler, but if she will handle well enough to tack and gybe smartly in a moderate breeze, she has a great advantage to the singlehanded man or do-it-all-myself owner.

While sailing, notice the course sailed when closehauled on each tack (by compass) and from this calculate how high she points *and still sails*. Don't expect her to point up within 45 degrees and still tramp along, but be critical of a boat which 'points but doesn't go'. Notice too how lively her helm is. A boat which flies around on the other tack the second the tiller is released is an annoying creature for the cruising man, but if she is so insensitive that the tiller feels sluggish she won't be much fun either.

Safety when going forward, ease of handling jib sheets, ease of starting engine and so on are all points to note as also is the accommodation layout when actually sailing. Locker doors which fly open, mattresses which slide off and so on should be checked. Consider chart work below, cooking and sleeping at sea, access below in wet weather and so on.

An engine trial is worth having if time allows. Stop her and let her drift to a standstill, then try backing and filling ahead and astern to make a tight turn. If there is a smart breeze try turning down-wind and then completing the full circle by heading into the wind to see whether her bow windage is excessive for the power available.

Make notes about everything you do for future reference. Measure windspeed if possible and speed of boat for sail area also roughly the angle of heel. Failing this and while moored alongside get everybody amidships and then put your full weight out by the shrouds on one side. Note the amount of freeboard remaining. When testing the next boat on the list repeat this dodge—a tender boat will be obvious to detect although bear in mind that according to hull form some have more initial stability than others. A cruiser that sails on her ear is a curse in any case. See how far you can steer her dead astern in a straight line.

If conditions, such as a narrow river, preclude much in the way of manoeuvre you will have to be content to note angle of heel for given wind, weather helm, etc. Tacking at normal speed teaches very little, but after a couple of normal tacks slow her right up by pinching her until she is barely moving and then see if she'll still go about. If she gets in stays so much the better. See how quickly you can recover control. On a reach let all sheets go and see if she lies quietly. Try bearing away with a tight mainsheet and anything else which is plainly unfair. A normal boat can't be blamed for misbehaving, but if she's unusually good it will be apparent.

The weather dictates the general programme. On a light air day one can only go through the basic drill of tacking and gybing, heaving to and manoeuvring under power, but the appropriate sails (biggest genoa) should be worn. Many small twin-keel cruisers are sluggish in light airs and give a poor impression of their qualities below Force 2. By the same token there is no hint concerning weather helm and in a stronger breeze they may gripe up hard as soon as they are heeled— they may also be tender. In such cases, it is better to try for a second trial at a later date if this is possible.

With anything of a working breeze general manoeuvrability may be tested by putting the boat about, leaving the jib sheets untouched and keeping the helm hard over so that she tacks, bears away, gybes, comes on the wind, tacks again and so on. A handy boat will often keep up this catch-my-tail routine indefinitely—she may be reluctant to bear away with the mainsail hardened in though. These tricks do more than to give a *feel* of the boat. She may still be hard of the helm on the wind. The important thing is to avoid a sail test which consists of a straight sail out and back again as this reveals very little.

In a fresher breeze weather helm can be assessed. No small cruiser should be so hard mouthed that the tiller needs to be hugged hard up against the chest. A pocket spring balance hooked over the tiller might show between 5 and 10 lbs. of pull required, which isn't *too* bad. Some need an 18 lb. pull and this is bad. Notice the stiffness of her too. In a Force 4 breeze she should have plenty of freeboard out of water under normal sail and depending on size, of course, a small cruiser may be better for a couple of rolls in the mainsail in winds approaching Force 5; she should still not be burying her rail.

Reefing is a sore defect in many new boats. The alloy boom of equal thickness for its whole length sags at the clew after 4–5 rolls have been taken in. The cure for this is to glue (Araldite) battens or 'whelps' to the outer end for about $\frac{1}{3}$ to $\frac{1}{2}$ its length, tapering forward to nothing, this causes the leech to build up a slightly larger roll than the luff and consequently lifts the boom end. On a sail test, and if time permits, try reefing her 5–6 rolls. Let the mainsheet fly, put her on a reach under the jib and let go of the tiller; she should sail herself. Keep the halliard taut and let the boom climb up the gooseneck track as it turns, paying out halliard as required. If a boat is hard to reef and a major defect is the cause this is a very serious disadvantage. Finally, be fair; you can't have everything and the perfect cruiser has yet to be designed. A good compromise for the size and the price is what you are looking for.

# Index